PHILOSOPHY, POLITICS AND SOCIETY

THIRD SERIES

Philosophy, Politics and Society

THIRD SERIES

A collection edited by
Peter Laslett and WGRunciman

BASIL BLACKWELL OXFORD 1978

© in this collection
Basil Blackwell 1967
Reprinted 1969, 1978

0 631 17730 2

Printed in Great Britain by
Billing & Sons Limited,
Guildford, London and Worcester

Contents

Introduction

Our last introduction was published in 1962. In it we proclaimed a modest revival in political philosophy since the declaration made in the original collection of 1956 that 'for the moment, anyway, political philosophy is dead'. At the same time, we ventured to predict that this revival would continue to display the characteristics which marked the contributions to the second volume. In putting together a third collection, therefore, we are at least to some degree publicly committed to putting our prediction to the test.

We suggested in 1962 that the revival of political philosophy was largely due to two separate but related influences. On the one hand, there was the renewed interest taken by philosophers in the prescriptive discussion of social and political issues. On the other hand, there was the much closer attention which was being accorded to the methods and results of the social sciences. We do not go so far as to claim that all the papers in the present volume reflect either or both of these influences. But both are readily visible at various points in the volume; and in general, it seemed to us that the revival, or in some cases continuance, of theoretical discussion falling under our broad title was sufficient to call for the preparation of a further collection.

Only two of the present papers have appeared in print before. Most of the remainder were either written at our request or else made available to us out of work in progress. One of these is by an author already represented in our last collection: Professor Rawls, whose article 'Justice as Fairness' we reprinted last time, has now made available to us a paper on 'Distributive Justice' in which he develops further the implications of a theory of justice which, we believe, promises to be a major contribution to contemporary political philosophy.[1] The other authors are all represented in the series for the first time. It has not become our policy to seek for original contributions rather than reprints, and the high proportion of them in this collection is fortuitous. But it may be worth remarking that there is not at present an academic journal published in Great Britain which can be called a journal of political philosophy. Collections of this kind are no substitute; but they do gain an added purpose because of this lack.

There is, however, more evidence than this volume for both the revival of political philosophy and also the increased interest of philosophers in general in the social sciences. Indeed, it includes

[1] See also his 'The Sense of Justice', *Philosophical Review* (1963), and 'Constitutional Liberty and the Concept of Justice', *Nomos* VI (1963).

several works recently published by our present contributors. Professor
Taylor, who here discusses what he calls the 'value-slope' in political
sociology, published in 1964 a book on *The Explanation of Behaviour*
which is one of the most interesting of recent contributions to the
perennial controversy over behaviourism. Professor Hare's *Freedom and
Reason* (1963) extends his earlier analysis of moral reasoning in *The
Language of Morals* into problems which bear directly on social and
political theory. Professor Macpherson's *The Political Theory of
Possessive Individualism*, which appeared in 1962, is not only an original
reinterpretation of Hobbes, Locke and others of the classical theorists,
but a contribution to political theory in its own right. Professor Arrow
brought out in 1963 a revised edition, with an additional chapter, of
his important monograph on *Social Choice and Individual Values*; his
present paper further elucidates his views on what is perhaps the most
important single problem in the difficult middle ground between
economics and political theory.

There have been other works also to which attention may be drawn.
The controversy started by Lord Devlin's Maccabaean lecture of
1959 on 'The Enforcement of Morals', to which we made reference in
the introduction to our last collection, has been continued in Professor
Hart's *Law, Liberty and Morality* (1963) and Lord Devlin's own
volume of collected papers published in 1965 under the title of his
Maccabaean lecture. Dr Brian Barry, in *Political Argument* (1965),
has set out explicitly to show the joint value of explanatory models and
analytical philosophy as applied to questions of practical politics.
Mr J. L. Lucas in *The Principles of Politics* (1966) has attempted to
construct a rational theory of obligation from first principles. In
the United States, Professors Buchanan and Tullock, in *The Calculus
of Consent* (1962), have put forward a controversial model of constitutional choice which attempts to replace orthodox majoritarianism with
a principle of unanimity after bargaining. Several useful collections
have also been published in the United States: a set of lectures on *Social
Justice* (1962) edited by Professor R. B. Brandt, and volumes in the
series *Nomos* on *Liberty, The Public Interest* and *Justice*. Apart from
these collections, there has been a small but continuing flow of articles
in the Anglo-American philosophical journals on concepts central to
the traditional concerns of the political theorist,[2] and an increasing

---

[2] For example: Richard Wasserstrom, 'Rights, Human
Rights and Racial Discrimination', *Journal of Philosophy* (1964);
R. B. Brandt, 'The Concepts of Obligation and Duty', *Mind*
(1964); H. J. McCloskey, 'Rights', *Philosophical Quarterly*
(1965); Joel Feinberg, 'Duties, Rights and Claims', *American
Philosophical Quarterly* (1966).

volume of discussion on problems in the philosophy of history and the logic of the social sciences. Finally, we may point to the works translated into English in the last few years, which have included, for example, Professor Sartori's *Democratic Theory* (1962) and Professor Perelman's *The Idea of Justice and the Problem of Argument* (1963).

There is thus little purpose in labouring the point that political philosophy in the English-speaking world is alive again. But there are perhaps one or two general conclusions to be drawn now that the impact of linguistic philosophy and behavioural science on social and political theory has been registered and to some extent absorbed. There has been little reversion to the sort of *a priori* sociology and disguised prescriptivism for which the traditional theorists have so often been criticized. But if we are to try to characterize the state of our social and political theory at the time of putting this volume together, it may be plausible to suggest that what is broadly happening is a holding operation, and at some points even a counter-attack, against positivism, whether derived from linguistic philosophy or from the behavioural sciences.

This generalization, however, needs qualification in its turn. Attacks on the assumptions alleged to underlie behaviouristic psychology have been answered with no less vigorous rebuttals. Those philosophers who have attempted to undermine the orthodox fact-value distinction have met with only limited success. And even if there has been a change of emphasis, if not of doctrine, among philosophers themselves it has not yet had effect on the greater part of the work done under the heading of political science, particularly in the United States. The earlier part of Professor Taylor's essay in this volume makes this quite clear. The reaction against positivism, therefore, may extend only as far as a greater wariness about either dismissing value-judgments too readily as arbitrary or assuming too easily that the methods and assumptions of the physical sciences can be applied without modification to the sciences of man.

Some philosophers would argue that such notions as intention, motive and choice are integral to the explanation of human behaviour and that for this reason the assimilation of the social sciences to the physical cannot be pressed too far. Others would deny that the accepted application of these terms is sufficient grounds for ruling out the possibility of establishing statistical generalizations and causal sequences of equivalent validity to those of the physical sciences. Professor Ayer, in his Comte lecture which is reprinted here, suggests that there is no good reason to suppose that the distinguishing features of human action should not as such form part of law-like explanatory statements. But there would seem to be a broad agreement not merely that the continuing task of the philosopher is the appraisal of conceptual schemes (for this, after all, applies in the physical just as much as the social sciences), but also that there is an inherent difference, which it is for the philosopher to try to elucidate, in the conceptual schemes which apply to the behaviour of man.

In the same way, the revival of interest in prescriptive discussion does not mean that philosophers would now credit judgments of value with the status of fact. Even those who, like Professor Macpherson in the book we have referred to, have protested against what they see as an arid and profitless preoccupation with the fact-value distinction, would not suggest that it has yet been overthrown. But Macpherson does go further than any of our contributors have yet done in his critique of our own existing economic and political system. Moreover, he attacks it on diametrically opposite grounds to those on which Professor Rawls bases his claim that a regulated competitive market can satisfy the requirements of distributive justice.

This disagreement might still be said to fall short of the kind of pre-scription which political philosophy once undertook to supply. But what is important is the way in which both Macpherson and Rawls argue from philosophical premises to clear, and incompatible, implica-tions for the organization of society. This sort of link between judgments of value and judgments of fact is particularly clear whenever the 'needs' of society are being discussed, and as Mr Lukes shows in his paper on 'Alienation and Anomie', it requires to be elucidated most of all where a wide-ranging social theory is built round a single influential and persuasive concept such as one of these. Analysis of this kind may be purely deductive, or it may involve an attempt to test the empirical assumptions on which the judgment of value is based, or it may consist in showing where and to what degree sociological and political terms are not reducible to definitions analogous to those of natural science. But its general moral is likely to be twofold: that prescriptive discussion of political issues is not meaningless, and that both deductive argument and empirical evidence can be brought to bear on it.

It may be that such discussion is not conducted with the range and confidence of the classical theorists, and that attempts to construct all-embracing systems of political morality or to resolve the deeper questions of personal commitment are still not being undertaken. But the moral to be drawn from this is that the joint correctives of the linguistic philosophers and the empirical sociologists have been, if sometimes exaggerated, nonetheless salutary. In qualifying the revival of political theory we are not implying that it either will or ought to become more grandiose. On the contrary, it is rather to be welcomed that it is at once more careful about its claims and more securely grounded in the established results of economics, psychology and political science.

We have not tried to represent in this volume continental political philosophy, although the same influences may to some degree be at work there. Nor have we included any contribution from the political anthropologists, although much of their work has, as we remarked in our last introduction, a considerable interest to political theorists.[3] We would obviously not want to pretend to be covering all the topics which might be subsumed under our title. We would claim, however, that Anglo-American political and social theory has indeed been revived, and that this revival has largely followed the course which we foresaw when we assembled our last collection.

Our particular thanks are due to Mr John Dunn, of King's College, Cambridge, for his help in preparing this collection.

[3] See for example the volume on *Political Systems and the Distribution of Power* published in 1965 by the Association of Social Anthropologists of the Commonwealth.

1 Man as a Subject for Science[1]

A J Ayer

'Oh, the monster!' exclaimed the Reverend Doctor Folliott
'he has made a subject for science of the only friend he had
in the world.' PEACOCK, 'CROTCHET CASTLE'.

Those who catch the allusion in my title may remember that the
science in question was anatomy. The devotees of science to whom
Peacock was referring were body-snatchers who provided medical
students with corpses for dissection: for in 1831, when *Crotchet Castle*
was published, it was still thought improper, mainly on religious
grounds, to treat even lifeless human beings as subjects for experiment.
But the march of mind, of which these criminals were supposed to be
the camp-followers, had far more ambitious aims than that which they
were serving. It was the belief of the positivists and utilitarians who
gave its progressive intellectual tone to the first half of the nineteenth
century that the science of nature which Newton had established was
due to be completed by a science of man. This was not merely a question
of supplementing physics with biology: the empire of science was to
be extended to every facet of man's nature; to the workings of men's
minds as well as their bodies and to their social as well as their individual
behaviour; law, custom, morality, religious faith and practice, political
institutions, economic processes, language, art, indeed every form of
human activity and mode of social organization, were to be explained
in scientific terms; and not only explained but transfigured. For Comte
and Bentham and their followers, no less than for the Marxists, the
point of understanding society was to change it; there was a rational
way of ordering human affairs, and it only required the application of
scientific method to discover it and put it into operation.

It is not an underestimate of what has been achieved in the social
sciences to say that these hopes have not been fulfilled. Auguste Comte
died in 1852, just a year after the opening of the Great Exhibition,
which expressed a faith in the power of science that has indeed been
justified; it has been more than a century of astonishing scientific
progress. But the progress has been in the physical and, to a rather lesser
but still very considerable extent, the biological sciences; the social
sciences have not kept pace. Admittedly they began this period in a very
much less favourable position; neither would it be fair to say that they

[1] This essay was delivered as the sixth Auguste Comte Memorial
Lecture at the London School of Economics in 1964.

have made no progress at all. How great this progress has been is not very easy to assess. A large body of economic doctrine has been built up, but the deductions which are made from it appear still to fit rather loosely to the facts; the emergence of psycho-analysis, particularly in its Freudian version, has had important social and literary effects; it would not be too much to say that our ideas of human nature have been transformed by it; even so the charge that psycho-analytical theories are not testable has not been effectively met, and so long as this is so their scientific value remains in doubt; in anthropology the reaction against the rather too facile acceptance of far-reaching theories has led to a puritanical distrust of generalization; the theoretical contribution of Marxism to the study of history, though not entirely negligible, falls a long way behind its practical influence. All in all, the stock of generally accredited and well-tested theories that the social sciences can muster is comparatively small. The social scientist may well look on the garden of the natural sciences as an intellectual paradise from which he has lamentably been excluded.

But why should this be so? Is it just that the factors which govern human behaviour are unmanageably complex? Is it that for moral and practical reasons there are rather narrow limits to the type and number of experiments that can be carried out on human beings? Have the wrong methods been pursued? Have the right questions not yet been asked? Are the social sciences merely waiting for their Galileo or their Newton? Or is there some more fundamental reason, some reason of principle, why the kind of success that the natural sciences have had is here unattainable? This is the first question that I wish to examine.

In whatever other ways they may differ, the various special sciences at least have this in common—that they contain a set of what are any-how provisionally taken to be valid generalizations. These generalizations may be more or less abstract; they may be causal or statistical in form; they may or may not be capable of being organized into a deductive system; they may be valued primarily for their own sakes or for the particular inferences which can be made from them, according to the character of the science and the view which is taken of it: all that I am now concerned with is that they must exist. Now it is characteristic of the social sciences that their stock of generalizations is relatively poor. For the most part the generalizations which they do claim to have established are lacking in precision and scope; and in some fields at least, they are not very well attested. This is sometimes taken merely as an indication that the social sciences are still in their infancy; they are still at the stage of building up the data from which a stock of fruitful generalizations will later spring. But may not the explanation be quite different? May it not be that there is something about the material on which these sciences have to work, something about the nature of men, which makes it impossible to generalize about them in any way comparable to that which has made the success of the natural sciences? If this were so, the rather poor showing which men have so far made as anything but purely biological subjects for science would be logically accounted for.

The idea that man somehow stands outside the order of nature is one that many people find attractive on emotional grounds, so that it has to be received with some caution. It is, however, fairly widely accepted nowadays, even by philosophers who are supposed to be able to discount their emotional prejudices, and this for various reasons. One of them is, of course, the belief in the freedom of the will. It is argued that since men are free to behave as they choose, they are always capable of nullifying any generalization about their conduct to which they are alleged to be subject. If any such generalization is produced, it is only to be expected that someone will proudly or perversely exercise his option of rendering it false.

The trouble with this argument is that it simply assumes the false-hood of the position which it is intended to demolish. If the attribution of free will is construed in such a way that a man can be said to have acted freely only if his action is not susceptible of any causal explanation, then there will indeed be no question but that if men ever act freely, their behaviour is not totally subject to causal law. This still allows for its being subject to statistical laws, but on the assumption, which the proponents of this view tacitly make, that a man is free on any given occasion to try to do anything whatsoever that he believes to be feasible, the possibility of there being even statistical laws about human be-haviour which would be of any scientific value is effectively excluded. But now it is surely fair to ask for some justification of these very strong assumptions. What reason have we for believing that men ever do act freely, in this sense? There may be a *prima facie* case for holding that men are capable of acting freely in some sense or other; but it is by no means clear that an action which passes this test of freedom, what-ever it may be, cannot also be governed by some causal law. Many philosophers have in fact held that what we ordinarily mean by speaking of an action as freely done is not incompatible with its being causally determined: some have gone even further to the point of holding that when we say that an action is free we actually imply, or presuppose, that it is determined; others who take the view that determinism excludes free will, as this is ordinarily understood, have concluded just for this reason that our ordinary notion of free will has no application. I do not myself think that we stand to gain very much by making a conscientious effort to discover what people ordinarily mean when they talk about free will: it might very well turn out that some people mean one thing by it, and some another, and that many people's idea of it is very confused. The important question, so far as we are concerned, is whether human behaviour is or is not entirely subject to law. If we conclude that it is, or even just that there is no good reason to suppose that it is not, then we may find it expedient to introduce a sense of acting freely which squares with these conclusions. We shall presumably want it to apply, so far as possible, to the same actions as those that most people would now regard as being free, though not necessarily with the same implications, but we shall rather be correcting ordinary usage than merely following it. If, on the other hand, our conclusion is that human behaviour is not entirely subject to law, then again we shall have to decide what provision, if any, this enables us to make for freedom of action; for example, if we make the absence of causal determination a necessary condition of an action's being freely done, we shall have to consider whether we can still preserve the connection between freedom and responsibility. But the point is that before we can usefully embark upon such matters, we must first decide the issue of determinism. How far and in what sense is man's behaviour subject to law?

It may appear, indeed, that this is not an issue which one could hope to settle *a priori*. Surely, it may be said, we can never be in a position to show that any piece of human conduct is inexplicable: the most that we can claim is that we have not been able to find any explanation for it, but this does not imply that there is no explanation, or even that the explanation is one which it will always be beyond our power to discover. But while this remark is perfectly sound, it may also be thought to miss the point. For what is most commonly maintained by those who wish to set limits to the extent to which men's actions are governed by law is not that these actions are inexplicable, but rather that the kinds of explanation which they call for do not conform to the scientific model. That is to say, they do not account for an action as resulting from the operation of a natural law. It is allowed that explanations of the scientific type are sometimes appropriate, as when we account for some piece of deviant behaviour by relating it to a disorder in the agent's constitution, but cases of this kind are said to be the exception rather than the rule. In the normal way we explain a man's action in terms of his intentions, or his motives, or his beliefs, or the social context in which the action takes place. Consider, for example, the simple action of drinking a glass of wine. As performed by different people in different circumstances, this may be an act of self-indulgence, an expression of politeness, a proof of alcoholism, a manifestation of loyalty, a gesture of despair, an attempt at suicide, the performance of a social rite, a religious communication, an attempt to summon up one's courage, an attempt to seduce or corrupt another person, the sealing of a bargain, a display of professional expertise, a piece of inadvertence, an act of expiation, the response to a challenge and many other things besides. All these are accepted as good explanations: if the circumstances are right, they render the performance of the action intelligible; but only in the case of the alcoholic is it clear that the explanation is of a scientific character. In the other cases we find the action intelligible because we are given a reason for its performance; it is explained in terms of the agent's purpose, or by reference to a social norm, or through some combination of these two.

This is a fair enough statement of the facts, but it raises a number of quite difficult questions which we shall have to examine rather carefully before we can draw any conclusions about the extent to which human conduct eludes the grasp of science. Exactly how do explanations in terms of purpose operate and in what way are they explanatory? In particular, how do they significantly differ from explanations in terms of causal laws? What kind of understanding of an action do we acquire when we are able to fit it into a social context, or see it as fulfilling a social norm? In what sense, again, is this an explanation of the action? And finally, even if a reason can be found for saying that explanations of these types are not, or not wholly scientific, does it follow that the actions which they explain cannot also be explained in a way which does confirm to the scientific model? Assuming that we do have to deal here with two or more radically different sorts of explanations, are we bound to conclude that they are mutually exclusive?

Let us begin then with the type of explanation in which an action is accounted for in terms of the agent's purpose. In the standard instance of this type, the agent has some end in view which he wishes to attain and believes that there is a causal connection between the performance of the action and the attainment of this end; he need not believe that the performance of the action is a necessary condition for the attainment of the end, since he may suppose that the end could come about, or even that he could bring it about, in other ways, and he need not believe it to be a uniquely sufficient condition, but he must at least regard it as part of a sufficient condition. This is most commonly expressed by saying that the agent takes the action to be a means towards the end in question. And correspondingly the end or rather, to speak more accurately, the agent's desire for the attainment of the end is said to be the motive for his action. It is not indeed essential that the motive should be conscious: we do sometimes explain a man's behaviour in terms of an end which he is not himself aware that he is pursuing. Sometimes we even discount the motive which he thinks he has in favour of the unconscious motive by which we judge that he is really actuated. However, the cases in which we speak of unconscious motives are modelled on those in which the motive is conscious. The reason why we credit a man with pursuing an end of which he is unaware is that his behaviour, in the given circumstances, not only indicates that he finds the end desirable but also resembles the behaviour which might be expected of one who was consciously pursuing it.

It is not necessary either that the agent's belief in the efficacy of the means should be fully articulated. That is to say, he does not have to formulate the proposition that such and such a course of action will conduce to his end. It is enough that he acts as though he took this proposition to be true and, in the case where his motive is conscious, that he assents to it if it is put to him. The proposition may on occasion be false, in the sense that the means which are supposed to be sufficient in the attendant circumstances for the production of the end do not in fact produce it; and it may also happen that the agent is mistaken about the circumstances. He may adopt a course of action which would have been sufficient for his purpose if the circumstances had been what he took them to be, but which is not sufficient as things actually are. This is a more common cause of failure than the other, but failure of any kind is less common than success. We should not be satisfied with the assignment of men's purposes as explanations for their actions, if they did not in general attain their ends.

The case which I have been taking as standard is that in which a man's action is directed on a particular occasion towards some specific end. In a situation of this kind, the action which the agent takes may not be the only one which he regards as suitable for his purpose, but the range of actions of which this is true is likely to be fairly narrow. There are, however, cases in which the assignment of a motive covers a rather wide range of behaviour, and these are usually also cases in which the end towards which the behaviour is directed is not very specific. I am thinking of the sort of actions which are done from what one might call a standing motive, a motive like that of ambition or avarice, or a love of learning. The end of being powerful or famous or rich or learned, or whatever it may be, is unspecific in the sense that it may take many different concrete forms and the means to it may be correspondingly various. The agent himself may not envisage at all clearly what form the achievement of his end will take, and he may even have no considered idea of the way in which he will set about pursuing it. His having the motive is rather a matter of his being disposed to accept whatever opportunity arises of achieving his end in one form or another. In cases where the motive is something like the love of learning, it may amount to little more than his seeking opportunities to engage in a certain sort of activity. It is, however, to be remembered that where an activity is mainly undertaken for its own sake, the description of it in terms of purposes or motives seems a little out of place. It is perhaps not incorrect to say that my motive for reading novels or playing bridge or going to the cinema is that I enjoy these pursuits, but if I were asked what my motive was for engaging in them I should be more inclined to answer that I had no motive at all.

In his book on *The Concept of Motivation*, Professor Peters goes much further than this. He not only allows that there can be voluntary behaviour which is not motivated, but he does not think it correct to talk of there being a motive even in all cases in which an agent takes means towards a further end. The cases which he wishes to exclude are those in which our actions are habitual or fit into some conventional pattern. He thinks that the word 'motive' is commonly 'used in contexts where conduct is being assessed and not simply explained, where there is a breakdown in conventional expectations', and therefore wishes to restrict its application to purposeful actions which are somehow out of the ordinary and in particular to those in which we are inclined to pass an adverse moral judgment. There is indeed some warrant for this restriction in ordinary usage, in the sense that we do not normally inquire into people's motives unless we are surprised by their conduct or think that they are called upon to justify it. I should think it strange if someone asked me what was my motive in putting on my overcoat to go out on a winter's day, and I might be inclined to take offence if someone asked me what was my motive in asking a friend to dinner. But the reason why such questions appear strange or offensive is not that conventional actions are not motivated, or that motives tend to be discreditable, but simply that we do not bother to ask questions to which we already know the answers. The desire to keep warm, or the desire to give pleasure to a friend or to enjoy his company are just as much motives for action as the more unusual desire to catch cold, say with a view to avoiding some disagreeable duty, or the desire to worm information out of a friend or to borrow money from him. There seems to be no good reason to exclude them merely because they are innocent and commonplace. It is not as if they functioned any differently as springs of actions from motives which are ulterior in the pejorative sense.

I do, however, agree with Professor Peters, as against, for example,

Professor Ryle, that for an action to be motivated it is at least necessary that it be directed to an end. Professor Ryle has gone astray, in my opinion, through concentrating, almost exclusively, on actions which are done from standing motives, where, as we have seen, the ends are relatively unspecific; so unspecific, in fact, that Ryle effectively ignores them.[2] In this way he comes to assimilate actions which are done from standing motives, like ambition, to actions like habitual chess playing which are not done in the pursuit of any further end at all, and so he finds himself able to conclude that motives can be wholly analysed in terms of dispositions, that to act from such and such a motive amounts to no more than being disposed to engage in behaviour of such and such a type. Accordingly he interprets explanation in terms of motives as if it were simply a matter of subsuming the particular under the general case, as when we say that a piece of glass has broken because it was brittle, or that a man is late on a particular occasion because he is habitually unpunctual. This is not even a very plausible account of explanation in terms of a standing motive, and quite obviously wrong when it is applied to actions which are explained in terms of the agent's aiming on a given occasion at some specific end. Indeed one of my reasons for giving central importance to actions which are done from occasional motives is that the element of directedness there stands out more clearly.

Of course Professor Ryle himself has a motive for dissolving motives into dispositions. It is an important part of his campaign against the idea of the ghost in the machine to dismember the mechanical model, in which motives are conceived as 'ghostly thrusts'. And whatever the deficiency of his tactics his strategy has been successful. Thanks to him and also to Wittgenstein it is now almost a commonplace among philosophers that motives are not causes. But this is not to say that it is true.

Why is it thought to be true? There are various reasons, not all of them of equal weight. The most simple of them is that motives operate *a fronte* whereas causes operate *a tergo*; to put it crudely, that causes push while motives pull. A more sophisticated argument is that cause and effect are distinct events: so, if the motive for an action caused it, it would have to be a separate occurrence which preceded the action or at any rate accompanied it; but in many, perhaps in most, cases of motivated actions, such separate occurrences are simply not discoverable; the specification of the motive is part of the description of the action, not a reference to anything outside it, and certainly not a reference to any distinct event. Thirdly, it is argued that in the

[2] See *The Concept of Mind*, ch. iv.

scientific sense of 'cause', which is what is here in question, even singular causal statements are implicitly universal; to say that one particular event is the cause of another is to imply that events of these types are invariably connected by a causal law: this is not true, however, of statements in which a motive is assigned for some particular action; such a statement does not imply that whenever people have motives of the kind in question they act in a similar manner, or that whenever actions of that type are performed they are done from the same sort of motive. Finally, a point is made of the fact that motivated action often consists in following or attempting to follow a rule; that is to say, the action may be one to which normative criteria are applicable; the question arises whether it has been performed correctly; but this means, so it is argued, that we somehow impoverish the motive if we regard it merely as a cause.

Let us now examine these arguments in turn. The first of them need not detain us long. If the contention is that purposive behaviour is to be accounted for, not as the response to any past or present stimulus, but rather in terms of the future state of affairs towards the realization of which the behaviour is directed, the argument fails for the simple reason that there may not in fact be any such state of affairs. Even if men generally succeed in fulfilling their purposes, they do sometimes fail, and the explanation of their embarking on the action must be the same whether the purpose is fulfilled or not. But this is enough to rule the end out of court as a determinant of the action. I do not share the qualms that some people feel about the idea of an event's being pulled into existence by one that does not yet exist, for these metaphors of pushing and pulling must not be taken too seriously; there is no great difficulty in regarding an earlier event as a function of a later one. But however little we are influenced by the metaphor, we cannot think it possible that an event may be pulled into existence by one that never exists at all.

But this, it may be said, is to take an unfairly naïve view of the argument. Its point is not that purposive behaviour is to be explained in terms of its actual achievement but rather that it has to be understood as tending towards a certain end, whether or not this end is actually attained. A general may not succeed in winning his battle, a chess player may not succeed in mating his opponent, but in order to make sense of their manoeuvres, we have to know that these are their aims. If we want to explain behaviour of this kind, the question which we have to ask is not what impels it but where it is directed; and the same applies at all levels down to the rat, or even the mechanical rat, in the maze.

This is all very well, but does it not concede the point at issue? For what is now singled out as the explanatory fact is not the end towards which the behaviour is directed, considered as a future event, but rather the agent's having this as his aim. The suggestion is that the agent behaves as he does because he has a conscious or unconscious need or desire for such and such a state of affairs to be realized. And why should not this be said to impel him?

At this point, the first argument dissolves into the second. For the answer which will be given to our last question is that very often these desires and needs do not exist independently of the behaviour which they are supposed to impel. No doubt there are cases in which a man is impelled to action by a felt desire for the end which he believes that the action will secure him, but even in many cases in which an agent would be said to be conscious of his purpose, his action is not preceded by any psychological occurrence which could figure as his desire for the end in question. His consciousness of his purpose, in so far as it is anything apart from his behaviour, may just consist in his ability to say what it is, if the occasion for this arises; it is not required that he should actually have formulated it even to himself. If the agent is not conscious of his purpose, it is still less likely that he will have had any distinctive experience which can be identified as the felt desire or need for the end towards which his action is directed. In such cases we may indeed conceive of the agent's desire as an unconscious mental state which drives him to act as he does; if we have a materialistic outlook, we may identify his desire or his need with some physical state of his organism; but to have recourse in this way to the unconscious or to physiology is to put up a theory which may account for the agent's having the motive that he has rather than to offer an analysis of what the motive is. What it provides at best is a problematic explanation of the existence of the motive; but what is wanted here, and what it does not provide, is an account of the motive as being itself an explanation of the action which it governs.

Again this is all quite true, but it proves very little. If one starts with the assumption that motives can cause the actions which they motivate only if they are 'ghostly thrusts', that is only if they take the form of distinctive experiences which precede or accompany the action, then indeed this argument will show that motives need not be causes. But the assumption is unjustified. It is true that a cause must be distinguishable from its effect, but there are other ways in which a motive can be independent of the action which it motivates than by figuring as a distinct experience, or even as an element in a psycho-analytical or physiological theory. The reason why we say that an action is done from such and such a motive may be no more than that the agent behaves or is disposed to behave in a certain fashion; but the point is that the description of the behaviour which constitutes his having the motive need not be identical with, or even include, a description of the action to which his having the motive leads him. On the contrary, if the assignment of the motive did not refer to something other than the action, if it did not associate the action with anything else at all, it is hard to see how it could have any explanatory force: merely to redescribe a phenomenon is not in any way to account for it. Yes it is, someone may say, if the redescription tells us more about the phenomenon; the assignment of a motive is explanatory in the sense that it enlarges our description of the action; it fills in an important gap in the story. But at this stage the dispute becomes merely verbal. If anyone wishes to give such a wide interpretation to the concept of an action that the motive from which the action is done is counted as a part of it, well and good: this is not perhaps a very felicitous usage, but it is manageable. The point still remains that if the initial description of the action does not include a reference to the motive, then the provision of this reference does link the behaviour which has been described to something beyond it, whether it be a distinctive experience or, as is more commonly the case, a further item or pattern of actual or potential behaviour; and it is only because it does this that the reference to the motive is explanatory. Indeed, this would seem to be the main characteristic of explanations in terms of motive, or more generally in terms of purpose. They serve to establish a lawlike connection between different pieces of behaviour.

This may operate in various ways. The simplest level of purposive behaviour is that which is ascribed to a homoeostatic system. The behaviour of the system on any given occasion is seen as exemplifying a uniform tendency to maintain equilibrium; it is purposive just in the sense that under varying conditions it operates so as to attain the same end-state. Much the same applies to the case of the animal, or the machine in the maze; what makes its behaviour purposive is that its agitation habitually continues until it emerges from the maze; in this instance the directional aspect of the behaviour is underlined by the fact that the individual trials may be stages in a process of learning, in which case they are related in a lawlike fashion to one another. If the animal is given a reward for its success, its appetite for the reward may be a measurable causal factor in the process of its training. The sense in which the animal looks for the reward, and so may be said to have this as its motive, is just that its behaviour would not be quite what it is if the reward had not been given to it on previous occasions. When it comes to simple human actions like putting on an overcoat to go out on a winter's day, our explanation derives its force from some such pre-supposition as that people in general under conditions of this kind do what they can to protect themselves against the cold. That this is the agent's motive on this particular occasion, rather than, say, a desire to appear well dressed, may indeed be discoverable only through his own avowal of it. But then his disposition to make this avowal, at any rate to himself, is a causal condition of his action. If he were not disposed to make it, then he would not in these circumstances be acting as he does. Otherwise there is no ground for concluding that this is his motive. In a more complicated case, like that of the general planning his battle, the general's desire for victory, if that is in fact his motive, may be exhibited in a fairly wide range of behaviour, apart from his conduct of this particular engagement. And here again, if the assignment of the motive is to have any explanatory force, we must be in a position to say that unless he behaved, or was disposed to behave, in these other ways he would not in the circumstances be planning the battle in the way that he does.

In all this there is little that is controversial. No one would deny that purposive behaviour fitted into some sort of pattern, and it seems pretty obvious that the assignment of motives could not be explanatory unless some lawlike connections were indicated by it. What may, however, still be disputed is that these connections are causal. It may be contended that the rough regularities in behaviour, which are all that we have seen to be required for the applicability of a purposive explanation, do not fit the standard model of the relation of cause and effect.

Once more this is partly a question of terminology. If we construe the causal relation in a strictly Humean fashion so that its terms can only be distinct events, then the objection holds. For we have seen that in many quite typical cases the motive may be present in the form of a disposition which, though distinct from the behaviour which it moti-vates, is still not exactly a distinct event. It seems to me, however, that even from the point of view of doing justice to the ordinary, let alone the scientific, use of causal language, this conception of the causal relation may be too restrictive. For one thing, we often want to be able to regard the absence of some circumstance as a causal factor, that is, to admit negative as well as positive conditions, and even this does not fit tidily into the Humean scheme. I have, of course, no quarrel with Hume's fundamental idea that causation must in the end be a matter of regular concomitance, but I suggest that causal relations should be regarded as holding between facts rather than events, where 'fact' is understood in the wide sense in which true propositions of any form can be taken as expressing facts. This involves no sacrifice, since in any cases where it is appropriate these causal statements about facts can be translated into statements about events; it merely extends the field of causal relations a little more widely. Then the sense in which an agent's motive may be said to be the cause of the action which it motivates is that given certain conditions the fact that the agent performs the action is inferable from the fact that he has the motive in virtue of a causal law.

But just as the first of the arguments which we listed dissolved into the second, so, if I am right in what I have just been saying, the second dissolves into the third; for now the question arises whether there really are such causal laws. On the face of it, it seems at least very doubtful. As I said when I first referred to this argument, it is surely possible for someone to act from a given motive on a particular occasion without its being the case either that whenever anyone has a motive of this kind he acts in this way, or that whenever anyone acts in this way he does so from this kind of motive. No doubt there must be some degree of regularity in the way in which motives lead to actions, for us to find the connection intelligible. If people hold very queer beliefs, they may indeed take means to a given end that others would not take; in this sense the connection between motive and action may even be quite idiosyncratic. It remains true, however, that people in general do what they believe will enable them to achieve their ends, and that these beliefs, though they may be false, are usually backed by a fair amount of evidence. The result is that there is at least a tendency for similar motives to be correlated with similar actions. This tendency is especially marked in the case of standing motives. The range of behaviour which we are prepared to ascribe to jealousy, or greed, or ambition is fairly narrow. Even so, it will be objected, such tendencies, at their very strongest, fall a long way short of being causal laws.

All this is true, but possibly not decisive; for it may be that we are looking for our causal laws in the wrong place. The point from which I think that we should start is that when a man is said to have acted in consequence of having such and such a motive, it is implied at least that if he had not had this motive he would not in the particular circumstances have acted as he did. But this is to say that the existence of the motive is taken to be a necessary condition of the action; not indeed a necessary condition of anyone's performing the action at any time, or even of the agent's performing it at any time, but a necessary condition of his performing it at just this juncture. The question then arises whether it is also taken to be part of a sufficient condition, and this is not easy to answer. The ground for arguing that it must be is that otherwise the ascription of the motive would not properly account for the action; we should have to allow that even granting the agent's motive and the rest of the attendant circumstances, including all the other aspects of the agent's mental and physical condition at that time, we could not entirely rely on the action's taking place; and to this extent its occurrence will still be unexplained and indeed inexplicable. There may, however, be those who are prepared to accept this consequence, so long as they can hold that there is a high probability in this situation of the action's taking place: that is, they may be satisfied with the hypothesis that if the situation were repeated a great number of times the action would take place very much more often than not. But since this leaves an element of arbitrariness, in that we have no answer to the question why it should ever not take place, it seems preferable to make the stronger claim, unless it can be shown to be untenable. The suggestion then would be that whenever an agent can properly be said to have acted exclusively from a given motive, the circumstances must be such that in any situation of this kind, indispensably including the presence of such a motive, an action of this kind invariably follows.

It is clear that if so strong a claim as this is to be made to appear even plausible, a great deal will have to be included in the situation, both in the way of positive and negative conditions. We must, however, avoid including so much detail in the description either of the situation or the action that our claim becomes trivial; our ground for saying that there is an invariable connection between situations and actions of the sorts in question must be not that either the situation or the action is unique. In other words, the types of fact which our laws connect must be envisaged as repeatable.

But where are these connections to be found? Surely it is idle to maintain that these laws exist if we are unable to produce any examples. Well, perhaps we can produce examples of a rather humble kind. Let us begin with the hypothesis that whenever a person has a desire for the existence of a state of affairs S and believes that it is immediately in his power to bring about S by performing the action A, but not by any other means, and there is no state of affairs S^1 such that he both prefers the existence of S^1 to that of S and believes it to be immediately in his power to bring about S^1, but not conjointly with S, then unless he is prevented he will perform the action A. This is not quite a tautology, since the existence of the agent's desire is supposed to be established independently of his taking any steps to satisfy it. On this account, indeed, it may even not be unconditionally true: there may be cases of inhibition which would have to be specially provided for. But even if this difficulty can be overcome, the hypothesis still falls short of what we want because its consequent is subject to a general proviso:

the person who satisfies the antecedent will perform the action A unless he is prevented. The question is whether this proviso can be dispensed with.

The way to dispense with it would be to list all the things that might prevent the action from being done, and insert them in the antecedent in the form of negative conditions. This would seem indeed to be an impossible undertaking at this level of generality: we could hardly hope to draw up an exhaustive list of negative conditions which would at this point apply to any action whatsoever. But in its application to particular instances, our general hypothesis will in any case dissolve into a number of more specific ones, according to the nature of the case: and once the relevant type of action and perhaps also certain features in the situation of the agent have been specified, it does not seem to me obvious that the list of negative conditions cannot be completed. Thus if the action is one which involves making a certain sort of hand move-ment, there may be a finite number of types of bodily disorder which would prevent it from being carried out; if it involves handling certain physical objects, there may be a finite number of ways in which they could become intractable; if the condition of the agent is specified, the types of psychological impediment to which he is then subject may again be finite in number: and if the number of these various factors is so limited, there seems to be no compelling reason to hold that they cannot be discovered and listed.

Of course we shall have no guarantee that the list is complete; but then we do not have such a guarantee in the case of laws of any other type. However carefully a generalization is formulated it must at least remain conceivable that it holds only under certain further conditions which we have failed to specify. Technically, if there are found to be such conditions, the generalization is falsified, though sometimes we prefer to regard it as having been incompletely stated. I do not, how-ever, agree with those who would read into every generalization of law a *ceteris paribus* clause which tacitly protects it from being falsified through the operation of factors which the proponent of the generaliza-tion did not foresee. No doubt it is too much to require, as John Stuart Mill did, that causal laws should hold unconditionally, if this is under-stood to imply that they would still be true no matter what else were true; for one law often depends upon others, so that its truth would not be preserved if these other laws were false. It is, however, not too much to require that the law should hold under any circumstances whatever that actually arise. If the field which it is designed to cover is restricted, this limitation can and should be made explicit.

If *ceteris paribus* clauses were allowable, the task of finding laws in the sphere of human action would be very much easier, but as our example has shown, these provisos would only increase the laws' security at the expense of their scientific interest. Even as it is, our hypothesis contained a stipulation which would often not be satisfied. It is by no means invariably true that when someone is aiming at a given end he believes that there is only one means of attaining it which it is immediately in his power to realize. Very often he will be presented with a choice of such means, so that it needs to be explained why he selects one of them rather than the others. I have no doubt that a number of examples could be found in which I should not know how this was to be done, but I suggest that quite a lot of cases would be covered by the following hypothesis: whenever the antecedent of our first hypothesis is satisfied, with the difference that the agent believes that it is immediately in his power to bring about S not only by performing the action A but also by performing the action A^1, but that he cannot perform both, then if he believes that A and A^1 are equally efficacious in bringing about S, but prefers what he expects to be the other consequences of A to those which he expects of A^1, he will, unless he is prevented, perform the action A. Again, if this is not to be tautologous, there must be evidence for his preferring the other expected consequences of A to those of A^1, independently of the fact that he does perform A, but I think it fair to assume that this will usually be available. Our hypothesis does not, of course, commit us to holding that whenever an agent has a choice between actions of the kind A and A^1 as means to a given type of end S, he will choose A. A man may well decide to walk to work on one occasion and take a taxi on another. But then the assumption is that there is a change in the circumstances, in the state of his health or his finances or the weather or some other combination of factors, which will sufficiently account for the variations in his preference. I admit, however, that until a set of such hypotheses has been formulated and tested, the degree of strength that we can attribute to generalizations about human conduct remains an open question.

The most that I would claim at this stage is that the difference between these generalizations and those that can be found to govern other natural phenomena is nowhere more than a difference of degree. What I have tried to show, in arguing that motives may be causes, is that there is no warrant for regarding explanation in terms of motives as something of a different order from the explanations that occur in the physical sciences. There is nothing about human conduct that would entitle us to conclude *a priori* that it was in any way less lawlike than any other sort of natural process.

But what of the argument that human actions conform to rules, that we are often more interested in judging whether and how far they are up to standard than in discovering how they came about? I cannot see that it is relevant. From the fact that we can estimate an action in terms of its conforming to a rule, it no more follows that the performance of the action is not causally explicable than it follows that the appearance of a rainbow is not causally explicable from the fact that it can be made the subject of an aesthetic judgment. To explain something causally does not preclude assessing it in other ways. But perhaps the suggestion is merely that to relate an action to a rule is one way of accounting for it, and, in the present state of our knowledge, a better way of accounting for it than trying to subsume it under dubious causal laws. I cannot even agree with this because I think that it presents us with a false antithesis. The only reason why it is possible to account for the performance of an action by relating it to a rule is that the recognition of the requirements of the rule is a factor in the agent's motivation. He may attach a value in itself to performing a certain sort of action correctly; he may see its correct performance as a means towards some further end; or it may be a combination of the two. In any event this is as much a causal explanation as any other explanation in terms of motive. The invocation of rules adds nothing to the general argument.

The same applies, in my view, to the argument that actions most often need to be understood in terms of their social contexts. A great deal is made by some philosophers of the fact that an action is not a mere physical movement. It has a significance which depends not only on the agent's intention and motive, but very frequently also on a complex of social factors. Think of the social norms and institutions that are involved in such commonplace actions as signing a cheque, signalling that one is going to turn when one is driving a car, saluting a superior officer, playing a card, shaking hands with someone to whom one has just been introduced, waving goodbye to a friend. To represent these merely as different sorts of hand-movements, which of course they also are, is to miss their significance; it is indeed to fail to represent them in their character as actions.

All this is true, except that it seems to be an arbitrary question what we are to regard as constituting an action: whether, for example, we choose to say that the motorist's action is one of putting out his hand or one of signalling that he is going to turn. Earlier on, I referred to the action of drinking a glass of wine as an instance of the way in which the same action can have a different significance in different social contexts: it would have been no less, but also no more correct if I had described this as an instance of the way in which the same physical process can in such different contexts become a different action.

Wherever we decide to draw the line between the characterization of an action and the assessment of its significance, the point remains that the physical movement has to be interpreted, and that in order to interpret it correctly it will often be necessary to understand its social as well as its personal implications.

But if we grant this point, what follows? Certainly not, as the philosophers who lay stress upon it seem to think, that these actions cannot be explained in causal terms. For when it comes to accounting for an action, the only way in which the social context enters the reckoning is through its influence upon the agent. The significance of the action is the significance that it has for him. That is to say, his idea that this is the correct, or expedient, or desirable thing to do in these circumstances is part of his motivation; his awareness of the social context and the effects which this has on him are therefore to be included in the list of initial conditions from which we seek to derive his performance of the action by means of a causal law. Whether such laws are discoverable or not may be an open question; but the fact that these items figure among the data has no important bearing on it.

That human behaviour has a point or meaning, in this sense, is not even an argument against the materialist thesis that it is all physiologically determined. This thesis is indeed highly speculative; we are very far from having a physiological theory which would account for people's actions in specific detail, let alone from being in a position to apply one. But if the motives which impel men to act are, let us say, projections of the state of their brains, there is no reason why this should not apply to their social responses as much as to anything else. But surely no purely physiological account could be an adequate description of an action. Obviously it could not; even if the study of the agent's brain could give us all the information that we needed beyond the observation of his physical movements, we should still have to decode it. But this is not an objection to holding that actions can be explained in these terms, any more than the fact that to talk about wave-lengths is not to describe colours is an objection to the science of optics. This also shows that even if I am wrong in assimilating motives to causes, it will not follow from this alone that human behaviour is not entirely subject to causal explanation. For the fact that we can explain an action in one manner by referring to the agent's motive leaves it a fully open question whether it cannot also be explained more scientifically in terms, say, of a physiological theory.

None of this settles the issue of determinism. I do not indeed think that it can be settled at this level, since I agree with those who hold that it should not be interpreted as an *a priori* question. It is of course true that not every event in human history could in fact be predicted. Not only would the making of each prediction itself then have to be predicted, and so *ad infinitum*, but as Professor Popper and others have rightly pointed out, it would follow that no one could ever have a new idea. But however comforting this may be to those who dislike conceiving of themselves as subjects for science, it does not go any way to prove that not all events in human history are susceptible of lawlike explanations. The strength of the determinists lies in the fact that there seems to be no reason why the reign of law should break down at this point, though this is an argument which seemed more convincing in the age of classical physics than it does today. The strength of the indeterminists lies in the fact that the specific theories which alone could vindicate or indeed give any substance to their opponents' case have not yet been more than sketched, though this is not to say that they never will be. Until such theories are properly elaborated and tested, I think that there is little more about this topic that can usefully be said.

A philosophical question which I have not here discussed, partly because I do not think that I have anything new to say about it, is whether the denial of determinism is implied in our usual ascriptions of moral and legal responsibility. In common with many other philosophers I used to hold that it was not, that in this respect the antithesis between the claims of free will and determinism was illusory, but in so far as this is a question of what people actually believe, I now think it more likely that I was wrong. This is indeed a matter for a social survey which, as I said before, would probably not yield a very clear result. I should, however, expect it to indicate that if it were shown to them that a man's action could be explained in causal terms, most people would take the view that he was not responsible for it. Since it is not at all clear why one's responsibility for an action should depend on its being causally inexplicable, this may only prove that most people are irrational, but there it is. I am indeed strongly inclined to think that our ordinary ideas of freedom and responsibility are very muddle-headed: but for what they are worth, they are also very firmly held. It would not be at all easy to estimate the social consequences of discarding them.

2 Neutrality in Political Science

Charles Taylor

I

1 A few years ago one heard it frequently said that political philosophy was dead, that it had been killed by the growth of science, the growth of positivism, the end of ideology, or some combination of these forces, but that, whatever the cause, it was dead. It is not my intention to rake over the coals of this old issue once more. I am simply using this as a starting point for a reflection on the relation between political science and political philosophy. For behind the view that political philosophy was dead, behind any view which holds that it *can* die, lies the belief that its fate can be separated from that of political science; for no one would claim that the science of politics is dead, however one might disapprove of this or that manner of carrying it on. It remains a perpetually possible, and indeed important enterprise.

The view was indeed that political science has come of age in freeing itself finally of the incubus of political philosophy. No more would its scope be narrowed and its work prejudiced by some value position which operated as an initial weight holding back the whole enterprise. The belief was that political science had freed itself from philosophy in becoming value-free and in adopting the scientific method. These two moves were felt to be closely connected; indeed, the second contains the first. For scientific method is, if nothing else, a dispassionate study of the facts as they are, without metaphysical presuppositions, and without value biases.

As Vernon van Dyke puts it:

> *science* and *scientific*, then, are words that relate to only one kind of knowledge, i.e., to knowledge of what is observable, and not to any other kinds of knowledge that may exist. They do not relate to alleged knowledge of the normative – knowledge of what ought to be. Science concerns what has been, is, or will be, regardless of the 'oughts' of the situation. (*Political Science*, p. 192.)

Those who could hold that political philosophy was dead, therefore, were those who held to a conception of the social sciences as *wertfrei*; like natural science, political science must dispassionately study the facts. This position received support from the views of the logical empiricists who had, for philosophers, an extraordinarily wide influence among scientists in general, and among the sciences of man in particular. Emboldened by their teaching, some orthodox political scientists tended to claim that the business of normative theory, making recommendations and evaluating different courses of action, could be entirely separated from the study of the facts, from the theoretical attempt to account for them.

Many, of course, had doubts; and these doubts seem to be growing today among political scientists. But they do not touch the thesis of the logical separation between fact and value. They centre rather around the possibility of setting one's values to one side when one undertakes the study of politics. The relation between factual study and normative beliefs is therefore thought of in the same traditional positivist way: that the relationship if any is from value to fact, not from fact to value. Thus, scientific findings are held to be neutral: that is, the facts as we discover them do not help to establish or give support to any set of values; we cannot move from fact to value. It is, however, often admitted that our values can influence our findings. This can be thought of as a vicious interference, as when we approach our work with bias which obscures the truth, or as something anodyne and inevitable, as when our values select for us the area of research on which we wish to embark. Or it can be thought of as a factor whose ill effects can be compensated by a clear consciousness of it: thus many theorists today recommend that one set out one's value position in detail at the beginning of a work so as to set the reader (and perhaps also the writer) on guard.

Value beliefs remain therefore as unfounded on scientific fact for the new generation of more cautious theorists as they were for the thinkers of the hey-day of 'value-freedom'. They arise, as it were, from outside factual study; they spring from deep choices which are independent of the facts. Thus David Easton, who goes on to attempt to show that

> whatever effort is exerted, in undertaking research we cannot shed our values in the way we remove our coats. (*The Political System*, p. 225.)

nevertheless states his acceptance at the outset of the 'working assumption' which is 'generally adopted today in the social sciences', and which

> holds that values can ultimately be reduced to emotional responses conditioned by the individual's total life-experiences. (p. 221.)

Thus there is no question of founding values on scientific findings. Emotional responses can be explained by life-experience, but not justified or shown to be appropriate by the facts about society:

> The moral aspect of a proposition ... expresses only the emotional
> response of an individual to a state of real or presumed facts. ...
> Although we can say that the aspect of a proposition referring to
> a fact can be true or false, it is meaningless to characterize the
> value aspect of a proposition in this way. (*Loc. cit.*)

The import of these words is clear. For, if value positions could be
supported or undermined by the findings of science, then they could
not simply be characterized as emotional responses, and we could not
say simply that it was *meaningless* (although it might be misleading)
to speak of them as true or false.

Political philosophy, therefore, as reasoned argument about fundamental political values, can be entirely separated from political science,
even on the mitigated positivist view which is now gaining ground
among political scientists. 'Values' steer, as it were, the process of
discovery, but they do not gain or lose plausibility by it. Thus although
values may be somehow ineradicable from political science, reasoned
argument concerning them would seem easily separable (though theorists
may differ as to whether this is wise or not: cf. Easton, *op. cit.*). Indeed,
it is hard to see in what such reasoned argument could consist. The
findings of science will be relevant to our values, of course, in this
sense, that they will tell us how to realize the goals we set ourselves.
We can reconstruct political science in the mould of a 'policy science',
like engineering and medicine, which shows us how to attain our goals.
But the goals and values still come from somewhere else; they are
founded on choices whose basis remains obscure.

The aim of this paper is to call into question this notion of the relation
of factual findings in politics to value positions, and thus the implied
relation between political science and political philosophy. In particular
my aim is to call into question the view that the findings of political
science leave us, as it were, as free as before, that they do not go some
way to establishing particular sets of values and undermining others.
If this view is shown to be mistaken, then we will have to recognize
a convergence between science and normative theory in the field of
politics.

It is usual for philosophers, when discussing this question, to
leave the realms of the sciences of man and launch into a study of
'good', or commending, or emotive meaning, and so on. I propose to
follow another course here, and to discuss the question first in connection with the disciplines in terms of which I have raised it, namely,
political philosophy and political science. When we have some understanding of the relations between these two on the ground, as it were,

it will be time to see if these are considered possible in the heaven of philosophy.

II   The thesis that political science is value neutral has maximum plausibility when we look at some of its detailed findings. That French workers tend to vote Communist may be judged deplorable or encouraging, but it does not itself determine us to accept either of these judgments. It stands as a fact, neutral between them.

If this were all there is to political science, the debate would end here. But it is no more capable than any other science of proceeding by the random collection of facts. At one time it was believed that science was just concerned with the correlation of observable phenomena – the observables concerned being presumed to lie unproblematically before our gaze. But this position, the offshoot of a more primitive empiricism, is abandoned now by almost everyone, even those in the empiricist tradition.

For the number of features which any given range of phenomena may exhibit, and which can thus figure in correlations, is indefinite; and this because the phenomena themselves can be classified in an indefinite number of ways. Any physical object can be classified according to shape, colour, size, function, aesthetic properties, relation to some process, etc.; when we come to realities as complex as political society, the case is no different. But among these features only a limited range will yield correlations which have some explanatory force.

Nor are these necessarily the most obtrusive. The crucial features, laws or correlations concerning which will explain or help to explain phenomena of the range in question, may at a given stage of the science concerned be only vaguely discerned if not frankly unsuspected. The conceptual resources necessary to pick them out may not yet have been elaborated. It is said, for instance, that the modern physical concept of mass was unknown to the ancients, and only slowly and painfully evolved through the searchings of the later middle ages. And yet it is an essential variable in the modern science. A number of more obtrusive features may be irrelevant; that is, they may not be such that they can be linked in functions explanatory of the phenomena. Obvious distinctions may be irrelevant, or have an entirely different relevance from that attributed to them, such as the distinction between Aristotle's 'light' and 'heavy' bodies.

Thus when we wish to go beyond certain immediate low-level correlations whose relevance to the political process is fairly evident, such as the one mentioned above; when we want to explain why French workers vote Communist, or why McCarthyism arises in the United

States in the late 'forties, or why the level of abstentionism varies
from election to election, or why new African regimes are liable
to military take-over, the features by reference to which we can explain
these results are not immediately in evidence. Not only is there a wide
difference of opinion about them, but we are not even sure that we have
as yet the conceptual resources necessary to pick them out. We may
easily argue that certain more obtrusive features, those pertaining, say,
to the institutional structure, are not relevant, while others less obtrusive, say, the character structure prevalent in certain strata of the society,
will yield the real explanation. We may, for instance, refuse to account
for McCarthyism in terms of the struggle between Executive and
Legislature, and look rather to the development of a certain personality
structure among certain sections of the American population. Or else
we may reject both these explanations and look to the role of a new
status group in American society, newly rich but excluded from the
Eastern Establishment. Or we may reject this, and see it as a result
of the new position of the United States in the world.

The task of theory in political science, one which cannot be foregone
if we are to elaborate any explanations worth the name, is to discover
what are the kinds of features to which we should look for explanations
of this kind. In which of the above dimensions are we to find an
explanation for McCarthyism? Or rather, since all of these dimensions
obviously have relevance, how are we to relate them in explaining the
political phenomena? The task of theory is to delineate the relevant
features in the different dimensions and their relation so that we have
some idea of what can be the cause of what, of how character affects
political process, or social structure affects character, or economic
relations affect social structure, or political process affects economic
relations, or vice versa; how ideological divisions affect party systems,
or history affects ideological divisions, or culture affects history, or
party systems affect culture, or vice versa. Before we have made some
at least tentative steps in this direction we don't even have an idea
where to look for our explanations; we don't know which facts to
gather.

It is not surprising, then, that political science should be the field
in which a great and growing number of 'theoretical frameworks'
compete to answer these questions. Besides the Marxist approach, and
the interest-group theory associated with the name of Bentley, we have
seen the recent growth of 'structural-functional' approaches under the
influence of systems theory; there have been approaches which have
attempted to relate the psychological dimension to political behaviour
(e.g. Lasswell), different applications of sociological concepts and

methods (e.g. Lipset and Almond), applications of game theory (e.g. Downs and Riker), and so on.

These different approaches are frequently rivals, since they offer different accounts of the features crucial for explanation and the causal relations which hold. We can speak of them, along with their analogues in other sciences, as 'conceptual structures' or 'theoretical frameworks', because they claim to delimit the area in which scientific enquiry will be fruitful. A framework does not give us at once all the variables which will be relevant and the laws which will be true, but it tells us what needs to be explained, and roughly by what kinds of factors. For instance, if we accept the principle of Inertia, certain ways of conceiving bodies and therefore certain questions are beyond the pale. To pursue them is fruitless, as was the search for what kept the cannon-ball moving in pre-Galilean physics. Similarly an orthodox Marxist approach cannot allow that McCarthyism can be explained in terms of early upbringing and the resultant personality structure.

But we can also see a theoretical framework as setting the crucial dimensions through which the phenomena can vary. For it sets out the essential functional relations by which they can be explained, while at the same time ruling out other functional relations belonging to other, rival frameworks. But the given set of functional relations defines certain dimensions in which the phenomena can vary; a given framework therefore affirms some dimensions of variation and denies others. Thus for a Marxist, capitalist societies do not vary as to who wields power, no matter what the constitution or the party in office; supposed variations in these dimensions, which are central to a great many theories, are sham; the crucial dimension is that concerning class structure.

In the more exact sciences theoretical discovery may be couched in the form of laws and be called principles, such as, e.g., of Inertia, or the Rectilinear Propagation of Light. But in the less exact, such as politics, it may consist simply of a general description of the phenomena couched in the crucial concepts. Or it may be implicit in a series of distinctions which a given theory makes (e.g. Aristotle's classification of the types of polity), or in a story of how the phenomena came to be (e.g. the myth of the Social Contract), or in a general statement of causal relations (e.g. Marx's Preface to *A Contribution to the Critique of Political Economy*).

But, however expressed, theoretical discovery can be seen as the delineating of the important dimensions of variation for the range of phenomena concerned.

III   Theoretical discovery of this kind is thus one of the concerns of modern political science, as we have seen. But it also is a traditional concern of what we call political philosophy, that is, normative political theory. It is not hard to see why. Normative theorists of the tradition have also been concerned with delineating crucial dimensions of variation – of course, they were looking for the dimensions which were significant for judging of the value of polities and policies rather than for explaining them. But the two types of research were in fact closely interwoven so that in pursuing the first they were also led to pursue the second.

Aristotle, for instance, is credited with a revision of Plato's threefold classification of political society which enhanced its explanatory value. He substituted for the number criterion a class criterion which gives a more revealing classification of the differences, and allows us to account for more: it made clear what was at stake between democracy and oligarchy; it opened up the whole range of explanations based on class composition, including the one for which Aristotle is known in history, the balancing role of the middle class.

But this revision was not unconnected with differences in the normative theory of the two thinkers. Plato attempted to achieve a society devoid of class struggle, either in the perfect harmony of the *Republic*, or in the single class state of the *Laws*. Aristotle is not above weaving the dream of the ideal state in one section of the *Politics*, but there is little connection between this and the political theory of the rest of the work. This latter is solidly based on the understanding that class differences, and hence divergence of interest and tension, are here to stay. In the light of this theory, Plato's idea in the *Republic* of overcoming class tension by discipline, education, a superior constitution, and so on, is so much pie-in-the-sky (not even very tasty pie in Aristotle's view, as he makes clear in Book II, but that is for other reasons).

Aristotle's insight in political science is incompatible with Plato's normative theory, at least in the *Republic*, and the *Politics* therefore takes a quite different line (for other reasons as well, of course). The difference on this score might perhaps be expressed in this way: both Plato and Aristotle held that social harmony was of crucial importance as a value. But Plato saw this harmony as achieved in the ending of all class conflict; Aristotle saw it as arising from the domestication of this conflict. But crucial to this dispute is the question of the causal relevance of class tension: is it an eradicable blot on social harmony, in the sense that one can say, for instance, that the violent forms of this conflict are? Or is it ineradicable and ever-present, only varying in its forms? In the first case one of the crucial dimensions of variation of our

32 *Charles Taylor*

explanatory theory is that concerning the presence or absence of class conflict. In the second case, this dimension is not even recognized as having a basis in fact. If this is so, then the normative theory collapses, or rather is shifted from the realm of political philosophy to that we call Utopia-building. For the idea of a society without class conflict would be one to which we cannot even approach. Moreover, the attempt to approach it would have all the dangerous consequences attendant on large-scale political changes based on illusory hopes.

Thus Plato's theory of the *Republic*, considered as the thesis that a certain dimension of variation is normatively significant, contains claims concerning the dimensions of variation which are relevant for explanation, for it is only compatible with those frameworks which concede the reality of the normatively crucial dimension. It is incompatible with any view of politics as the striving of different classes, or interest groups, or individuals against one another.

It is clear that this is true of any normative theory, that it is linked with certain explanatory theory or theories, and incompatible with others. Aristotle's dimension whereby different constitutions were seen as expressing and moulding different forms of life disappears in the atomistic conception of Hobbes. Rousseau's crucial dimension of the *Social Contract*, marking a sharp discontinuity between popular sovereignty and states of dependence of one form or another, could not survive the validation of the theories of Mosca, or Michels or Pareto.

Traditional political philosophy was thus forced to engage in the theoretical function that we have seen to be essential to modern political science; and the more elaborate and comprehensive the normative theory, the more complete and defined the conceptual framework which accompanied it. That is why political science can learn something still from the works of Aristotle, Hobbes, Hegel, Marx, and so on. In the tradition one form of enquiry is virtually inseparable from the other.

II

1   This is not a surprising result. Everyone recognized that political philosophers of the tradition were engaged in elaborating on, at least embryonic, political science. But, one might say, that is just the trouble; that is why political science was so long in getting started. Its framework was always set in the interests of some normative theory. In order to progress science must be liberated from all *parti pris* and be value-neutral. Thus if normative theory requires political science and cannot

be carried on without it, the reverse is not the case; political science can and should be separated from the older discipline. Let us examine some modern attempts to elaborate a science of politics to see if this is true.

Let us look first at S. M. Lipset's *Political Man*. In this work Lipset sets out the conditions for modern democracy. He sees societies as existing in two dimensions – conflict and consensus. Both are equally necessary for democracy. They are not mere opposites as a simple-minded view might assume. Conflict here is not seen as a simple divergence of interest, or the existence of objective relations of exploitation, but as the actual working out of these through the struggle for power and over policy.

> Surprising as it may sound, a stable democracy requires the manifestation of conflict or cleavage so that there will be struggle over ruling positions, challenges to parties in power, and shifts of parties in office; but without consensus – a political system allowing the peaceful 'play' of power, the adherence by the 'outs' to decisions made by the 'ins', and the recognition by the 'ins' of the rights of the 'outs' – there can be no democracy. The study of the conditions encouraging democracy must therefore focus on the sources of both cleavage and consensus. (*Political Man*, p. 21.)

And again,

> Cleavage – where it is legitimate – contributes to the integration of societies and organizations. (*Loc. cit.*)

The absence of such conflict, such as where a given group has taken over, or an all-powerful state can produce unanimity, or at least prevent diversity from expressing itself, is a sign that the society is not a free one. De Tocqueville feared (*Political Man*, p. 27) that the power of the state would produce apathy and thus do away even with consensus.

> Democracy in a complex society may be defined as a political system which supplies regular constitutional opportunities for changing the governing officials, and a social mechanism which permits the largest possible part of the population to influence major decisions by choosing among contenders for political office. (*Op. cit.*, p. 45.)

Such a society requires the organization of group interests to fight for their own goals – provided that this is done in a peaceful way, within the rules of the game, and with the acceptance of the arbiter in the form of elections by universal suffrage. If groups are not organized, they have no real part, their interests are neglected, and they cannot have their share of power; they become alienated from the system.

Now this view can at once be seen to conflict with a Rousseauian view which disapproves of the organization of 'factions', and which sees consensus as arising out of isolated individuals. It also goes against the modern conservative view that to organize people on a class basis gratuitously divides the society. In face of Rousseau, Lipset holds that the absence of close agreement among all concerning the general will is not a sign that something has gone wrong. There are ineradicable basic divergences of interest; they have to be adjusted. If we get to some kind of conflictless state, this can only be because some of the parties have been somehow done down and prevented from competing. For Lipset, absence of conflict is a sure sign that some groups are being excluded from the public thing.

This difference closely parallels the one mentioned above between Plato and Aristotle. Indeed, Lipset points out on several occasions the similarity between his position and that of Aristotle. And it is clear that it is a difference of the same kind, one in which a normative theory is undermined because the reality of its crucial dimension of variation is challenged. A similar point can be made concerning the difference with conservatives who allow for divergence in the state, but resist class parties. Here the belief is that the divergence is gratuitous, that the real differences lie elsewhere, either in narrower or in broader interests, and that these are obfuscated and made more difficult of rational adjustment by class divisions. More, the state can be torn apart if these divisions are played up. Conservatives tend to feel about class in politics as liberals do about race in politics. Once again, Lipset's view would undermine the position, for he holds that class differences are at the centre of politics, and cannot be removed except by reducing the number of players, as it were. They are therefore the very stuff of democratic politics, provided they are moderately and peacefully expressed. The struggle between rich and poor is ineradicable; it can take different forms, that's all.

Attempts to break outside of this range are thus irrational and dysfunctional. Irrational, because based on false premises; and dysfunctional, because the goal of conflictlessness or absence of class tension can only be achieved at the expense of features of the system which most will accept as valuable; by oppressing some segment of the population, or by its apathy and lack of organization. This is, of course, the usual fate of theories with a false factual base in politics; as was remarked above, they are not just erroneous, but positively dangerous.

It can be seen that the value consequences of Lipset's theory are fairly widespread even restricting ourselves to the alternatives which it negates or undermines. An examination of some of the factors which tend to strengthen democracy according to the theory will increase this list of rejected alternatives. Lipset holds that economic development is conducive to the health of democracy, in that, *inter alia*, it narrows gaps in wealth and living standards, tends to create a large middle class, and increases the 'cross-pressures' working to damp down class conflict. For a society cannot function properly as a democracy unless, along with an articulation of class differences, there is some consensus which straddles them. Now Lipset's 'cross-pressures' – typically exercised by religious affiliation, for instance, which cuts across class barriers – are the 'opiates' of a strict Marxist. For they are integrators which prevent the system coming apart at the social seam, and thus prevent the class war from coming to a head. But we are not dealing here simply with two value-judgments about the same facts understood in the same way. The crucial difference is that for Lipset the stage beyond the class struggle doesn't and cannot exist; the abolition of the conflict in unanimity is impossible; his view is: 'the rich ye have always with you'. But in this case the integrating factors cease to be 'opiates', breeding false consciousness and hiding the great revolutionary potentiality. There is nothing there to hide. Lipset's view therefore negates revolutionary Marxism in a direct way – in the same way as it negates the views above – by denying that the crucial dimensions of variation have reality.

But if we examine this last example a little more closely, we can see even wider normative consequences of Lipset's view. For if we rule out the transformation to the classless society, then we are left with the choice between different kinds of class conflict: a violent kind which so divides society that it can only survive under some form of tyranny, or one which can reach accommodations in peace. This choice, set out in these terms, virtually makes itself for us. We may point out that this does not cover the range of possibility, since there are also cases in which the class conflict is latent, owing to the relative absence of one party. But this is the result of underdevelopment, of a lack of education, or knowledge, or initiative on the part of the underprivileged. Moreover, it unfailingly leads to a worsening of their position relative to the privileged. As Lipset says in the statement of his political position which forms the introduction to the Anchor Edition of *Political Man*,

> I believe with Marx that all privileged classes seek to maintain and *enhance* their advantages against the desire of the under-privileged to reduce them. (Anchor Edition, p. xxii, emphasis in original.)

Thus, for Lipset, the important dimension of variation for political societies can be seen as L-shaped, as it were. On one end lie societies where the divisions are articulated but are so deep that they cannot be contained without violence, suppression of liberty and despotic rule; on the other end lie societies which are peaceful but oligarchic and which are therefore run to secure the good of a minority ruling group. At the angle are the societies whose differences are articulated but which are capable of accommodating them in a peaceful way, and which therefore are characterized by a high degree of individual liberty and political organization.

Faced with this choice, it is hard to opt for anywhere else but the angle. For to do so is either to choose violence and despotism and suppression over peace, rule by consent and liberty, or to choose a society run more for the benefit of a minority over a society run more for the benefit of all, a society which exploits and/or manipulates over a society which tends to secure the common good as determined by the majority. Only in the angle can we have a society really run for the common good, for at one end is oligarchy based on an unorganized mass, at the other despotism.

Lipset himself makes this option explicit:

> A basic premise of this book is that democracy is not only or even primarily a means through which different groups can attain their ends or seek the good society; it is the good society itself in operation. Only the give-and-take of a free society's internal struggles offers some guarantee that the products of the society will not accumulate in the hands of a few power-holders, and that men may develop and bring up their children without fear of persecution. (p. 403.)

This is a succinct statement of the value position implicit in *Political Man*, but it is wrongly characterized as a 'premise'. The use of this term shows the influence of the theory of value-neutrality, but it is misplaced. It would be less misleading to say 'upshot', for the value position flows out of the analysis of the book. Once we accept Lipset's analysis concerning the fundamental role of class in politics, that it always operates even when division is not overt, and that it can never be surmounted in unanimity, then we have no choice but to accept democracy as he defines it, as a society in which most men are doers, take their fate in their own hands, or have a hand in determining it, and at least reduce the degree to which injustice is done to them, or their interests are unfavourably handled by others, as the good society.

11   But now we have gone far beyond the merely negative consequences noted above for Marxism, conservatism or Rousseau's general will. We are saying that the crucial dimensions of variation of Lipset's theory not only negate dimensions crucial to other normative theories but support one of their own, which is implicit in the theory itself.

But this conclusion, if true, goes against the supposed neutrality of scientific fact. Let us examine it a bit more closely.

We have said above that faced with the choice between a regime based on violence and suppression, and one based on consent, between regimes which serve the interests more or less of all versus regimes which serve the interests only of a minority, the choice is clear. Is this simply a rhetorical flourish, playing on generally accepted values among readers? Or is the connection more solid?

Granted that we wish to apply 'better' and 'worse' to regimes characterized along this dimension, can one conceive of reversing what seemed above to be the only possible judgment? Can one say: yes, a regime based on minority rule with violent suppression of the majority is better than one based on general consensus, where all have a chance to have their interests looked to? Certainly this is not a logically absurd position in itself. But if someone accepted the framework of Lipset and proceeded to make this judgment, surely we would expect him to go on and mention some other considerations which led him to this astounding conclusion. We might expect him to say, that only minorities are creative, that violence is necessary to keep men from stagnating, or something of this kind. But supposing he said nothing of the sort? Supposing he just maintained that violence was better than its opposite, not qua stimulus to creativity, or essential element in progress, but just qua violence; that it was better that only the minority interest be served, not because the minority would be more creative but just because it was a minority? A position of this kind would be unintelligible. We could understand that the man was dedicating himself to the furtherance of such a society, but the use of the words 'good' or 'better' would be totally inappropriate here, for there would be no visible grounds for applying them. The question would remain open whether the man had understood these terms, whether, e.g., he hadn't confused 'good' with 'something which gives me a kick', or 'aesthetically pleasing'.

But, it might be argued, this is not a fair example. Supposing our unorthodox thinker did adduce other grounds for preferring violence and majority rule? Surely, then, he would be permitted to differ from us? Yes, but then it is very dubious whether he could still accept Lipset's framework. Suppose, for instance, that one believed (as Hegel did about war) that violence was morally necessary from time to time for the well-being of the state. This would not be without effect on one's conception of political science; the range of possible regimes would be different from that which Lipset gives us; for peaceful democratic regimes would suffer a process of stagnation which would render them less viable; they would not in fact be able to maintain themselves, and thus the spectrum of possible regimes would be different from the one Lipset presents us with; the most viable regime would be one which was able to ration violence and maintain it at a non-disruptive level without falling over into stagnation and decay.

But why need this change of values bring along with it a change in explanatory framework? We seem to be assuming that the evils of internal peace must be such as to have a political effect, to undermine the viability of the political society. Is this assumption justified? Normally, of course, we would expect someone putting forward a theory of this kind to hold that inner violence is good because it contributes to the dynamism, or creativity of people, or progress of the society, or something of the kind which would make peaceful societies less viable. But supposing he chose some other benefits of violence which had nothing to do with the survival or health of political society? Let us say that he held that violence was good for art, that only in societies rent by internal violence could great literature, music, painting be produced? The position, for instance, of Harry Lime in *The Third Man?*

This certainly is a possible case. But let us examine it more closely. Our hypothetical objector has totally forsaken the ground of politics, and is making his judgment on extraneous (here aesthetic) grounds. He cannot deny that, setting these grounds aside, the normal order of preference is valid. He is saying in effect that, although it is better abstracting from aesthetic considerations that society be peaceful, nevertheless this must be overridden in the interests of art.

This distinction is important. We must distinguish between two kinds of objection to a given valuation. It may be that the valuation is accepted, but that its verdict for our actual choices is overridden, as it were, by other more important valuations. Thus we may think that freedom of speech is always a good, while reluctantly conceding that it must be curtailed in an emergency because of the great risks it would entail here. We are in this case self-consciously curtailing a good. The other kind of objection is the one which undermines the valuation itself, seeks to deprive the putative good of its status. This is what Lipset does, for instance, to spiritual followers of Rousseau in showing that their harmony can only be the silence of minority rule.[1] In one case we are conceding that the thing in question does really have the properties which its proponents attribute to it (e.g., that free speech does contribute to justice, progress, human development, or whatever), but we are adding that it also has other properties which force us to

---

[1] Of course, Rousseau's general will may remain a value in the hypothetical world he casts for it, but that concerns Utopia building, not political philosophy.

proceed against it (e.g., it is potentially disruptive) temporarily or permanently. In the other case, we are denying the condition in question the very properties by which it is judged good (e.g., that the legislation of the society without cleavage emanates from the free conscious will of all its citizens). Let us call these two objections respectively overriding and undermining.

Now what is being claimed here is that an objection which undermines the values which seem to arise out of a given framework must alter the framework; that in this sense the framework is inextricably connected to a certain set of values; and that if we can reverse the valuation without touching the framework, then we are dealing with an overriding.

To go back to the example above. In order to undermine the judgment against violence we would have to show that it does not have the property claimed for it. Now obviously violence has the property of killing and maiming which goes some way towards putting it in the list of undesirables, one might think irrevocably; so that it could only be overridden. But here we are not dealing with a judgment about violence *per se*, but rather with one concerning the alternative of peace and violence; and the judgment rests on the ground that violence has properties which peace has not, that the evils obviously attributed to violence are effectively avoided by peace. But if one can show that peace leads to stagnation, and thus to breakdown (and hence eventual chaos or violence) or foreign conquest, then the supposed gap between the two narrows. On the contrary, one is presented with a new alternative, that between more or less controlled violence and the destructive uncontrolled kind associated with internal breakdown or foreign conquest. What the undermining job has done is to destroy the alternative on which the original judgment was based, and thus deprive the previously preferred alternative of its differential property for which it was valued.

But any undermining of this kind is bound to alter the explanatory framework of which the original alternative was an essential part. If we cannot maintain a peaceful polity, then the gamut of possibilities is very different, and Lipset is guilty of neglecting a whole host of factors, to do with the gamut tension-stagnation.

To take the other example, let our objector make a case for rule by the minority. Let him claim that only the minority are creative, that if they are not given preference, then they will not produce, and then everyone will suffer. Thus the supposed difference between rule for the minority and that for all, viz., that the ordinary bloke gets something out of the second that he doesn't out of the first, is set aside; rather the opposite turns out to be the case. The value is undermined. But so is the political framework altered, for now we have an élitist thesis about the importance of minority rule; another variable has entered the picture which was not present in the previous framework and which cuts across it, in so far as the previous framework presented the possibility of good progressive societies run for all.

Let us hold, however, that violence or élite rule is good for painting, and we have an over-ruling; for it remains the case that it would be better to have no violence and everybody getting a square deal, but alas. . . .

Thus the framework does secrete a certain value position, albeit one that can be overridden. In general we can see this arising in the following way: the framework gives us as it were the geography of the range of phenomena in question, it tells us how they can vary, what are the major dimensions of variation. But since we are dealing with matters which are of great importance to human beings, a given map will have, as it were, its own built-in value-slope. That is to say, a given dimension of variation will usually determine for itself how we are to judge of good and bad, because of its relation to obvious human wants and needs.

Now this may seem a somewhat startling result, since it is well known that there are wide differences over what human needs, desires and purposes are. Not that there is not a wide area of agreement over basic things like life; but this clearly breaks down when one tries to extend the list. There can thus be great disagreement over the putative human need for self-expression or for autonomous development, both of which can and do play important parts in debates and conflicts over political theory.

Does this mean, therefore, that we can reject the previous result and imagine a state of affairs where we could accept the framework of explanation of a given theory, and yet refuse the value-judgments it secretes, because we took a different view of the schedule of human needs?[2] Or, to put it another way, does this mean that the step between accepting a framework of explanation and accepting a certain notion of the political good is mediated by a premise concerning human needs,

---

[2] This could involve either an undermining or an over-riding of the value-judgment. For we can deny something, a condition or outcome, the property by which it is judged good not only by denying it a property by which it fulfils certain human needs, wants or purposes, but also by denying that these needs, wants or purposes exist. And we can over-ride the judgment that it is good by pointing to other needs, wants or purposes that it frustrates.

which may be widely enough held to go unnoticed, but which nevertheless can be challenged, thus breaking the connection? The answer is no. For the connection between a given framework of explanation and a certain notion of the schedule of needs, wants and purposes which seems to mediate the inference to value theory is not fortuitous. If one adopted a quite different view of human need, one would upset the framework. Thus to pursue another example from Lipset, stable democracies are judged better than stable oligarchies, since the latter can only exist where the majority is so uneducated and tradition-bound or narrowed that it has not yet learned to demand its rights. But suppose we tried to upset this judgment by holding that underdevelopment is good for men, that they are happier when they are led by some unquestioned norms, don't have to think for themselves, and so on? One would then be reversing the value-judgment. But at the same time one would be changing the framework. For we are introducing a notion of anomie here, and we cannot suppose this factor to exist without having some important effect on the working of political society. If anomie is the result of the development of education and the breakdown of tradition, then it will affect the stability of the societies which promote this kind of development. They will be subject to constant danger of being undermined as their citizens, suffering from anomie, look for havens of certainty. If men are made unhappy by democracy, then undoubtedly it is not as good as its protagonists make out, but it is not so viable either.

The view above that we could accept the framework of explanation and reject the value conclusion by positing a different schedule of needs cannot be sustained. For a given framework is linked to a given conception of the schedule of human needs, wants and purposes, such that, if the schedule turns out to have been mistaken in some significant way, the framework itself cannot be maintained. This is for the fairly obvious reason that human needs, wants and purposes have an important bearing on the way people act, and that therefore one has to have a notion of the schedule which is not too wildly inaccurate if one is to establish the framework for any science of human behaviour, that of politics not excepted. A conception of human needs thus enters into a given political theory, and cannot be considered something extraneous which we later add to the framework to yield a set of value-judgments.

This is not to say that there cannot be needs or purposes which we might add to those implicit in any framework, and which would not alter the framework since their effect on political events might be marginal. But this would at most give us the ground of an over-ruling, not for an undermining. In order to undermine the valuation we would have to show that the putative need fulfilled was not a need, or that what looked like fulfilling a need, or a want or a human purpose was really not so, or really did the opposite. Now even an over-ruling might destroy the framework, if a new need were introduced which was important enough motivationally to dictate quite different behaviour. But certainly an undermining, which implies that one has misidentified the schedule of needs, would do so.

III   It would appear from the above example that the adoption of a framework of explanation carries with it the adoption of the 'value-slope' implicit in it, although the valuations can be over-ruled by considerations of an extra-political kind. But it might be objected that the study of one example is not a wide enough base for such a far-reaching conclusion. The example might even be thought to be peculiarly inappropriate because of Lipset's closeness to the tradition of political philosophy, and particularly his esteem for Aristotle.

If we wish, however, to extend the range of examples, we can see immediately that Lipset's theory is not exceptional. There are, for instance, a whole range of theories in which the connection between factual base and valuation is built-in, as it were, to the conceptual structure. Such is the case of many theories which make use of the notion of function. To fulfil a function is to meet a requirement of some kind, and when the term is used in social theory, the requirement concerned is generally connected with human needs, wants and purposes. The requirement or end concerned may be the maintenance of the political system which is seen as essential to man, or the securing of some of the benefits which political systems are in a position to attain for men – stability, security, peace, fulfilment of some wants, and so on. Since politics is largely made up of human purposeful activity a characterization of political societies in terms of function is not implausible. But in so far as we characterize societies in terms of their fulfilling in different ways and to different degrees the same set of functions, the crucial dimension of variation for explanatory purposes is also a normatively significant one. Those societies which fulfil the functions more completely are *pro tanto* better.

We can take as an example the 'structural-functional' theory of Gabriel Almond as outlined in his *Politics of the Developing Areas*. Among the functions Almond outlines that all polities must fulfil is that of 'interest articulation'. It is an essential part of the process by which the demands, interests and claims of members of a society can be brought to bear on government and produce some result. Almond sees four main types of structures as involved in interest articulation.³ Of three of these (institutional, non-associational and anomic interest groups), he says that a prominent role for them in interest articulation tends to indicate poor 'boundary maintenance', between society and polity. Only the fourth (associational interest groups) can carry the main burden of interest articulation in such a way as to maintain a smooth-running system 'by virtue of the regulatory role of associational interest groups in processing raw claims or interest articulations occurring elsewhere in the society and the political system, and directing them in an orderly way and in aggregable form through the party system, legislature, and bureaucracy'.⁴

The view here is of a flow of raw demands which have to be processed by the system before satisfaction can be meted out. If the processing is inefficient, then the satisfaction will be less, the system will increase frustration, uncertainty, and often as a consequence instability. In this context boundary maintenance between society and polity is important for clarity and efficiency. Speaking of the functions of articulation and aggregation together, Almond says:

> Thus, to attain a maximum flow of inputs of raw claims from the society, a low level of processing into a common language of claims is required which is performed by associational interest groups. To assimilate and transform these interests into a relatively small number of alternatives of policy and personnel, a middle range of processing is necessary. If these two functions are performed in substantial part before the authoritative governmental structures are reached, then the output functions of rule-making and rule application are facilitated, and the political and governmental processes become calculable and responsible. The outputs may be related to and controlled by the inputs, and thus circulation becomes relatively free by virtue of good boundary maintenance or division of labour.⁵

Thus in characterizing different institutions by the way they articulate or aggregate interests, Almond is also evaluating them. For obviously a society with the above characteristics is preferable to one without, where, that is, there is less free circulation, where 'outputs' correspond less to 'inputs' (what people want, claim or demand), where government is less responsible, and so on. The characterization of the system in terms of function contains the criteria of 'eufunction' and 'dysfunction', as they are sometimes called. The dimension of variation leaves only one answer to the question, which is better?, because of the clear relation in which it stands to men's wants and needs.

³ *Politics of the Developing Areas*, p. 33.
⁴ *Ibid.*, pp. 35–36.
⁵ *Ibid.*, p. 39.

Theories of this kind include not only those which make explicit use of 'function', but also other derivatives of systems theory and frameworks which build on the analogy with organisms. This might be thought to include, for instance, David Easton (cf. *A Framework for Political Analysis* and *A Systems Analysis of Political Life*) and Karl Deutsch (*The Nerves of Government*). For the requirements by which we will judge the performance of different political systems are explicit in the theory.

But what about theories which set out explicitly to separate fact from evaluations, to 'state conditions' without in any way 'justifying preferences'? What about a theory of the 'behavioural' type, like that of Harold Lasswell?

IV   Harold Lasswell is clearly a believer in the neutrality of scientific findings. Lasswell is openly committed to certain values, notably those of the democratic society as he defines it, a society 'in which human dignity is realized in theory and fact'.[6] He believes that scientific findings can be brought to bear on the realization of these goals. A science so oriented is what he calls a 'policy science'. But this does not affect the neutrality of the findings: a policy science simply determines a certain grouping and selection of findings which help us to encompass the goal we have set. It follows that if there are policy sciences of democracy, 'there can also be a policy science of tyranny'.[7]

In Lasswell's 'configurative analysis', then, both fact and valuation enter; but they remain entirely separable. The following passage from the introduction of *Power and Society* makes the point unambiguously:

> The present conception conforms . . . to the philosophical tradition in which politics and ethics have always been closely associated. But it deviates from the tradition in giving full recognition to the existence of two distinct components in political theory – the empirical propositions of political science and the value judgments of political doctrine. Only statements of the first kind are formulated in the present work. (p. xiii.)

Yet the implied separation between factual analysis and evaluation is belied by the text itself. In the sections dealing with different types of polity,[8] the authors introduce a number of dimensions of variation of political society. Politics vary (1) as to the allocation of power (between autocracy, oligarchy, republic), (2) as to the scope of power (society either undergoes greater regimentation or liberalization), (3) as to the

---

[6] 'The Democratic Character,' in *Political Writings*, p. 473.
[7] *Ibid.*, p. 471n.
[8] *Power and Society*, ch. 9, sections 3 and 4.

concentration or dispersion of power (taking in questions concerning the separation of powers, or federalism), (4) as to the degree to which a rule is equalitarian (the degree of equality in power potential), (5) the degree to which it is libertarian or authoritarian, (6) the degree to which it is impartial, (7) and the degree to which it is juridical or tyrannical. Democracy is defined as a rule which is libertarian, juridical and impartial.

It is not surprising to find one's sympathies growing towards democracy as one ploughs through this list of definitions. For they leave us little choice. Dimension (5) clearly determines our preference. Liberty is defined not just in terms of an absence of coercion, but of genuine responsibility to self. 'A rule is libertarian where initiative, individuality and choice are widespread; authoritarian, if obedience, conformity and coercion are characteristic.'[9] Quoting Spinoza with approval, Lasswell and Kaplan come down in favour of a notion of liberty as the capacity to 'live by . . . free reason'. 'On this conception, there is liberty in a state only where each individual has sufficient self-respect to respect others.'[10]

Thus it is clear that liberty is preferable to its opposite. Many thinkers of the orthodox school, while agreeing with this verdict, might attribute it simply to careless wording on the author's part, to a temporary relaxation of that perpetual vigil which must be maintained against creeping value bias. It is important to point out therefore that the value force here is more than a question of wording. It lies in the type of alternative which is presented to us: on one hand, a man can be manipulated by others, obeying a law and standards set up by others which he cannot judge; on the other hand, he is developed to the point where he can judge for himself, exercise reason and apply his own standards; he comes to respect himself and is more capable of respecting others. If this is really the alternative before us, how can we fail to judge freedom better (whether or not we believe there are overriding considerations)?

Dimension (6) also determines our choice. 'Impartiality' is said to 'correspond in certain ways to the concepts of "justice" in the classical tradition',[11] and an impartial rule is called a 'commonwealth', 'enhancing the value position of all members of the society impartially, rather than that of some restricted class'.[12] Now if the choice is simply between a régime which works for the common good and a régime which works

[9] *Power and Society*, p. 228.
[10] *Ibid.*, p. 229.
[11] *Ibid.*, p. 231.
[12] *Loc. cit.*

46   *Charles Taylor*

for the good of some smaller group, there is no doubt which is better in the absence of any overriding considerations.

Similarly dimension (7) is value-determinate. 'Juridical' is opposed to 'tyrannical' and is defined as a state of affairs where 'decisions are made in accord with specified rules . . . rather than arbitrarily'[13] or where a 'decision is challenged by an appraisal of it in terms of . . . conditions, which must be met by rulers as well as ruled'. Since the alternative presented here is *arbitrary* decision, and one which cannot be checked by any due process, there is no question which is preferable. If we had wanted to present a justification of rule outside law (such as Plato did), we would never accept the adjective 'arbitrary' in our description of the alternative to 'juridical'.

As far as the other dimensions are concerned, the authors relate them to these three key ones, so that they too cannot be seen as neutral, although their value relevance is derivative. Thus voluntarization is better for liberty than regimentation, and the dispersion of power can be seen as conducive to juridicalness. In short, we come out with a full-dress justification of democracy, and this in a work which claims neutrality. The work, we are told in the introduction, 'contains no elaborations of political doctrine, of what the state and society *ought* to be'.[14] Even during the very exposition of the section on democracy, there are ritual disclaimers: for instance, when the term 'justice' is mentioned, a parenthesis is inserted: 'the present term, however, is to be understood altogether in a descriptive, non-normative sense';[15] and at the end of the chapter: 'the formulations throughout are descriptive rather than normatively ambiguous'.[16]

But neutral they are not, as we have seen: we cannot accept these descriptions and fail to agree that democracy is a better form of government than its opposite (a 'tyrannical', 'exploitative', 'authoritarian' rule: you can take your choice). Only the hold of the neutrality myth can hide this truth from the authors.

Of course these sections do not represent adequately Lasswell's total work. Indeed, one of the problems in discussing Lasswell is that he has espoused a bewildering variety of conceptual frameworks of explanation. This is evident from a perusal of *Power and Society* alone, quite apart from his numerous other works. These may all cohere in some unified system, but if this is the case, it is far from obvious. Yet the link between factual analysis and evaluation reappears in each of the

[13] *Power and Society*, p. 232.
[14] *Ibid.*, p. xi.
[15] *Ibid.*, p. 231.
[16] *Ibid.*, p. 239.

different approaches. There is not space to cover them all; one further example will have to suffice here.

In the later psychiatrically oriented works, such as *Power and Personality*, or "The Democratic Character',[17] the goal explicitly set for policy science is democracy. But the implication that this is a goal chosen independently of what is discovered to be true about politics is belied all along the line. For the alternative to a society where people have a 'self-system' which suits the democratic character is one in which various pathologies, often of a dangerous kind, are rampant. The problem of democracy is to create, among other things, a self-system which is 'multi-valued, rather than single-valued, and . . . disposed to share rather than to hoard or to monopolize'.[18] One might have some quarrel with this: perhaps single-minded people are an asset to society. But after seeing the alternative to multi-valuedness as set out in the 'Democratic Character',[19] one can understand why Lasswell holds this view. Lasswell lays out for us a series of what he describes frankly at one point as 'character deformations'.[20] In talking about the *homo politicus* who concentrates on the pursuit of power, he remarks

> The psychiatrist feels at home in the study of ardent seekers after power in the arena of politics because the physician recognizes the extreme egocentricity and sly ruthlessness of some of the paranoid patients with whom he has come in contact in the clinic. (p. 498.)

The point here is not that Lasswell introduces valuation illegitimately by the use of subtly weighted language, or unnecessarily pejorative terms. Perhaps politicians do tend to approximate to unbalanced personalities seeking to make up deprivation by any means. The point is that, if this is true, then some important judgments follow about political psychiatry. And these are not, as it were, suspended on some independent value-judgment, but arise from the fact themselves. There *could* be a policy science of tyranny, but then there could also be a medical science aimed at producing disease (as when nations do research into bacteriological warfare). But we couldn't say that the second was more worthy of pursuit than the first, unless we advanced some very powerful overriding reasons (which is what proponents of bacteriological warfare try – unsuccessfully – to do). The science of health, however, needs no such special justification.

[17] *Political Writings.*
[18] *Ibid.*, pp. 497–8.
[19] *Ibid.*, pp. 497–502.
[20] *Ibid.*, p. 500.

III

1   The thesis we have been defending, however plausible it may appear
in the context of a discussion of the different theories of political
science, is unacceptable to an important school of philosophy today.
Throughout the foregoing analysis, philosophers will have felt uneasy.
For this conclusion tells against the well-entrenched doctrine according
to which questions of value are independent of questions of fact; the
view which holds that before any set of facts we are free to adopt an
indefinite number of value positions. According to the view defended
here, on the other hand, a given framework of explanation in political
science tends to support an associated value position, secretes its own
norms for the assessment of polities and policies.

It is of course this philosophical belief which, because of its immense
influence among scientists in general and political scientists as well,
has contributed to the cult of neutrality in political science, and the
belief that genuine science gives no guidance as to right and wrong.

It is time, therefore, to come to grips with this philosophical view.

There are two points about the use of 'good' which are overlooked
or negated by the standard 'non-naturalist' view: (1) to apply 'good'
may or may not be to commend, but it is always to claim that there are
reasons for commending whatever it is applied to, (2) to say of something
that it fulfils human needs, wants or purposes always constitutes a
prima facie reason for calling it 'good', that is, for applying the term in
the absence of overriding considerations.[21]

Now the non-naturalist view, as expressed, for instance, by Hare
or Stevenson, denies both these propositions. Its starting point is the
casting of moral argument in deductive form – all the arguments against
the so-called 'naturalistic fallacy' have turned on the validity of deductive inference. The ordinary man may think that he is moving from a
factual consideration about something to a judgment that it is good or
bad, but in fact one cannot deduce a statement concerning the goodness
or badness of something from a statement attributing some descriptive
property to it. Thus the ordinary man's argument is really an enthy-
meme: he is assuming some major premise: when he moves from 'X
will make men happy' to 'X is good', he is operating with the suppressed

---

[21] We might also speak of 'interests' here, but this can be
seen as included in 'wants' and 'needs'. Interest may deviate
from want, but can only be explicited in terms of such concepts
as 'satisfaction', 'happiness', 'unhappiness', etc., the criteria for
whose application are ultimately to be found in what we want.

premise 'What makes men happy is good', for only by adding this can one derive the conclusion by valid inference.

To put the point in another way: the ordinary man sees 'X will make men happy' as the reason for his favourable verdict on it. But on the non-naturalist view, it is a reason only because he accepts the suppressed major premise. For one could, logically, reject this premise, and then the conclusion wouldn't follow at all. Hence, that something is a reason for judging X good depends on what values the man who judges holds. Of course, one can find reasons for holding these values. That is, facts from which we could derive the major premise, but only by adopting a higher major which would allow us to derive our first major as a valid conclusion. Ultimately, we have to decide beyond all reasons, as it were, what our values are. For at each stage where we adduce a reason, we have already to have accepted some value (enshrined in a major premise) in virtue of which this reason is valid. But then our ultimate major premises stand without reasons; they are the fruit of a pure choice.

Proposition (1) above, then, is immediately denied by non-naturalism. For in the highest major premises 'good' is applied to commend without the claim that there are reasons for this commendation. And (2) also is rejected, for nothing can claim always to constitute a reason for calling something good. Whether it does or not depends on the decisions a man has made about his values, and it is not logically impossible that he should decide to consider human needs, wants and purposes irrelevant to judgments about good and bad. A reason is always a reason-for-somebody, and has this status because of the values he has accepted.

The question at issue, then, is first whether 'good' can be used where there are no reasons, either evident or which can be cited for its application.[22] Consider the following case:[23] There are two segregationists who disapprove of miscegenation. The first claims that mixing races will produce general unhappiness, a decline in the intellectual capacity and moral standards of the race, the abolition of a creative tension, and so on. The second, however, refuses to assent to any of these beliefs: the race will not deteriorate, men may even be happier; in any case they will be just as intelligent, moral, etc. But, he insists, miscegenation is bad. When challenged to produce some substitute reason

[22] In what follows I am indebted to the arguments of Mrs P. Foot, e.g. to her 'When is a principle a moral principle?' in *Supplementary Vol. of Aristotelian Society*, 1954, and her 'Moral Arguments' in *Mind*, 1958, although I do not know whether she would agree with the conclusions I draw from them.

[23] Borrowed with changes from Hare's *Freedom and Reason*.

for this judgment, he simply replies: 'I have no reasons; everyone is entitled, indeed has to accept some higher major premise and stop the search for reasons somewhere. I have chosen to stop here, rather than seeking grounds in such fashionable quarters, as human happiness, moral stature, etc.' Or supposing he looked at us in puzzlement and said: 'Reasons? why do you ask for reasons? Miscegenation is just bad.'

Now no one would question that the first segregationist was making the judgment 'miscegenation is bad'. But in the case of the second, a difficulty arises. This can be seen as soon as we ask the question: how can we tell whether the man is really making a judgment about the badness of miscegenation and not just, say, giving vent to a strongly felt repulsion, or a neurotic phobia against sexual relations between people of different races? Now it is essential to the notions 'good' and 'bad' as we use them in judgments that there be a distinction of this kind between these judgments and expressions of horror, delight, liking, disliking and so on. It is essential that we be able, e.g. to correct a speaker by saying: 'What you want to say would be better put as "miscegenation horrifies me", or "miscegenation makes me go all creepy inside".' Because it is an essential part of the grammar of 'good' and 'bad' that they claim more than is claimed by expressions of delight, horror, etc. For we set aside someone's judgment that X is good when we say: 'All you're saying is that you *like* X.' To which the man can hotly reply: 'I don't like X any more than you do, but I recognize that it's good.'

There must therefore be criteria of distinction between these two cases if 'good' and 'bad' are to have the grammar that they have. But if we allow that our second segregationist is making the judgment 'miscegenation is bad', then no such distinction can be made. A judgment that I like something doesn't need grounds. That is, the absence of grounds doesn't undermine the claim 'I like X' (though other things, e.g. in my behaviour, may undermine it). But unless we adduce reasons for it (and moreover reasons of a certain kind as we shall see below) we cannot show that our claim that X is good says more than 'I like X'. Thus a man can only defend himself against the charge that all he's saying is that he likes X by giving his grounds. If there are no grounds, then judgment becomes indistinguishable from expression; which means that there are no more judgments of good and bad, since the distinction is essential to them as we have seen.

Those who believe in the fact-value dichotomy have naturally tried to avoid this conclusion; they have tried to distinguish the two cases by fastening on the use made of judgments of good and bad in commending, prescribing, expressing approval and so on. Thus, no matter what a man's grounds, if any, we could know that he was making a judgment of good and bad by the fact that he was commending, prescribing or committing himself to pursue the thing in question, or something of the kind. But this begs the question, for we can raise the query: what constitutes commending, or prescribing, or committing myself, or expressing approval, or whatever? How does one tell whether a man is doing one of these things as against just giving vent to his feelings?

If we can say that we can tell by what the man accepts as following from his stand – whether he accepts that he should strive to realize the thing in question – then the same problem breaks out afresh: how do we distinguish his accepting the proposition that he should seek the end and his just being hell-bent on seeking this end? Presumably, both our segregationists would agree that they should fight miscegenation, but this would still leave us just as puzzled and uncertain about the position of the second. Perhaps we can tell by whether they are willing to universalize their prescription? But here again we have no touchstone, for both segregationists would assent that everyone should seek racial purity, but the question would remain open whether this had a different meaning in the two cases. Perhaps the second one just means that he can't stand inter-racial mating, whether done by himself or by anyone else. Similarly, a compulsive may keep his hands scrupulously clean and feel disgust at the uncleanliness of others, even plead with them to follow his example; but we still want to distinguish his case from one who had judged that cleanliness was good.

Can we fall back on behavioural criteria, meaning by 'behaviour' what a man does in contrast to how he thinks about what he does? But there is no reason why a man with a neurotic phobia against X shouldn't do all the things which the man who judges X is bad does, i.e., avoiding X himself, trying to stop others from doing it, and so on.

Thus the non-naturalists would leave us with no criteria except what the man was willing to say. But then we would have no way of knowing whether the words were correctly applied or not, which is to say that they would nave no meaning. All that we achieve by trying to mark the distinction by what follows from the judgment is that the same question which we raised about 'X is bad' as against 'X makes me shudder' can be raised about the complex 'X is bad, I/you shouldn't do X' as against the complex 'X makes me shudder, please I/you don't do X'. We simply appeal from what the man is willing to say on the first question to what he is willing to say on the second. The distinction can only be properly drawn if we look to the reasons for the judgment, and this is why a judgment without reasons cannot be allowed, for it can no longer be distinguished from an expression of feeling.[24]

II This analysis may sound plausible for 'miscegenation is bad', but how about 'anything conducive to human happiness is good'? What can we say here, if asked to give grounds for this affirmation? The answer is that we can say nothing, but also we need say nothing. For that something conduces to human happiness is already an adequate ground for judging it good – adequate, that is, in the absence of counter-vailing considerations. We come, then to the second point at issue, the claim that to say of something that it fulfils human needs, wants or purposes always constitutes a *prima facie* reason for calling it 'good'.

For in fact it is not just necessary that there be grounds for the affirmation if we are to take it at its face value as an attribution of good or bad, they must also be grounds of a certain kind. They must be grounds which relate in some intelligible way to what men need, desire or seek after. This may become clearer if we look at another example. Suppose a man says: 'To make medical care available to more people is good'; suppose, then, that another man wishes to deny this. We could, of course, imagine reasons for this: world population will grow too fast, there are other more urgent claims on scarce resources, the goal can only be obtained by objectionable social policies, such as socialized medicine, and so on. The espousal of any of these would make the opposition to the above judgment intelligible, even it not acceptable, and make it clear that it was *this* judgment that was being denied, and not just, say, an emotional reaction which was being countered with another. If, however, our objector said nothing, and claimed to have nothing to say, his position would be unintelligible, as we have seen;

[24] We may use behaviour, of course, to judge which of the two constructions to put on a man's words, but the two are not distinguished by behavioural criteria alone, but also by what a man thinks and feels. It is possible, of course, to challenge a man's even sincere belief that he is judging of good and bad, and to disvalue it on the grounds that one holds it to be based largely on irrational prejudice or unavowed ambitions or fears. Thus our first segregationist may be judged as not too different from our second. For there is some evidence that segregationist ideas can at least partly be assimilated to neurotic phobias in their psychological roots. But this is just why many people look on the judgments of segregationists as self-deception and unconscious sham. 'Really', they are just expressions of horror. But this respects the logic of 'good' as we have outlined it: for it concludes that if the rational base is mere show, then the judgment is mere show. Segregationists, for their part, rarely are of the second type, and pay homage to the logic of 'good' by casting about for all sorts of specious reasons of the correct form.

or else we would construe his words as expressing some feeling of distaste or horror or sadness at the thought.

But supposing he was willing to give grounds for his position, but none of the above or their like, saying instead, for instance, 'There would be too many doctors', or 'Too many people would be dressed in white'? We would remain in doubt as to how to take his opposition, for we would be led to ask of his opposition to the increase of doctors, say, whether he was making a judgment concerning good and bad or simply expressing a dislike. And we would decide this question by looking at the grounds he adduced for *this* position. And if he claimed to have nothing to say, his position would be unintelligible in exactly the same way as if he had decided to remain silent at the outset and leave his original statement unsupported. 'What's this?' we would say, 'You are against an increase in medical services, because it would increase the number of doctors? But are you just expressing the feelings of dislike that doctors evoke in you or are you really trying to tell us that the increase is bad?' In the absence of any defence on his part, we would take the first interpretation.

It is clear that the problem would remain unsolved, if our opponent grounded his opposition to doctors on the fact that they generally wore dark suits, or washed their hands frequently. We might at this point suspect him of having us on. So that the length or elaboration of the reasoning has nothing to do with the question one way or another.

What would make his position intelligible, and intelligible as a judgment of good and bad, would be his telling us some story about the evil influence doctors exercise on society, or the sinister plot they were hatching to take over and exploit the rest of mankind, or something of the kind. For this would relate the increase of doctors in an intelligible way to the interests, needs or purposes of men. In the absence of such a relation, we remain in the dark, and are tempted to assume the worst.

What is meant by 'intelligibility' here is that we can understand the judgment as a use of 'good' and 'bad'. It is now widely agreed that a word gets its meaning from its place in the skein of discourse; we can give its meaning, for instance, by making clear its relations to other words. But this is not to say that we can give the meaning in a set of logical relations of equivalence, entailment, and so on, that an earlier positivism saw as the content of philosophical endeavour. For the relation to other terms may pass through a certain context. Thus, there is a relation between 'good' and commending, expressing approval, and so on. But this is not to say that we can construe 'X is good', for instance, as *meaning* 'I commend X'.[25] Rather, we can say that 'good' can be used for commending, that to apply the word involves being ready to commend in certain circumstances, for if you aren't then you are shown to have been unserious in your application of it, and so on.[26]

The relation between 'good' and commending, expressing approval, persuading, and so on, has been stressed by non-naturalist theorists of ethics (though not always adequately understood, because of the narrow concentration on logical relations), but the term has another set of relations, to the grounds of its predication, as we have tried to show. These two aspects correspond respectively to what has often been called the evaluative, emotive or prescriptive meaning on one hand (depending on the theory) and the 'descriptive' meaning on the other. For half a century an immense barrage of dialectical artillery has been trained on the so-called 'naturalistic fallacy' in an effort to prize 'good' loose from any set range of descriptive meanings. But this immense effort has been beside the point, for it has concentrated on the non-existence of logical relations between descriptive predicates and evaluative terms. But the fact that one cannot find equivalences, make valid deductive argument, and so on, may show nothing about the relation between a given concept and others.

Just as with the 'evaluative' meaning above, so with the 'descriptive' meaning: 'good' doesn't *mean* 'conducive to the fulfilment of human wants, needs or purposes'; but its use is unintelligible outside of any relationship to wants, needs and purposes, as we saw above. For if we abstract from this relation, then we cannot tell whether a man is using 'good' to make a judgment, or simply express some feeling; and it is an essential part of the meaning of the term that such a distinction can be made. The 'descriptive'[27] aspects of 'good's' meaning can rather be shown

[25] Cf. John Searle's 'Meaning and Speech Acts', *Philosophical Review*, October 1962.
[26] Thus, if I say, 'This is a good car,' and then my friend comes along and says, 'Help me choose a car,' I have to eat my words if I am not willing to commend the car to him, *unless* I can adduce some other countervailing factor such as price, my friend's proclivity to dangerous driving, or whatever. But this complex relationship cannot be expressed in an equivalence, e.g. 'This is a good car' entails 'If you are choosing a car, take this'.
[27] The terms 'descriptive meaning' and 'evaluative meaning' can be seen to be seriously misleading, as is evident from the discussion. For they carry the implication that the meaning is 'contained' in the word, and can be 'unpacked' in statements of logical equivalence. There is rather a descriptive aspect and an evaluative aspect of its role or use, which are, moreover, connected, for we cannot see whether a use of the term carries

in this way: 'good' is used in evaluating, commending, persuading and so on by a race of beings who are such that through their needs, desires, and so on, they are not indifferent to the various outcomes of the world-process. A race of inactive, godless angels, as really disinterested spectators, would have no use for it, could not make use of it, except in the context of cultural anthropology, just as human anthropologists use 'mana'. It is because 'good' has this use, and can only have meaning because there is this role to fill in human life, that it becomes unintelligible when abstracted from this role. Because its having a use arises from the fact that we are not indifferent, its use cannot be understood where we cannot see what there is to be not-indifferent about, as in the strange 'grounds' quoted by our imaginary opponent above. Moreover, its role is such that it is supposed to be predicated on general grounds, and not just according to the likes and dislikes or feelings of individuals. This distinction is essential since (among other things) the race concerned spends a great deal of effort achieving and maintaining consensus within larger or smaller groups, without which it would not survive. But where we cannot see what the grounds could be, we are tempted to go on treating the use of 'good' as an expression of partiality, only of the more trivial, individual kind.

We can thus see why, for instance, 'anything conducive to human happiness is good' doesn't need any further grounds to be adduced on its behalf. In human happiness, which by definition men desire, we have an adequate ground. This doesn't mean that all argument is foreclosed. We can try to show that men degenerate in various ways if they seek only happiness, and that certain things which also make men unhappy are necessary for their development. Or we can try to show that there is a higher and a lower happiness, that most men seek under this title only pleasure, and that this turns them away from genuine fulfilment; and so on. But unless we can bring up some countervailing consideration, we cannot deny a thesis of this kind. The fact that we can always bring up such countervailing considerations means that we can never say that 'good' *means* 'conducive to human happiness', as Moore saw. But that something is conducive to human happiness, or in general to the fulfilment of human needs, wants and purposes, is a *prima facie* reason for calling it good, which stands unless countered.

Thus the non-neutrality of the theoretical findings of political science need not surprise us. In setting out a given framework, a theorist is also setting out the gamut of possible polities and policies. But a

the evaluation force of 'good' unless we can also see whether it enters into the skein of relations which constitute the descriptive dimension of its meaning.

political framework cannot fail to contain some, even implicit, conception of human needs, wants and purposes. The context of this conception will determine the value-slope of the gamut, unless we can introduce countervailing considerations. If these countervailing factors are motivationally marginal enough not to have too much relevance to political behaviour, then we can speak of the original valuation as being only over-ridden. For that part of the gamut of possibilities which we originally valued still has the property we attributed to it and thus remains valuable for us in one aspect, even if we have to give it low marks in another. For instance, we still will believe that having a peaceful polity is a good, even if it results in bad art. But if the countervailing factor is significant for political behaviour, then it will lead us to revise our framework and hence our views about the gamut of possible polities and policies; this in turn will lead to new valuations. The basis of the old values will be undermined. Thus, if we believe that an absence of violence will lead to stagnation and foreign conquest or breakdown, then we change the gamut of possibility: the choice no longer lies between peace and violence, but between, say, controlled violence and greater uncontrolled violence. Peace ceases to figure on the register: it is not a good we can attain.

Of course, the countervailing factor may not revise our gamut of choices so dramatically. It may simply show that the values of our originally preferred régime cannot be integrally fulfilled or that they will be under threat from a previously unsuspected quarter, or that they will be attended with dangers or disadvantages or disvalues not previously taken into account, so that we have to make a choice as in the peace-versus-good-art case above. Thus not all alterations of the framework will undermine the original values. But we can see that the converse does hold, and all undermining will involve a change in the framework. For if we leave the original framework standing, then the values of its preferred régime will remain as fully realizable goods, even if they are attended with certain evils which force on us a difficult choice, such as that between peace and good art, or progress and psychic harmony, or whatever.

In this sense we can say that a given explanatory framework secretes a notion of good, and a set of valuations, which cannot be done away with – though they can be over-ridden – unless we do away with the framework. Of course, because the values can be over-ridden, we can only say that the framework tends to support them, not that it establishes their validity. But this is enough to show that the neutrality of the findings of political science is not what it was thought to be. For establishing a given framework restricts the range of value positions which can be defensibly adopted. For in the light of the framework certain goods can be accepted as such without further argument, whereas other rival ones cannot be adopted without adducing over-riding considerations. The framework can be said to distribute the onus of argument in a certain way. It is thus not neutral.

The only way to avoid this while doing political science would be to stick to the narrow gauge discoveries which, just because they are, taken alone, compatible with a great number of political frameworks, can bathe in an atmosphere of value neutrality. That Catholics in Detroit tend to vote Democrat can consort with almost anyone's conceptual scheme, and thus with almost anyone's set of political values. But to the extent that political science cannot dispense with theory, with the search for a framework, to that extent it cannot stop developing normative theory.

Nor need this have the vicious results usually attributed to it. There is nothing to stop us making the greatest attempts to avoid bias and achieve objectivity. Of course, it is hard, almost impossible, and precisely because our values are also at stake. But it helps, rather than hinders, the cause to be aware of this.

3 Distributive Justice[1]

John Rawls

I

We may think of a human society as a more or less self-sufficient association regulated by a common conception of justice and aimed at advancing the good of its members. As a co-operative venture for mutual advantage, it is characterized by a conflict as well as an identity of interests. There is an identity of interests since social co-operation makes possible a better life for all than any would have if everyone were to try to live by his own efforts; yet at the same time men are not indifferent as to how the greater benefits produced by their joint labours are distributed, for in order to further their own aims each prefers a larger to a lesser share. A conception of justice is a set of principles for choosing between the social arrangements which determine this division and for underwriting a consensus as to the proper distributive shares.

Now at first sight the most rational conception of justice would seem to be utilitarian. For consider: each man in realizing his own good can certainly balance his own losses against his own gains. We can impose a sacrifice on ourselves now for the sake of a greater advantage later. A man quite properly acts, as long as others are not affected, to achieve his own greatest good, to advance his ends as far as possible. Now, why should not a society act on precisely the same principle? Why is not that which is rational in the case of one man right in the case of a group of men? Surely the simplest and most direct conception of the right, and so of justice, is that of maximizing the good. This assumes a prior understanding of what is good, but we can think of the good as already given by the interests of rational individuals. Thus just as the principle of individual choice is to achieve one's greatest good, to advance so far as possible one's own system of rational desires, so the principle of social choice is to realize the greatest good (similarly defined) summed over all the members of society. We arrive at the principle of utility in a natural way: by this principle a society is rightly

[1] In this essay I try to work out some of the implications of the two principles of justice discussed in 'Justice as Fairness' which first appeared in the *Philosophical Review*, 1958, and which is reprinted in *Philosophy, Politics and Society*, Series II, pp. 132–57.

ordered, and hence just, when its institutions are arranged so as to realize the greatest sum of satisfactions.

The striking feature of the principle of utility is that it does not matter, except indirectly, how this sum of satisfactions is distributed among individuals, any more than it matters, except indirectly, how one man distributes his satisfactions over time. Since certain ways of distributing things affect the total sum of satisfactions, this fact must be taken into account in arranging social institutions; but according to this principle the explanation of common-sense precepts of justice and their seemingly stringent character is that they are those rules which experience shows must be strictly respected and departed from only under exceptional circumstances if the sum of advantages is to be maximized. The precepts of justice are derivative from the one end of attaining the greatest net balance of satisfactions. There is no reason in principle why the greater gains of some should not compensate for the lesser losses of others; or why the violation of the liberty of a few might not be made right by a greater good shared by many. It simply happens, at least under most conditions, that the greatest sum of advantages is not generally achieved in this way. From the standpoint of utility the strictness of common-sense notions of justice has a certain usefulness, but as a philosophical doctrine it is irrational.

If, then, we believe that as a matter of principle each member of society has an inviolability founded on justice which even the welfare of everyone else cannot over-ride, and that a loss of freedom for some is not made right by a greater sum of satisfactions enjoyed by many, we shall have to look for another account of the principles of justice. The principle of utility is incapable of explaining the fact that in a just society the liberties of equal citizenship are taken for granted, and the rights secured by justice are not subject to political bargaining nor to the calculus of social interests. Now, the most natural alternative to the principle of utility is its traditional rival, the theory of the social contract. The aim of the contract doctrine is precisely to account for the strictness of justice by supposing that its principles arise from an agreement among free and independent persons in an original position of equality and hence reflect the integrity and equal sovereignty of the rational persons who are the contractees. Instead of supposing that a conception of right, and so a conception of justice, is simply an extension of the principle of choice for one man to society as a whole, the contract doctrine assumes that the rational individuals who belong to society must choose together, in one joint act, what is to count among them as just and unjust. They are to decide among themselves once and for all what is to be their conception of justice. This decision is thought

of as being made in a suitably defined initial situation one of the significant features of which is that no one knows his position in society, nor
even his place in the distribution of natural talents and abilities. The
principles of justice to which all are forever bound are chosen in the
absence of this sort of specific information. A veil of ignorance prevents
anyone from being advantaged or disadvantaged by the contingencies of
social class and fortune; and hence the bargaining problems which
arise in everyday life from the possession of this knowledge do not
affect the choice of principles. On the contract doctrine, then, the
theory of justice, and indeed ethics itself, is part of the general theory
of rational choice, a fact perfectly clear in its Kantian formulation.

Once justice is thought of as arising from an original agreement of
this kind, it is evident that the principle of utility is problematical. For
why should rational individuals who have a system of ends they wish
to advance agree to a violation of their liberty for the sake of a greater
balance of satisfactions enjoyed by others? It seems more plausible to
suppose that, when situated in an original position of equal right, they
would insist upon institutions which returned compensating advantages
for any sacrifices required. A rational man would not accept an institution merely because it maximized the sum of advantages irrespective of
its effect on his own interests. It appears, then, that the principle of
utility would be rejected as a principle of justice, although we shall not
try to argue this important question here. Rather, our aim is to give a
brief sketch of the conception of distributive shares implicit in the
principles of justice which, it seems, would be chosen in the original
position. The philosophical appeal of utilitarianism is that it seems to
offer a single principle on the basis of which a consistent and complete
conception of right can be developed. The problem is to work out a
contractarian alternative in such a way that it has comparable if not all
the same virtues.

II

In our discussion we shall make no attempt to derive the two principles of justice which we shall examine; that is, we shall not try to show that they would be chosen in the original position.[2] It must suffice that it is plausible that they would be, at least in preference to the standard forms of traditional theories. Instead we shall be mainly concerned with three questions: first, how to interpret these principles so that they define a consistent and complete conception of justice; second, whether it is possible to arrange the institutions of a constitutional democracy so that these principles are satisfied, at least approximately; and third, whether the conception of distributive shares which they define is compatible with common-sense notions of justice. The significance of these principles is that they allow for the strictness of the claims of justice; and if they can be understood so as to yield a consistent and complete conception, the contractarian alternative would seem all the more attractive.

The two principles of justice which we shall discuss may be formulated as follows: first, each person engaged in an institution or affected by it has an equal right to the most extensive liberty compatible with a like liberty for all; and second, inequalities as defined by the institutional structure or fostered by it are arbitrary unless it is reasonable to expect that they will work out to everyone's advantage and provided that the positions and offices to which they attach or from which they may be gained are open to all. These principles regulate the distributive

[2] This question is discussed very briefly in 'Justice as Fairness', see pp. 138–41. The intuitive idea is as follows. Given the circumstances of the original position, it is rational for a man to choose as if he were designing a society in which his enemy is to assign him his place. Thus, in particular, given the complete lack of knowledge (which makes the choice one under uncertainty), the fact that the decision involves one's life-prospects as a whole and is constrained by obligations to third parties (e.g. one's descendants) and duties to certain values (e.g. to religious truth), it is rational to be conservative and so to choose in accordance with an analogue of the maximin principle. Viewing the situation in this way, the interpretation given to the principles of justice in Section IV is perhaps natural enough. Moreover, it seems clear how the principle of utility can be interpreted: it is the analogue of the Laplacean principle for choice uncertainty. (For a discussion of these choice criteria, see R. D. Luce and H. Raiffa, *Games and Decisions* (1957), pp. 275–98).

aspects of institutions by controlling the assignment of rights and duties throughout the whole social structure, beginning with the adoption of a political constitution in accordance with which they are then to be applied to legislation. It is upon a correct choice of a basic structure of society, its fundamental system of rights and duties, that the justice of distributive shares depends.

The two principles of justice apply in the first instance to this basic structure, that is, to the main institutions of the social system and their arrangement, how they are combined together. Thus this structure includes the political constitution and the principal economic and social institutions which together define a person's liberties and rights and affect his life-prospects, what he may expect to be and how well he may expect to fare. The intuitive idea here is that those born into the social system at different positions, say in different social classes, have varying life-prospects determined, in part, by the system of political liberties and personal rights, and by the economic and social opportunities which are made available to these positions. In this way the basic structure of society favours certain men over others, and these are the basic inequalities, the ones which affect their whole life-prospects. It is inequalities of this kind, presumably inevitable in any society, with which the two principles of justice are primarily designed to deal.

Now the second principle holds that an inequality is allowed only if there is reason to believe that the institution with the inequality, or permitting it, will work out for the advantage of every person engaged in it. In the case of the basic structure this means that all inequalities which affect life-prospects, say the inequalities of income and wealth which exist between social classes, must be to the advantage of everyone. Since the principle applies to institutions, we interpret this to mean that inequalities must be to the advantage of the representative man for each relevant social position; they should improve each such man's expectation. Here we assume that it is possible to attach to each position an expectation, and that this expectation is a function of the whole institutional structure: it can be raised and lowered by reassigning rights and duties throughout the system. Thus the expectation of any position depends upon the expectations of the others, and these in turn depend upon the pattern of rights and duties established by the basic structure. But it is not clear what is meant by saying that inequalities must be to the advantage of every representative man, and hence our first question.

III

One possibility is to say that everyone is made better off in comparison with some historically relevant benchmark. An interpretation of this kind is suggested by Hume.[3] He sometimes says that the institutions of justice, that is, the rules regulating property and contracts, and so on, are to everyone's advantage, since each man can count himself the gainer on balance when he considers his permanent interests. Even though the application of the rules is sometimes to his disadvantage, and he loses in the particular case, each man gains in the long-run by the steady administration of the whole system of justice. But all Hume seems to mean by this is that everyone is better off in comparison with the situation of men in the state of nature, understood either as some primitive condition or as the circumstances which would obtain at any time if the existing institutions of justice were to break down. While this sense of everyone's being made better off is perhaps clear enough, Hume's interpretation is surely unsatisfactory. For even if all men including slaves are made better off by a system of slavery than they would be in the state of nature, it is not true that slavery makes everyone (even a slave) better off, at least not in a sense which makes the arrangement just. The benefits and burdens of social co-operation are unjustly distributed even if everyone does gain in comparison with the state of nature; this historical or hypothetical benchmark is simply irrelevant to the question of justice. In fact, any past state of society other than a recent one seems irrelevant offhand, and this suggests that we should look for an interpretation independent of historical comparisons altogether. Our problem is to identify the correct hypothetical comparisons defined by currently feasible changes.

Now the well-known criterion of Pareto[4] offers a possibility along these lines once it is formulated so as to apply to institutions. Indeed, this is the most natural way of taking the second principle (or rather the first part of it, leaving aside the requirement about open positions). This criterion says that group welfare is at an optimum when it is impossible to make any one man better off without at the same time making at least one other man worse off. Applying this criterion to allocating a given bundle of goods among given individuals, a particular allocation yields an optimum if there is no redistribution which would

---

[3] For this observation I am indebted to Brian Barry.
[4] Introduced by him in his *Manuel d'économie politique* (1909) and long since a basic principle of welfare economics.

improve one individual's position without worsening that of another. Thus a distribution is optimal when there is no further exchange which is to the advantage of both parties, or to the advantage of one and not to the disadvantage of the other. But there are many such distributions, since there are many ways of allocating commodities so that no further mutually beneficial exchange is possible. Hence the Pareto criterion, as important as it is, admittedly does not identify the best distribution, but rather a class of optimal, or efficient, distributions. Moreover, we cannot say that a given optimal distribution is better than any non-optimal one; it is only superior to those which it dominates. The criterion is at best an incomplete principle for ordering distributions.

Pareto's idea can be applied to institutions. We assume, as remarked above, that it is possible to associate with each social position an expectation which depends upon the assignment of rights and duties in the basic structure. Given this assumption, we get a principle which says that the pattern of expectations (inequalities in life-prospects) is optimal if and only if it is impossible to change the rules, to redefine the scheme of rights and duties, so as to raise the expectations of any representative man without at the same time lowering the expectations of some other representative man. Hence the basic structure satisfies this principle when it is impossible to change the assignment of fundamental rights and duties and to alter the availability of economic and social opportunities so as to make some representative man better off without making another worse off. Thus, in comparing different arrangements of the social system, we can say that one is better than another if in one arrangement all expectations are at least as high, and some higher, than in the other. The principle gives grounds for reform, for if there is an arrangement which is optimal in comparison with the existing state of things, then, other things equal, it is a better situation all around and should be adopted.

The satisfaction of this principle, then, defines a second sense in which the basic structure makes everyone better off; namely, that from the standpoint of its representative men in the relevant positions, there exists no change which would improve anyone's condition without worsening that of another. Now we shall assume that this principle would be chosen in the original position, for surely it is a desirable feature of a social system that it is optimal in this sense. In fact, we shall suppose that this principle defines the concept of efficiency for institutions, as can be seen from the fact that if the social system does not satisfy it, this implies that there is some change which can be made which will lead people to act more effectively so that the expectations of some at least can be raised. Perhaps an economic reform will lead to an increase in production with given resources and techniques, and with greater output someone's expectations are raised.

It is not difficult to see, however, that while this principle provides another sense for an institution's making everyone better off, it is an inadequate conception of justice. For one thing, there is the same incompleteness as before. There are presumably many arrangements of an institution and of the basic structure which are optimal in this sense. There may also be many arrangements which are optimal with respect to existing conditions, and so many reforms which would be improvements by this principle. If so, how is one to choose between them? It is impossible to say that the many optimal arrangements are equally just, and the choice between them a matter of indifference, since efficient institutions allow extremely wide variations in the pattern of distributive shares.

Thus it may be that under certain conditions serfdom cannot be significantly reformed without lowering the expectations of some representative man, say that of landowners, in which case serfdom is optimal. But equally it may happen under the same conditions that a system of free labour could not be changed without lowering the expectations of some representative man, say that of free labourers, so that this arrangement likewise is optimal. More generally, whenever a society is relevantly divided into a number of classes, it is possible, let's suppose, to maximize with respect to any one of its representative men at a time. These maxima give at least this many optimal positions, for none of them can be departed from to raise the expectations of any man without lowering those of another, namely, the man with respect to whom the maximum is defined. Hence each of these extremes is optimal. All this corresponds to the obvious fact that, in distributing particular goods to given individuals, those distributions are also optimal which give the whole stock to any one person; for once a single person has everything, there is no change which will not make him worse off.

We see, then, that social systems which we should judge very differently from the standpoint of justice may be optimal by this criterion. This conclusion is not surprising. There is no reason to think that, even when applied to social systems, justice and efficiency come to the same thing. These reflections only show what we knew all along, which is that we must find another way of interpreting the second principle, or rather the first part of it. For while the two principles taken together incorporate strong requirements of equal liberty and equality of opportunity, we cannot be sure that even these constraints are sufficient to make the social structure acceptable from the standpoint of justice. As they stand the two principles would appear to place the burden of ensuring justice entirely upon these prior constraints and to leave indeterminate the preferred distributive shares.

IV

There is, however, a third interpretation which is immediately suggested by the previous remarks, and this is to choose some social position by reference to which the pattern of expectations as a whole is to be judged, and then to maximize with respect to the expectations of this representative man consistent with the demands of equal liberty and equality of opportunity. Now, the one obvious candidate is the representative man of those who are least favoured by the system of institutional inequalities. Thus we arrive at the following idea: the basic structure of the social system affects the life-prospects of typical individuals according to their initial places in society, say the various income classes into which they are born, or depending upon certain natural attributes, as when institutions make discriminations between men and women or allow certain advantages to be gained by those with greater natural abilities. The fundamental problem of distributive justice concerns the differences in life-prospects which come about in this way. We interpret the second principle to hold that these differences are just if and only if the greater expectations of the more advantaged, when playing a part in the working of the whole social system, improve the expectations of the least advantaged. The basic structure is just throughout when the advantages of the more fortunate promote the well-being of the least fortunate, that is, when a decrease in their advantages would make the least fortunate even worse off than they are. The basic structure is perfectly just when the prospects of the least fortunate are as great as they can be.

In interpreting the second principle (or rather the first part of it which we may, for obvious reasons, refer to as the difference principle), we assume that the first principle requires a basic equal liberty for all, and that the resulting political system, when circumstances permit, is that of a constitutional democracy in some form. There must be liberty of the person and political equality as well as liberty of conscience and freedom of thought. There is one class of equal citizens which defines a common status for all. We also assume that there is equality of opportunity and a fair competition for the available positions on the basis of reasonable qualifications. Now, given this background, the differences to be justified are the various economic and social inequalities in the basic structure which must inevitably arise in such a scheme. These are the inequalities in the distribution of income and wealth and the distinctions in social prestige and status which attach to the various positions and classes. The difference principle says that these inequalities are just if and only if they are part of a larger system in which they work out to the advantage of the most unfortunate representative man. The just distributive shares determined by the basic structure are those specified by this constrained maximum principle.

Thus, consider the chief problem of distributive justice, that concerning the distibution of wealth as it affects the life-prospects of those starting out in the various income groups. These income classes define the relevant representative men from which the social system is to be judged. Now, a son of a member of the entrepreneurial class (in a capitalist society) has a better prospect than that of the son of an unskilled labourer. This will be true, it seems, even when the social injustices which presently exist are removed and the two men are of equal talent and ability; the inequality cannot be done away with as long as something like the family is maintained. What, then, can justify this inequality in life-prospects? According to the second principle it is justified only if it is to the advantage of the representative man who is worst off, in this case the representative unskilled labourer. The inequality is permissible because lowering it would, let's suppose, make the working man even worse off than he is. Presumably, given the principle of open offices (the second part of the second principle), the greater expectations allowed to entrepreneurs has the effect in the longer run of raising the life-prospects of the labouring class. The inequality in expectation provides an incentive so that the economy is more efficient, industrial advance proceeds at a quicker pace, and so on, the end result of which is that greater material and other benefits are distributed throughout the system. Of course, all of this is familiar, and whether true or not in particular cases, it is the sort of thing which must be argued if the inequality in income and wealth is to be acceptable by the difference principle.

We should now verify that this interpretation of the second principle gives a natural sense in which everyone may be said to be made better off. Let us suppose that inequalities are chain-connected: that is, if an inequality raises the expectations of the lowest position, it raises the expectations of all positions in between. For example, if the greater expectations of the representative entrepreneur raises that of the unskilled labourer, it also raises that of the semi-skilled. Let us further assume that inequalities are close-knit: that is, it is impossible to raise (or lower) the expectation of any representative man without raising (or lowering) the expectations of every other representative man, and in particular, without affecting one way or the other that of the least fortunate. There is no loose-jointedness, so to speak, in the way in which expectations depend upon one another. Now, with these assumptions, everyone does benefit from an inequality which satisfies the difference principle, and the second principle as we have formulated it reads correctly. For the representative man who is better off in any pairwise comparison gains by being allowed to have his advantage, and the man who is worse off benefits from the contribution which all inequalities make to each position below. Of course, chain-connection and close-knitness may not obtain; but in this case those who are better off should not have a veto over the advantages available for the least advantaged. The stricter interpretation of the difference principle should be followed, and all inequalities should be arranged for the advantage of the most unfortunate even if some inequalities are not to the advantage of those in middle positions. Should these conditions fail, then, the second principle would have to be stated in another way.

It may be observed that the difference principle represents, in effect, an original agreement to share in the benefits of the distribution of natural talents and abilities, whatever this distribution turns out to be, in order to alleviate as far as possible the arbitrary handicaps resulting from our initial starting places in society. Those who have been favoured by nature, whoever they are, may gain from their good fortune only on terms that improve the well-being of those who have lost out. The naturally advantaged are not to gain simply because they are more gifted, but only to cover the costs of training and cultivating their endowments and for putting them to use in a way which improves the position of the less fortunate. We are led to the difference principle if we wish to arrange the basic social structure so that no one gains (or loses) from his luck in the natural lottery of talent and ability, or from his initial place in society, without giving (or receiving) compensating advantages in return. (The parties in the original position are not said to be attracted by this idea and so agree to it; rather, given the symmetries of their situation, and particularly their lack of knowledge, and so on, they will find it to their interest to agree to a principle which can be understood in this way.) And we should note also that when the difference principle is perfectly satisfied, the basic structure is optimal by the efficiency principle. There is no way to make anyone better off without making someone else worse off, namely, the least fortunate representative man. Thus the two principles of justice define distributive shares in a way compatible with efficiency, at least as long as we move on this highly abstract level. If we want to say (as we do, although it cannot be argued here) that the demands of justice have an absolute weight with respect to efficiency, this claim may seem less paradoxical when it is kept in mind that perfectly just institutions are also efficient.

V

Our second question is whether it is possible to arrange the institutions of a constitutional democracy so that the two principles of justice are satisfied, at least approximately. We shall try to show that this can be done provided the government regulates a free economy in a certain way. More fully, if law and government act effectively to keep markets competitive, resources fully employed, property and wealth widely distributed over time, and to maintain the appropriate social minimum, then if there is equality of opportunity underwritten by education for all, the resulting distribution will be just. Of course, all of these arrangements and policies are familiar. The only novelty in the following remarks, if there is any novelty at all, is that this framework of institutions can be made to satisfy the difference principle. To argue this, we must sketch the relations of these institutions and how they work together.

First of all, we assume that the basic social structure is controlled by a just constitution which secures the various liberties of equal citizenship. Thus the legal order is administered in accordance with the principle of legality, and liberty of conscience and freedom of thought are taken for granted. The political process is conducted, so far as possible, as a just procedure for choosing between governments and for enacting just legislation. From the standpoint of distributive justice, it is also essential that there be equality of opportunity in several senses. Thus, we suppose that, in addition to maintaining the usual social overhead capital, government provides for equal educational opportunities for all either by subsidizing private schools or by operating a public school system. It also enforces and underwrites equality of opportunity in commercial ventures and in the free choice of occupation. This result is achieved by policing business behaviour and by preventing the establishment of barriers and restriction to the desirable positions and markets. Lastly, there is a guarantee of a social minimum which the government meets by family allowances and special payments in times of unemployment, or by a negative income tax.

In maintaining this system of institutions the government may be thought of as divided into four branches. Each branch is represented by various agencies (or activities thereof) charged with preserving certain social and economic conditions. These branches do not necessarily overlap with the usual organization of government, but should be understood as purely conceptual. Thus the allocation branch is to keep the economy feasibly competitive, that is, to prevent the formation of unreasonable market power. Markets are competitive in this sense when they cannot be made more so consistent with the requirements of efficiency and the acceptance of the facts of consumer preferences and geography. The allocation branch is also charged with identifying and correcting, say by suitable taxes and subsidies wherever possible, the more obvious departures from efficiency caused by the failure of prices to measure accurately social benefits and costs. The stabilization branch strives to maintain reasonably full employment so that there is no waste through failure to use resources and the free choice of occupation and the deployment of finance is supported by strong effective demand. These two branches together are to preserve the efficiency of the market economy generally.

The social minimum is established through the operations of the transfer branch Later on we shall consider at what level this minimum should be set, since this is a crucial matter; but for the moment, a few general remarks will suffice. The main idea is that the workings of the transfer branch take into account the precept of need and assign it an appropriate weight with respect to the other common-sense precepts of justice. A market economy ignores the claims of need altogether. Hence there is a division of labour between the parts of the social system as different institutions answer to different common-sense precepts. Competitive markets (properly supplemented by government operations) handle the problem of the efficient allocation of labour and resources and set a weight to the conventional precepts associated with wages and earnings (the precepts of each according to his work and experience, or responsibility and the hazards of the job, and so on), whereas the transfer branch guarantees a certain level of well-being and meets the claims of need. Thus it is obvious that the justice of distributive shares depends upon the whole social system and how it distributes total income, wages plus transfers. There is with reason strong objection to the competitive determination of total income, since this would leave out of account the claims of need and of a decent standard of life. From the standpoint of the original position it is clearly rational to insure oneself against these contingencies. But now, if the appropriate minimum is provided by transfers, it may be perfectly fair that the other part of total income is competitively determined. Moreover, this way of dealing with the claims of need is doubtless more efficient, at least from a theoretical point of view, than trying to regulate prices by minimum wage standards and so on. It is preferable to handle these claims by a separate branch which supports a social minimum. Henceforth, in considering whether the second principle of justice is satisfied, the answer turns on whether the total income of the least advantaged, that is, wages plus transfers, is such as to maximize their long-term expectations consistent with the demands of liberty.

Finally, the distribution branch is to preserve an approximately just distribution of income and wealth over time by affecting the background conditions of the market from period to period. Two aspects of this branch may be distinguished. First of all, it operates a system of inheritance and gift taxes. The aim of these levies is not to raise revenue, but gradually and continually to correct the distribution of wealth and to prevent the concentrations of power to the detriment of liberty and equality of opportunity. It is perfectly true, as some have said,[5] that unequal inheritance of wealth is no more inherently unjust than unequal inheritance of intelligence; as far as possible the inequalities founded on either should satisfy the difference principle. Thus, the inheritance of greater wealth is just as long as it is to the advantage of the worst off and consistent with liberty, including equality of opportunity. Now by the latter we do not mean, of course, the equality of expectations between classes, since differences in life-prospects arising from the basic structure are inevitable, and it is precisely the aim of the second principle to say when these differences are just. Instead, equality of opportunity is a certain set of institutions which assures equally good education and chances of culture for all and which keeps open the competition for positions on the basis of qualities reasonably related to performance, and so on. It is these institutions which are put in jeopardy when inequalities and concentrations of wealth reach a certain limit; and the taxes imposed by the distribution branch are to prevent this limit from being exceeded. Naturally enough where this limit lies is a matter for political judgment guided by theory, practical experience, and plain hunch; on this question the theory of justice has nothing to say.

The second part of the distribution branch is a scheme of taxation for raising revenue to cover the costs of public goods, to make transfer payments, and the like. This scheme belongs to the distribution branch since the burden of taxation must be justly shared. Although we cannot examine the legal and economic complications involved, there are several points in favour of proportional expenditure taxes as part of an ideally

[5] See for example F. von Hayek, *The Constitution of Liberty* (1960), p. 90.

just arrangement. For one thing, they are preferable to income taxes at the level of common-sense precepts of justice, since they impose a levy according to how much a man takes out of the common store of goods and not according to how much he contributes (assuming that income is fairly earned in return for productive efforts). On the other hand, proportional taxes treat everyone in a clearly defined uniform way (again assuming that income is fairly earned) and hence it is preferable to use progressive rates only when they are necessary to preserve the justice of the system as a whole, that is, to prevent large fortunes hazardous to liberty and equality of opportunity, and the like. If proportional expenditure taxes should also prove more efficient, say because they interfere less with incentives, or whatever, this would make the case for them decisive provided a feasible scheme could be worked out.[6] Yet these are questions of political judgment which are not our concern; and, in any case, a proportional expenditure tax is part of an idealized scheme which we are describing. It does not follow that even steeply progressive income taxes, given the injustice of existing systems, do not improve justice and efficiency all things considered. In practice we must usually choose between unjust arrangements and then it is a matter of finding the lesser injustice.

Whatever form the distribution branch assumes, the argument for it is to be based on justice: we must hold that once it is accepted the social system as a whole – the competitive economy surrounded by a just constitutional and legal framework – can be made to satisfy the principles of justice with the smallest loss in efficiency. The long-term expectations of the least advantaged are raised to the highest level consistent with the demands of equal liberty. In discussing the choice of a distribution scheme we have made no reference to the traditional criteria of taxation according to ability to pay or benefits received; nor have we mentioned any of the variants of the sacrifice principle. These standards are subordinate to the two principles of justice; once the problem is seen as that of designing a whole social system, they assume the status of secondary precepts with no more independent force than the precepts of common sense in regard to wages. To suppose otherwise is not to take a sufficiently comprehensive point of view. In setting up a just distribution branch these precepts may or may not have a place depending upon the demands of the two principles of justice when applied to the entire system.

---

[6] See N. Kaldor, *An Expenditure Tax* (1955).

VI

Our problem now is whether the whole system of institutions which we have described, the competitive economy surrounded by the four branches of government, can be made to satisfy the two principles of justice. It seems intuitively plausible that this can be done, but we must try to make sure. We assume that the social system as a whole meets the demands of liberty; it secures the rights required by the first principle and the principle of open offices. Thus the question is whether, consistent with these liberties, there is any way of operating the four branches of government so as to bring the inequalities of the basic structure in line with the difference principle.

Now, quite clearly the thing to do is to set the social minimum at the appropriate level. So far we have said nothing about how high this minimum should be. Common sense might be content to say that the right level depends on the average wealth of the country, and that, other things equal, the minimum should be higher if this average is higher; or it might hold that the proper level depends on customary expectations. Both of these ideas are unsatisfactory. The first is not precise enough since it does not state how the minimum should depend on wealth and it overlooks other relevant considerations such as distribution; and the second provides no criterion for when customary expectations are themselves reasonable. Once the difference principle is accepted, however, it follows that the minimum should be set at the level which, taking wages into account, maximizes the expectations of the lowest income class. By adjusting the amount of transfers, and the benefits from public goods which improve their circumstances, it is possible to increase or decrease the total income of the least advantaged (wages plus transfers plus benefits from public goods). Controlling the sum of transfers and benefits, thereby raising or lowering the social minimum, gives sufficient leeway in the whole scheme to satisfy the difference principle.

Now, offhand it might appear that this arrangement requires a very high minimum. It is easy to imagine the greater wealth of those better off being scaled down until eventually all stand on nearly the same level. But this is a misconception. The relevant expectation of the least advantaged is their long-term expectation extending over all generations; and hence over any period of time the economy must put aside the appropriate amount of real capital accumulation. Assuming for the moment that this amount is given, the social minimum is determined in the following way. Suppose, for simplicity, that transfer payments and the benefits from public goods are supported by expenditure (or income) taxes. Then raising the minimum entails raising the constant proportion at which consumption (or income) is taxed. Now presumably as this proportion is increased there comes a point beyond which one of two things happens: either the savings required cannot be made or the increased taxes interfere so much with the efficiency of the economy that the expectations of the lowest class for that period no longer improve but begin to decline. In either case the appropriate level for the minimum has been reached and no further increase should be made.

In order to make the whole system of institutions satisfy the two principles of justice, a just savings principle is presupposed. Hence we must try to say something about this difficult question. Unfortunately there are no very precise limits on what the rate of saving should be; how the burden of real saving should be shared between generations seems to admit of no definite answer. It does not follow, however, that certain general bounds cannot be prescribed which are ethically significant. For example, it seems clear that the classical principle of utility, which requires us to maximize total well-being over all generations, results in much too high a rate of saving, at least for the earlier generations. On the contract doctrine the question is approached from the standpoint of the parties in the original position who do not know to which generation they belong, or what comes to the same thing, they do not know the stage of economic advance of their society. The veil of ignorance is complete in this respect. Hence the parties ask themselves how much they would be willing to save at each stage on the assumption that other generations save at the same rates. That is, a person is to consider his willingness to save at every phase of development with the understanding that the rates he proposes will regulate the whole span of accumulation. Since no one knows to which generation he belongs, the problem is looked at from the standpoint of each. Now it is immediately obvious that all generations, except possibly the first, gain from a reasonable rate of accumulation being maintained. Once the saving process is begun, it is to the advantage of all later generations. Each generation passes on to the next a fair equivalent in real capital as defined by a just savings principle, this equivalent being in return for what is received from previous generations and enabling the later ones to have a higher standard of life than would otherwise be possible. Only those in the first generation do not benefit, let's suppose; while they begin the whole process, they do not share in the fruits of their provision. At this initial stage, then, in order to obtain unanimity from the point of view of generations, we must assume that fathers, say, are willing to save for the sake of their sons, and hence that, in this case at least, one generation cares for its immediate descendants. With these suppositions, it seems that some just savings principle would be agreed to.

Now a just savings principle will presumably require a lower rate of saving in the earlier stages of development when a society is poor, and a greater rate as it becomes wealthier and more industrialized. As their circumstances become easier men would find it reasonable to agree to save more since the real burden is less. Eventually, perhaps, there will come a point beyond which the rate of saving may decline or stop altogether, at least if we suppose that there is a state of affluence when a society may concentrate on other things and it is sufficient that improvements in productive techniques be introduced only to the extent covered by depreciation. Here we are referring to what a society must save as a matter of justice; if it wishes to save for various grand projects, this is another matter.

We should note a special feature of the reciprocity principle in the case of just savings. Normally this principle applies when there is an exchange of advantages, that is, when each party gives something to the other. But in the accumulation process no one gives to those from whom he has received. Each gives to subsequent generations and receives from his predecessors. The first generation obtains no benefits at all, whereas the last generations, those living when no further saving is required, gain the most and give the least. Now this may appear unjust; and contrary to the formulation of the difference principle, the worst off save for those better off. But although this relation is unusual, it does not give rise to any difficulty. It simply expresses the fact that generations are spread out in time and exchanges between them can take place only in one direction. Therefore, from the standpoint of the original position, if all are to gain, they must agree to receive from their predecessors and to pass along a fair equivalent to those who come after them. The criterion of justice is the principle which would be chosen in the original position; and since a just savings principle would, let's suppose, be agreed to, the accumulation process is just. The savings principle may be reconciled with the difference principle by assuming that the representative man in any generation required to save belongs to the lowest income class. Of course, this saving is not done so much, if at all, by taking an active part in the investment process; rather it takes the form of approving of the economic arrangements which promote accumulation. The saving of those worse off is undertaken by accepting, as a matter of political judgment, those policies designed to improve the standard of life, thereby abstaining from the immediate advantages which are available to them. By supporting these arrangements and policies the appropriate savings can be made, and no representative man regardless of generation can complain of another for not doing his part.

Of the nature of the society at which the saving process aims we can give only the most general description. It is a society of persons with the greatest equal talent enjoying the benefits of the greatest equal liberty under economic conditions reached immediately after the highest average income *per capita* at which any saving at all is required. There is no longer a lowest income class in the traditional sense; such differences in wealth as exist are freely chosen and accepted as a price of doing things less in demand. All of this is, unfortunately, terribly vague. But, in any case, this general conception specifies a horizon of sorts at which the savings process aims so that the just savings principle is not completely indeterminate. That is, we suppose that the intention is to reach a certain social state, and the problem of the proper rate of accumulation is how to share fairly in the burdens of achieving it. The contractarian idea is that if we look at this question from the perspective of those in the original position, then, even though the savings principle which results is inevitably imprecise, it does impose ethically significant bounds. What is of first importance is that the problem of just savings be approached in the right way; the initial conception of what we are to do determines everything else. Thus, from the standpoint of the original position, representatives of all generations, so to speak, must agree on how to distribute the hardships of building and preserving a just society. They all gain from adopting a savings principle, but also they have their own interests which they cannot sacrifice for another.

VII

The sketch of the system of institutions satisfying the two principles of justice is now complete. For once the just rate of savings is determined, at least within broad limits, we have a criterion for setting the level of the social minimum. The sum of transfers should be that which maximizes the expectations of the lowest income class consistent with the appropriate saving being undertaken and the system of equal liberties maintained. This arrangement of institutions working over time results in a definite pattern of distributive shares, and each man receives a total income (wages plus transfers) to which he is entitled under the rules upon which his legitimate expectations are founded. Now an essential feature of this whole scheme is that it contains an element of pure procedural justice. That is, no attempt is made to specify the just distribution of particular goods and services to particular persons, as if there were only one way in which, independently of the choices of economic agents, these things should be shared. Rather, the idea is to design a scheme such that the resulting distribution, whatever it is, which is brought about by the efforts of those engaged in co-operation and elicited by their legitimate expectations, is just.

The notion of pure procedural justice may be explained by a comparison with perfect and imperfect procedural justice. Consider the simplest problem of fair division. A number of men are to divide a cake: assuming that a fair division is an equal one, which procedure will give this outcome? The obvious solution is to have the man who divides the cake take the last piece. He will divide it equally, since in this way he assures for himself as large a share as he can. Now in this case there is an independent criterion for which is the fair division. The problem is to devise a procedure, a set of rules for dividing the cake, which will yield this outcome. The problem of fair division exemplifies the features of perfect procedural justice. There is an independent criterion for which the outcome is just;—and we can design a procedure guaranteed to lead to it.

The case of imperfect procedural justice is found in a criminal trial. The desired outcome is that the defendant should be declared guilty if and only if he has committed the offence as charged. The trial procedure is framed to search for and to establish this result, but we cannot design rules guaranteed to reach it. The theory of trial procedures examines which rules of evidence, and the like, are best calculated to advance this purpose. Different procedures may reasonably be expected in different circumstances to yield the right result, not always, but at least most of the time. Hence a trial is a case of imperfect procedural justice. Even though the law may be carefully followed, and the trial fairly and properly conducted, it may reach the wrong outcome. An innocent man may be found guilty, a guilty man may be set free. In such cases we speak of a miscarriage of justice: the injustice springs from no human fault but from a combination of circumstances which defeats the purpose of the rules.

The notion of pure procedural justice is illustrated by gambling. If a number of persons engage in a series of fair bets, the distribution of cash after the last bet is fair, or at least not unfair, whatever this distribution is. (We are assuming, of course, that fair bets are those which define a zero expectation, that the bets are made voluntarily, that no one cheats, and so on.) Any distribution summing to the initial stock of cash held by everyone could result from a series of fair bets; hence all of these distributions are, in this sense, equally fair. The distribution which results is fair simply because it is the outcome. Now when there is pure procedural justice, the procedure for determining the just result must actually be carried out; for in this case there is no independent criterion by reference to which an outcome can be known to be just. Obviously we cannot say that a particular state of affairs is just because it could have been reached by following a just procedure. This would permit far too much and lead to absurdly unjust consequences. In the case of gambling, for example, it would entail that any distribution whatever could be imposed. What makes the final outcome of the betting fair, or not unfair, is that it is the one which has arisen after a series of fair gambles.

In order, therefore, to establish just distributive shares a just total system of institutions must be set up and impartially administered. Given a just constitution and the smooth working of the four branches of government, and so on, there exists a procedure such that the actual distribution of wealth, whatever it turns out to be, is just. It will have come about as a consequence of a just system of institutions satisfying the principles to which everyone would agree and against which no one can complain. The situation is one of pure procedural justice, since there is no independent criterion by which the outcome can be judged. Nor can we say that a particular distribution of wealth is just because it is one which could have resulted from just institutions although it has not, as this would be to allow too much. Clearly there are many distributions which may be reached by just institutions, and this is true whether we count patterns of distributions among social classes or whether we count distributions of particular goods and services among particular individuals. There are indefinitely many outcomes and what makes one of these just is that it has been achieved by actually carrying out a just scheme of co-operation as it is publicly understood. It is the result which has arisen when everyone receives that to which he is entitled given his and others' actions guided by their legitimate expectations and their obligations to one another. We can no more arrive at a just distribution of wealth except by working together within the framework of a just system of institutions than we can win or lose fairly without actually betting.

This account of distributive shares is simply an elaboration of the familiar idea that economic rewards will be just once a perfectly competitive price system is organized as a fair game. But in order to do this we have to begin with the choice of a social system as a whole, for the basic structure of the entire arrangement must be just. The economy must be surrounded with the appropriate framework of institutions, since even a perfectly efficient price system has no tendency to determine just distributive shares when left to itself. Not only must economic activity be regulated by a just constitution and controlled by the four branches of government, but a just saving-function must be adopted to estimate the provision to be made for future generations. Thus, we cannot, in general, consider only piecewise reforms, for unless all of these fundamental questions are properly handled, there is no assurance that the resulting distributive shares will be just; while if the correct initial choices of institutions are made, the matter of distributive justice may be left to take care of itself. Within the framework of a just system men may be permitted to form associations and groupings as they please so long as they respect the like liberty of others. With social ingenuity it should be possible to invent many different kinds of economic and social activities appealing to a wide variety of tastes and talents; and as long as the justice of the basic structure of the whole is not affected, men may be allowed, in accordance with the principle of free association, to enter into and to take part in whatever activities they wish. The resulting distribution will be just whatever it happens to be. The system of institutions which we have described is, let's suppose, the basic structure of a well-ordered society. This system exhibits the content of the two principles of justice by showing how they may be perfectly satisfied; and it defines a social ideal by reference to which political judgment among second-bests, and the long range direction of reform, may be guided.

VIII

We may conclude by considering the third question: whether this conception of distributive shares is compatible with common-sense notions of justice. In elaborating the contract doctrine we have been led to what seems to be a rather special, even eccentric, conception the peculiarities of which centre in the difference principle. Clear statements of it seem to be rare, and it differs rather widely from traditional utilitarian and intuitionist notions.[7] But this question is not an easy

[7] The nearest statement known to me is by Santayana. See the last part of ch. IV in *Reason and Society* (1906) on the aristocratic ideal. He says, for example, '. . . an aristocratic regimen can only be justified by radiating benefit and by proving that were less given to those above, less would be attained by those beneath them'. But see also Christian Bay, *The Structure of Freedom* (1958), who adopts the principle of maximizing freedom, giving special attention to the freedom of the marginal, least privileged man. Cf. pp. 59, 374f.

one to answer, for philosophical conceptions of justice, including the one we have just put forward, and our common-sense convictions, are not very precise. Moreover, a comparison is made difficult by our tendency in practice to adopt combinations of principles and precepts the consequences of which depend essentially upon how they are weighted; but the weighting may be undefined and allowed to vary with circumstances, and thus relies on the intuitive judgments which we are trying to systematize.

Consider the following conception of right: social justice depends positively on two things, on the equality of distribution (understood as equality in levels of well-being) and total welfare (understood as the sum of utilities taken over all individuals). On this view one social system is better than another without ambiguity if it is better on both counts, that is, if the expectations it defines are both less unequal and sum to a larger total. Another conception of right can be obtained by substituting the principle of a social minimum for the principle of equality; and thus an arrangement of institutions is preferable to another without ambiguity if the expectations sum to a larger total and it provides for a higher minimum. The idea here is to maximize the sum of expectations subject to the constraint that no one be allowed to fall below some recognized standard of life. In these conceptions the principles of equality and of a social minimum represent the demands of justice, and the principle of total welfare that of efficiency. The principle of utility assumes the role of the principle of efficiency the force of which is limited by a principle of justice.

Now in practice combinations of principles of this kind are not without value. There is no question but that they identify plausible standards by reference to which policies may be appraised, and given the appropriate background of institutions, they may give correct conclusions. Consider the first conception: a person guided by it may frequently decide rightly. For example, he would be in favour of equality of opportunity, for it seems evident that having more equal chances for all both improves efficiency and decreases inequality. The real question arises, however, when an institution is approved by one principle but not by the other. In this case everything depends on how the principles are weighted, but how is this to be done? The combination of principles yields no answer to this question, and the judgment must be left to intuition. For every arrangement combining a particular total welfare with a particular degree of inequality one simply has to decide, without the guidance from principle, how much of an increase (or decrease) in total welfare, say, compensates for a given decrease (or increase) in equality.

Anyone using the two principles of justice, however, would also appear to be striking a balance between equality and total welfare. How do we know, then, that a person who claims to adopt a combination of principles does not, in fact, rely on the two principles of justice in weighing them, not consciously certainly, but in the sense that the weights he gives to equality and total welfare are those which he would give to them if he applied the two principles of justice? We need not say, of course, that those who in practice refer to a combination of principles, or whatever, rely on the contract doctrine, but only that until their conception of right is completely specified the question is still open. The leeway provided by the determination of weights leaves the matter unsettled.

Moreover, the same sort of situation arises with other practical standards. It is widely agreed, for example, that the distribution of income should depend upon the claims of entitlement, such as training and experience, responsibility and contribution, and so on, weighed against the claims of need and security. But how are these common-sense precepts to be balanced? Again, it is generally accepted that the ends of economic policy are competitive efficiency, full employment, an appropriate rate of growth, a decent social minimum, and a more equal distribution of income. In a modern democratic state these aims are to be advanced in ways consistent with equal liberty and equality of opportunity. There is no argument with these objectives; they would be recognized by anyone who accepted the two principles of justice. But different political views balance these ends differently, and how are we to choose between them? The fact is that we agree to little when we acknowledge precepts and ends of this kind; it must be recognized that a fairly detailed weighting is implicit in any complete conception of justice. Often we content ourselves with enumerating, sense precepts and objectives of policy, adding that on particular questions we must strike a balance between them having studied the relevant facts. While this is sound practical advice, it does not express a conception of justice. Whereas on the contract doctrine all combinations of principle, precepts, and objectives of policy are given a weight in maximizing the expectations of the lowest income class consistent with making the required saving and maintaining the system of equal liberty and equality of opportunity.

Thus despite the fact that the contract doctrine seems at first to be a somewhat special conception, particularly in its treatment of inequalities, it may still express the principles of justice which stand in the background and control the weights expressed in our everyday judgments.

Whether this is indeed the case can be decided only by developing the consequences of the two principles in more detail and noting if any discrepancies turn up. Possibly there will be no conflicts; certainly we hope there are none with the fixed points of our considered judgments. The main question perhaps is whether one is prepared to accept the further definition of one's conception of right which the two principles represent. For, as we have seen, common sense presumably leaves the matter of weights undecided. The two principles may not so much oppose ordinary ideas as provide a relatively precise principle where common sense has little to say.

Finally, it is a political convention in a democratic society to appeal to the common good. No political party would admit to pressing for legislation to the disadvantage of any recognized social interest. But how, from a philosophical point of view, is this convention to be understood? Surely it is something more than the principle of efficiency (in its Paretian form) and we cannot assume that government always affects everyone's interests equally. Yet since we cannot maximize with respect to more than one point of view, it is natural, given the ethos of a democratic society, to single out that of the least advantaged and maximize their long-term prospects consistent with the liberties of equal citizenship. Moreover, it does seem that the policies which we most confidently think to be just do at least contribute positively to the well-being of this class, and hence that these policies are just throughout. Thus the difference principle is a reasonable extension of the political convention of a democracy once we face up to the necessity of choosing a complete conception of justice.

4 The Maximization of Democracy

C B Macpherson

This paper sketches an analysis of the justifying theory of Western democracy which I hope may be useful in identifying fundamental defects and in suggesting the kind of rebuilding that is possible and needed. I shall argue that the justifying theory of our Western democracies rests on two maximizing claims – a claim to maximize individual utilities and a claim to maximize individual powers; that neither of these claims can be made good, partly because of inherent defects, partly because of changed circumstances; and that the changed circumstances both permit and require a change in some of the theory's assumptions.

Changed circumstances have created new difficulties for democratic theory because of the very breadth of its claims. One of the central values of our democratic theory has been the surpassing importance of freedom of choice. We have claimed a sort of political consumer's sovereignty which ensures that the society will respond to changes in consumer preference, just as the market economy on which our Western democracies are based responds to changes in effective demand. But what is not often noticed in this connection is that, in what might be called the world-wide political market, consumers' preferences are rapidly changing. We in the West have still the same predominant preference for a 'free society', but the other two-thirds of the world – the communist nations and the newly independent underdeveloped countries which are neither communist nor liberal-democratic – have now become global effective demanders, and are demanding something different. If we believe in consumers' sovereignty we must be prepared to let the new effective demand take its course and to admit that it has moral claims. To grant this is not to demonstrate that we should abandon our cherished theory: it is at most an argument for coexistence of theories.

But our situation is both worse and better than this suggests. Worse, in that the appearance of serious competitors to liberal-democratic society has stiffened the requirements of a justifying theory. Better, in that certain twentieth-century developments have opened a possibility of avoiding the main fault in the justifying theory we inherited from the nineteenth century. Whether twentieth-century developments also make possible a sufficiently fundamental change in our institutions this paper does not attempt to explore.

I

The main elements of the justifying theory of our Western or liberal democracies – I use the terms interchangeably, for reasons that will be apparent[1] – can, I suggest, be stated as two maximizing claims: the claim to maximize individual utilities, and the claim to maximize individual powers. The first claim is familiar to students of political theory in its nineteenth-century Utilitarian form. The second, less immediately familiar, is, I suggest, a useful and revealing way of formulating the extra-Utilitarian claims that were built into the liberal theory as soon as it became liberal-democratic, say from John Stuart Mill on. Both claims are made in the name of individual personality. The argument in both cases is that the liberal society provides for the greatest measure of realization of human personality, though in the two cases the essential character of that personality is seen differently, and the different views have different historical roots. Before examining the two claims it may be useful to place them, provisionally at least, in the Western intellectual tradition.

The first claim is that the liberal-democratic society, by instituting a wider freedom of individual choice than does any non-liberal society, maximizes individual satisfactions or utilities. The claim is not only that it maximizes the aggregate of satisfactions, but that it does so equitably: that it maximizes the satisfactions to which, on some concept of equity, each individual is entitled. This claim implies a particular concept of man's essence. To treat the maximization of utilities as the ultimate justification of a society is to view man as essentially a consumer of utilities. It is only when man is seen as essentially a bundle of appetites demanding satisfaction that the good society is the one which maximizes satisfactions. This view of man, dominant in Benthamism, goes back beyond the classical political economists. It is firmly embedded in the liberal tradition and has remained a considerable part of the case for the liberal-democratic society today.

The second claim is that the liberal-democratic society maximizes men's powers, that is, their potential for using and developing their uniquely human capacities. This claim is based on a view of man's essence not as a consumer of utilities but as a doer, a creator, an enjoyer of his human attributes. These attributes may be variously listed and

---

[1] On the distinction between liberal-democracy and other types, see my *The Real World of Democracy* (Oxford, Clarendon Press, 1966).

assessed: they may be taken to include the capacity for rational understanding, for moral judgment and action, for aesthetic creation or contemplation, for the emotional activities of friendship and love, and, sometimes, for religious experience. Whatever the uniquely human attributes are taken to be, in this view of man their exertion and development is seen as an end in itself, a satisfaction in itself, not simply a means to consumer satisfactions. It is better to travel than to arrive. Man is not a bundle of appetites seeking satisfaction but a bundle of conscious energies seeking to be exerted.

This is almost an opposite view of the essence of man from that of the Utilitarians. It came, indeed, as a reaction against the crude Benthamite view of man as consumer. Benthamism provoked in the nineteenth century a variety of reactions – conservative, radical, and middle of the road – ranging from Carlyle and Nietzsche, through John Stuart Mill, to Ruskin and Marx. All these thinkers brought back, in one way or another, the idea of the essence of man as activity rather than consumption. I say brought back, because it is an old idea in the Western humanist tradition. From Aristotle until the seventeenth century it was more usual to see the essence of man as purposeful activity, as exercise of one's energies in accordance with some rational purpose, than as the consumption of satisfactions. It was only with the emergence of the modern market society, which we may put as early as the seventeenth century in England, that this concept of man was narrowed and turned into almost its opposite. Man was still held to be essentially a purposive, rational creature, but the essence of rational behaviour was increasingly held to lie in unlimited individual appropriation, as a means of satisfying unlimited desire for utilities. Man became an infinite appropriator and an infinite consumer; an infinite appropriator because an infinite desirer. From Locke to James Mill this concept of man became increasingly prevalent. The nineteenth-century reaction against it, radical, moderate, and conservative, was an attempt to reclaim and restate the much older tradition. But the Utilitarian concept was by then too deeply rooted in the market society to be driven out of the liberal tradition, while too clearly inadequate to be allowed any longer to dominate it. The result can be seen in John Stuart Mill and T. H. Green and the whole subsequent liberal-democratic tradition: an uneasy compromise between the two views of man's essence, and, correspondingly, an unsure mixture of the two maximizing claims made for the liberal-democratic society.

It is not surprising that the two concepts of man, and the two maximizing claims, were brought together. For the problem which the first liberal-*democratic* thinkers faced, in the nineteenth century, was to find a way of accommodating the pre-democratic liberal tradition of the previous two centuries to the new moral climate of democracy. The liberal tradition had been built in a market society, whose ethos was competitive maximization of utilities. The liberal thinkers of the seventeenth and eighteenth centuries had assumed, quite correctly, that the society they were talking about was a market society operating by contractual relations between free individuals who offered their powers, natural and acquired, in the market with a view to getting the greatest return they could. A man's powers, in this view, were not of his essence but were merely instrumental: they were, in Hobbes' classic phrase, 'his present means to obtain some future apparent good'. Powers were a way of getting utilities.[2] The society was permeated with utility-maximizing behaviour. Liberal thinkers could not abandon the implicit concept of man as a maximizer of utilities without abandoning all the advantages they found in the liberal society.

Why, then, was it necessary for liberal-democratic thinkers to add the other concept of man and the other maximizing claim? Two reasons are fairly evident. One was the repugnance of men like John Stuart Mill to the crass materialism of the market society, which had by then had time to show what it could do. It clearly had not brought that higher quality of life which the earlier liberals had counted on its bringing. A second reason may be seen in the belief of mid-nineteenth-century liberals that the democratic franchise could not be withheld much longer. Given this conviction, it seemed urgent to moralize the society before the mass took control. It was thus necessary to present an image of liberal-democratic society which could be justified by something more morally appealing (to the liberal thinker and, hopefully, to the new democratic mass) than the old utilitarianism. This could be done, consonantly with the liberal commitment to individual freedom, by offering as the rationale of liberal-democratic society its provision of freedom to make the most of oneself. Thus individual freedom to maximize one's powers could be added to the freedom to maximize utilities. A newly moralized liberal-democratic society could claim, as a market society, to maximize individuals' chosen utilities, and, as a free society, to maximize their powers. Neither claim has stood up very well.

[2] This is of course a very different view of a man's powers from that contained in the liberal-democratic (and the pre-seventeenth-century) notion of maximization of human powers. For the importance of the distinction, see below, section III.

II

The claim that the liberal-democratic society maximizes individual utilities (and does so equitably) may be reduced to an economic claim. It is in substance a claim that the market economy of individual enterprise and individual rights of unlimited appropriation, i.e. the capitalist market economy, with the requisite social and political institutions, maximizes individual utilities and does so equitably. To reduce the utility-maximizing claim to economic terms is not to exclude from liberal-democratic claims the value attached to other liberal institutions. Civil and political liberties are certainly held to have a value apart from their instrumental economic value. But they are less often thought of as *utilities* than as prerequisite conditions for the exertion and development of individual *powers*. We may therefore exclude them here and consider them under the other maximizing heading.

The claim that the capitalist market economy maximizes individual utilities has already been pretty well destroyed by twentieth-century economists, although few political theorists seem to realize this. For one thing, the claim to maximize the aggregate of individual utilities involves an insuperable logical difficulty. The satisfactions that different individuals get from particular things cannot be compared on a single measuring scale. Therefore they cannot be added together. Therefore it cannot be shown that the set of utilities which the market actually produces is greater than some other set that might have been produced by some other system. Therefore it cannot be shown that the market maximizes aggregate utility.

The claim that the market maximizes utilities equitably runs into even greater difficulties. Equity here refers to the distribution of the aggregate among the individual members of the society. Equity has, in the liberal tradition, generally been held to require distribution in proportion to the contributions made by each to the aggregate product. How is it claimed that the market does this? Economists can demonstrate that, assuming some specific distribution of resources or income, the operation of the perfectly free competitive market will give each the maximum satisfaction to which his contribution entitles him. But unless it can be shown that the given distribution of resources or income is just, the claim of equitable maximization is not sustained. The most that can be shown by the economists' model is that the pure competitive market gives everyone a reward proportional to what he contributes by way of any resources he owns, whether his energy and skill, his capital, or his land or other resources. But this leaves open the question whether the actual pattern of ownership of all these resources is equitable. If equity is held to require rewards proportional to the individual energy and skill expended – which was John Stuart Mill's 'equitable principle' of property – the market model can be demonstrated to be inequitable. For it distributes rewards proportionally to other owned resources, as well as energy and skill, however the ownership of the other resources was acquired, and no one argues that the ownership of the other resources is in proportion to the energy and skill exerted by their owners.

The market, then, does not maximize utilities equitably according to work. Nor does it maximize equitably according to need, on any egalitarian concept of need. Bentham, indeed, had made the egalitarian assumption that individuals have equal capacities for pleasure, and hence have equal need, and had argued that in calculating aggregate utility each individual should count as one and no one as more than one. He then demonstrated that, by the law of diminishing utility, utility would be maximized by an absolutely equal distribution of wealth. He then pointed out that equal distribution would be totally incompatible with security of property, including profit, which he saw as the indispensable incentive to productivity. He concluded that the claims of equality must yield to the claims of security, in order to maximize the aggregate production of utilities. What Bentham showed with admirable clarity was that, as soon as you make the market assumption about profit incentives, you must abandon the possibility of weighting each individual equally in calculating the maximum utility. Bentham did not claim that the market maximizes utilities equitably according to his concept of equity; he demonstrated, rather, that the market cannot do so.

Other concepts of equity than the two we have just examined – distribution according to work, and distribution according to assumed equal need – are possible, but none that is consistent with the minimum egalitarian assumptions of a democratic theory provides a demonstration that the market maximizes utilities equitably.

Thus the claim to maximize utilities, and the claim to do so equitably, both fail, even on the assumption of perfect competition. There is the further difficulty that the capitalist market economy moves steadily away from perfect competition towards oligopoly, monopoly, and managed prices and production. In the measure that it does so, its claim to maximize utilities fails on yet another ground.

III

The claim that the liberal-democratic society maximizes men's powers is more complex, though the basic conception is clear enough. To collect into this one principle – maximization of individual powers – all the main claims of liberal-democracy other than the utility-maximizing one is no doubt a considerable simplification, but it has the merit of drawing attention to fundamental factors which are often overlooked. The power-maximizing principle is offered here as a reformulation of the extra-Utilitarian principles that were built into the liberal theory in the nineteenth century in order to make it democratic, and as a way of linking them with the pre-liberal (or pre-market) Western tradition. Whether that Western tradition is traced back to Plato or Aristotle or to Christian natural law, it is based on the proposition that the end or purpose of man is to use and develop his uniquely human attributes or capacities. His potential use and development of these may be called his human powers. A good life is one which maximizes these powers. A good society is one which maximizes (or permits and facilitates the maximization of) these powers, and thus enables men to make the best of themselves.

It is important to notice that this concept of powers is an ethical one, not a descriptive one. A man's powers, in this view, are his potential for realizing the essential human attributes said to have been implanted in him by Nature or God, not (as with Hobbes) his present means, however acquired, to ensure future gratification of his appetites. The difference is important. It may be stated as a difference in what is included in each concept.

The ethical concept of a man's powers, being a concept of a potential for realizing some human end, necessarily includes in a man's powers not only his natural capacities (his energy and skill) but also his *ability* to exert them. It therefore includes *access* to whatever things outside himself are requisite to that exertion. It must therefore treat as a diminution of a man's powers whatever stands in the way of his realizing his human end, including any limitation of that access.

The descriptive concept of a man's powers, on the other hand, includes his natural capacities *plus* whatever additional power (means to ensure future gratifications) he has acquired by getting command over the energies and skill of other men, or *minus* whatever part of his energies and skill he has lost to some other men. This concept of powers does not stipulate that a man shall have the ability to use his human capacities fully. It does not require that a man shall have free access to that which he needs in order to use his capacities. It therefore does not treat as a diminution of a man's powers anything that stands in the way of his using his human capacities fully, or any limitation of his access to what he needs for that purpose. A man's powers on this view are the powers he has, not the powers he needs to have in order to be fully human. One man's powers, defined as his present means to get what he wants in the future, will include the command he has acquired over other men's energies and skills; another's will include merely what is left of his energy and skill after some of it has been transferred to others. On this concept of powers there is no diminution of a man's powers in denying him access to that which he needs in order to use his capacities, for his powers are measured after any such diminution has taken place.

One of the ways of transferring another man's powers to oneself is by denying him free access to what he needs in order to use his capacities, and making him pay for access with part of his powers. In any society where limitation of access has taken place on a large scale the resulting situation will appear differently depending on which concept of a man's powers is being used. On the ethical concept, there will be a continuous net transfer of part of the powers of some men to others, and a diminution of the human essence of those from whom power is being transferred. On the descriptive concept, there will be no net transfer of powers (since powers are defined as the means each man has acquired or has been left with), and no diminution of human essence (since the only idea of human essence that is at all implied in this concept of powers is that of man as consumer of satisfactions).

It was, I suggest, the ethical concept of a man's powers that was reintroduced into the Western tradition in the nineteenth century, and its reintroduction was what converted the liberal into the liberal-democratic theory. It is clearly apparent in T. H. Green, slightly less clearly in John Stuart Mill (who had, after all, to fight his way out of the Benthamite, i.e. Hobbesian, position). When this ethical concept was reintroduced in the nineteenth century it contained a more specific egalitarian assumption than it had contained in its ancient and mediaeval forms. It assumed not only that each individual was equally entitled to the opportunity to realize his human essence, but also (as against the Greeks) that men's capacities were substantially equal, and (as against the mediaeval tradition) that they were entitled to equal opportunity in this world.

Thus, when this ethical concept was reintroduced in the nineteenth century, by those who were seeking to humanize the market society and the pre-democratic liberal theory, it became a claim that the liberal-democratic society maximizes each individual's powers in the sense of maximizing each man's ability to use and develop his essentially human attributes or capacities.

This concept of maximizing men's human powers does not encounter the logical difficulty that besets the notion of maximizing utilities. Here there is no problem of measuring and comparing the utilities or satisfactions derived by different individuals from the receipt and consumption of the same things. True, the enjoyment one man gets from the use and development of his energies is incommensurable with the enjoyment every other man gets from his. But what is being claimed here is simply that the liberal-democratic society does provide the maximum freedom to each to use and develop what natural capacities he has. There is no need to compare incommensurable quantities of utility.

The difficulty in this claim lies deeper. It lies in the facts that the liberal-democratic society is a capitalist market society,[3] and that the latter by its very nature compels a continual net transfer of part of the power of some men to others, thus diminishing rather than maximizing the equal individual freedom to use and develop one's natural capacities which is claimed.

It is easy to see how this comes about. The capitalist market society operates necessarily by a continual and ubiquitous exchange of individual powers. Most men sell the use of their energy and skill on the market, in exchange for the product or the use of others' energy and skill. They must do so, for they do not own or control enough capital or other resources to work on, it being the nature of a capitalist society that the capital and other resources are owned by relatively few, who are not responsible (to the whole society or any section of it) for anything except the endeavour to increase their capitals. The more they increase their capitals, the more control they have over the terms on which those without capital may have access to it. Capital and other material resources are the indispensable means of labour: without access to them one cannot use one's skill and energy in the first business of life, which is to get a living, nor, therefore, in the real business of life, which (on the second view of the essence of man) is to enjoy and develop one's powers. One must have something to work on. Those without something of their own to work on, without their own means of labour, must pay for access to others'. A society in which a man cannot use his skill and energy without paying others, for the benefit of those others, for access to something to use them on, cannot be said to maximize each man's powers (on the ethical concept of a man's powers).

The reason why this has not generally been seen should be clear from

[3] I argue at the end of this section that the rise of the welfare state has not altered this equation.

our analysis of the two concepts of a man's powers. It has not been seen because the two concepts have been confused. Twentieth-century economists (and most political writers) see no net transfer of powers in a perfectly competitive capitalist market society. They do not see it because, as heirs of the Hobbes-to-Bentham concept of man, they define a man's powers, in the way we have seen, to be whatever means a man has to procure satisfactions, that is, as much power as a man has already acquired, by his acquisition of land or capital, or as little as he is left with (his own capacity to labour) when others have acquired the land and capital. When powers are so defined there is no net transfer of powers in the labour-capital relation.

But this definition of powers is, as we have seen, quite inconsistent with the ethical definition of a man's powers, and it is the latter on which the claim of liberal-democracy to maximize individual powers must logically be based.[4]

If then a man's powers must, in the context of the liberal-democratic maximizing claim, be taken to include his ability to use his natural capacities, it follows that the capitalist market society, which operates by a continual net transfer of part of the powers of some men to others, for the benefit and enjoyment of the others, cannot properly claim to maximize each individual's powers.

It may be objected that while the capitalist market model does necessarily contain a continuous net transfer of powers, our present Western liberal-democracies do not do so because they have moved some distance away from the capitalist model. One result, it is commonly held, of the operation of the democratic franchise has been the emergence of the welfare state, whose characteristic feature is the massive continuous transfer payments from owners to non-owners, by way of state provision of free or subsidized services. It may thus be argued that the modern welfare state has, or can, offset the transfer of powers from non-owners that must exist in the capitalist model of society.

This argument cannot be sustained. We need not enter into the question whether the transfer payments of the welfare state have in fact altered the previously prevailing distribution of the whole social product between classes. We need only notice that the modern welfare state does still rely on capitalist incentives to get the main productive work of the society done, and that so long as this is so, any welfare state transfers from owners to non-owners cannot offset the original and continuing

[4] It would take too long here to demonstrate, what I hope to demonstrate in a subsequent study of nineteenth-century theory, that the same confusion between the two concepts of powers is the root of the inadequacy of Mill's and Green's theories.

transfer in the other direction. This is fully appreciated by the strongest defenders of capitalism, who point out, quite rightly, that if welfare transfers were so large as to eat up profits there would be no incentive to capitalist enterprise, and so no capitalist enterprise. We may conclude, therefore, that the existence of the welfare state does not cancel and cannot substantially alter the net transfer of powers from non-owners to owners which we have seen to be inherent in the capitalist model. The claim that the liberal-democratic welfare-state society maximizes human powers is therefore still unsustained.

IV

Our analysis of the maximization-of-powers claim so far has disclosed an inherent defect. The powers which liberal-democratic society actually and necessarily maximizes are different from the powers it claims to maximize, and the maximization it achieves is inconsistent with the maximization that is claimed. The powers which it claims to maximize are every man's potential of using and developing his human capacities; the powers it does maximize are some men's means of obtaining gratifications by acquiring some of the powers of other men as a continued net transfer. This defect can be seen to be inherent when the liberal-democratic claim is taken in isolation.

We must, however, go on to look at the liberal-democratic claim comparatively, for the problem in the twentieth century is the confrontation of liberal-democratic claims with other claims. And the liberal-democratic claim to maximize human powers is, after all, a comparative claim: it is a claim that the liberal-democratic market society provides, in greater measure than any other society, the possibility of every individual realizing his human essence. This claim could still be sustained, even granting the continued net transfer of powers from non-owners to owners in our society, if it could be shown that a similar transfer is inherent in any possible society. The transfer of powers would then be irrelevant to any comparison between societies, and a case could be made that the liberal-democratic market society gives the individual a better chance than could any other society. The important question, then, is whether such a continued net transfer is inherent in any possible society.

Since the transfer is a payment for access to the means of labour, the question is whether free access would be possible in any society. Two models of society giving free access to the means of labour come to mind at once: neither of them, for different reasons, can settle our problem, but we should notice them if only to point the way to a further line of enquiry.

One model is a society of independent producers where everyone owns or has the free use of as much land or other resources as he wishes to use. Such was the hypothetical position in the first stage of Locke's state of nature, where everyone had as much land as he could use and there was still 'enough and as good' for others. Whether a society of independent producers is envisaged as a pure household economy where nothing is produced for exchange, or as a simple exchange economy where products but not labour are put on the market, there is no net transfer of powers.

But although such a society is conceivable, and although approximations to it have existed at times when there was more free land than the population could use, no one would think that such a society is now generally possible. Advanced industrial societies cannot go back to handicraft and peasant production. They could not so sustain their present populations; probably not at all, certainly not at the material level of life their members expect. And the world's present underdeveloped societies, which until now have generally remained at a level of handicraft and peasant production (except for such large-scale production as was organized by and for outside capital), have recently formed a new level of expectations and are therefore determined not merely to reduce the transfer of powers involved in outside ownership but also to move beyond their own peasant and handicraft production. We may therefore say that a society of independent producers each owning his own means of labour is now out of the question.

The other model of society in which no net transfer of powers is necessary is the socialist model, in which no individuals own the means of labour of the whole society, and in which, therefore, no class of owners automatically gets a net transfer of some of the powers of the others. Such a society would, of course, be no more possible than the one we have just rejected unless it could sustain all its members at the material level which they have come to expect. But the reason why a society of independent producers could not now do this does not apply to any other societies. The society of independent producers has a built-in limit on its productivity, for by definition it cannot use any technology which requires larger units of capital equipment than each independent producer can operate by himself. A society not confined to independent producers is not subject to this limit; it can take full advantage of technological advances in productivity.

It must, like any society, ensure that a part of the powers of its members is spent on replacing and even increasing the social capital which is required to maintain or improve the level of production. But this is not in itself a transfer of powers from some men to others for the benefit of the others: it does not in itself, therefore, diminish anyone's human essence.

However, the fact that a socialist model contains no necessary transfer of powers does not in itself settle our problem. For we do not know and cannot demonstrate whether or not a socialist society necessarily contains some other diminution of each man's powers equal to or greater than the market society's diminution of powers. When we bring back into account what we set aside earlier in considering the utility-maximizing claim of liberal-democratic society, namely, the civil and political liberties which have been won in the market society and which have not been won so far in the practising socialist societies, the balance of advantage in terms of maximization of power is substantially altered. And whether civil and political liberties are considered as utilities, or whether they are considered as contributing directly to the opportunity to maximize individual powers, they clearly must be weighed in any judgment about the maximizing claims of a society.

The absence or severe restriction of civil and political liberties must be held, on the ethical concept of powers, to diminish men's powers more than does the market transfer of powers. But while the comparative record of liberal-democratic and practising socialist societies on civil and political liberties is clear enough, we cannot demonstrate that the lack of civil and political liberties in the socialist societies is inherent rather than attributable to the circumstances in which those societies were born and have developed.

Moreover we must weigh not only civil and political liberties but all the other freedoms which, on the ethical concept of powers, make up the total opportunity each man has to exert and develop all his natural capacities. One of the freedoms which is said to do this in the market society (and which does do it there for successful men), namely, the right of unlimited appropriation, is clearly not present in a socialist model. But this is a freedom for some which reduces the freedom for others, hence its absence is not obviously a net loss of freedom. The Marxian vision of the ultimately free classless society offers, of course, the greatest conceivable opportunity for each individual to use and develop his human attributes. But no society built on a Marxian revolution has yet achieved this vision, and we do not know if it can be done. And no liberal-democratic society, however politically strong a socialist movement there may be within it, has yet moved beyond the welfare state into a socialist model far enough for any judgment on the possibility that the diminution of human powers inherent in the market society can be discarded without losing other freedoms which are important in the maximizing of human powers.

In short, experience so far can neither validate nor invalidate the claim of liberal-democratic society to maximize men's powers in comparison with any other possible kind of society.

The analysis so far has proceeded on the assumption that it is theoretically possible to compare and weigh the claims of different kinds of society to maximize individual powers, on the ethical concept of powers. The difficulty has been our lack of knowledge about the inherent properties of the socialist model. This difficulty is insuperable at the present stage of our knowledge. We may therefore drop the assumption that an objective comparison is possible, and consider instead the subjective judgments about the comparative merit of liberal-democratic society that are actually made by the members of those societies.

The people in liberal-democratic societies have voted pretty consistently for a market society rather than a socialist society. It is worth considering on what judgments this choice may possibly have been based, and whether any of the judgments are likely to change.

Three possible bases for this choice, in increasing order of rationality, may be considered. First, the choice may be founded on nothing more than a failure to recognize the fact of the net transfer of powers in the market society. The transfer is likely to be, in the more affluent societies, obscured and overlaid by an appreciation of the comparatively high material productivity of those market societies. That it is so obscured is suggested by the negative correlation between the strength of socialist and communist votes in, and the affluence of, various Western nations. If this is the case, the voters' judgment can be expected to change in the measure that the material productivity of the most advanced socialist countries catches up with that of the capitalist countries.

Or, secondly, the choice of the voters in the liberal-democracies may be founded on a value judgment that the civil and political liberties which they enjoy are worth more than any gain in their powers to be expected from the cancellation of the transfer of powers in a socialist society, and on the empirical judgment that they might lose those liberties in a socialist society. This judgment also may be expected to change, if and to the extent that the practising socialist societies find themselves able to institute more civil and political liberties as their ability to meet the material expectations of their peoples increases.

Or, thirdly, the choice of voters in the liberal-democracies may be based on a value judgment that, while the transfer of powers is inevitable in a full market society, market freedoms (including freedom of enterprise and freedom of appropriation) are nevertheless a prerequisite of, or a substantial part of, the full enjoyment and development of the human essence. This is the most rational basis for that choice. Yet this judgment may also change if it appears that the assumptions on which it is based are of only transitory validity. I think it can be shown that this is so.

I want now to argue that the net transfer of powers in a free society is necessary only when the society has made certain assumptions about scarcity and desire, and that these assumptions have been historically necessary in liberal societies down to the present but are now becoming unnecessary and unrealistic.

V

To argue this case we must begin by looking more closely into the causes of the net transfer of powers. We must try to establish the set of factors whose conjuncture has historically required, and does logically require, a net transfer of powers. We are concerned only with the transfer in a free society. There is obviously a transfer also in slave societies, in feudal societies, and in colonial and other dependent societies which are tributary to an imperial power, but in all these cases the transfer can be explained simply as the result of superior military force. Our question is, how does the transfer come about in a free society, where no class or group is using open force to keep down another, and where everyone is free to make the best bargain he can in the market for his powers?

The immediate cause of the transfer in such a society is, as we have seen, that one set of people has got virtually all the capital and other resources, access to which is necessary for anyone to use and develop his human capacities. But when and how does this distribution of resources come about in a free society? It comes when the society has set up, as an incentive to get the productive work of the society done, the individual right to unlimited, or virtually unlimited, accumulation of property. It is then, and only then, that the natural inequality of individual capacities leads to the accumulation of virtually all the resources – the means of labour – in the hands of one set of people.

When, and why, does a society set up the right of unlimited accumulation as an incentive to production? The question needs to be asked, because, taking the world as a whole and through history, the right of unlimited individual appropriation has been the exception rather than the rule. A society sets up this right, I suggest, when the people (or the most active classes) make two value judgments. One (which is already included in our hypothesis of a free society, but may be restated here for completeness) is the preference for individual freedom of choice of work and reward rather than authoritative allocation of work and reward: without this value judgment men would be content with a hierarchical customary society. The other value judgment is the elevation to the position of one of the highest values, if not the highest value – as one of the chief purposes, if not the chief purpose, of man – of an endless increase in productivity, or, which comes to the same thing, an endless battle against scarcity. Without this value judgment men would be content with a less strenuous society, and one with more moderate incentives.

The second value judgment, which I find implicit in Locke, became increasingly articulate in the eighteenth and nineteenth centuries.[5] What was new in this value judgment was the assumption of the rationality of unlimited desire. There had always been scarcity: men had always had to struggle with Nature to get a living. What was new was the assumption that the scarcity against which man was pitted was scarcity in relation to unlimited desire, which was itself rational and natural. Moral and political philosophers had from the earliest times recognised in mankind a strain of unlimited desire, but most of them had deplored it as avarice and had believed that it could, and urged that it should, be fought down. What was new, from the seventeenth century onwards, was the prevalence of the assumption that unlimited desire was rational and morally acceptable. When this assumption is made, the real task of man becomes the overcoming of scarcity in relation to infinite desire. Our second value judgment, then, can be stated as the assumption of the rationality and naturalness of unlimited desire.

It was this assumption, along with the other value judgment about freedom, which led, I suggest, to the setting up of the right to unlimited individual appropriation. For the only way that a free society could call forth the effort required in the unending battle against scarcity was the carrot, not the stick. And the right of unlimited individual appropriation was an admirable carrot. It moved man, the infinitely desirous creature, to continuous effort by giving him the prospect of unlimited command over things to satisfy his desire as consumer. Moreover, it could be seen as a way of moving man as a doer, an exerter of powers, for it

---

[5] Hume, for instance, held that what distinguished man from other animals was 'the numberless wants and necessities with which [nature] has loaded him, and . . . the slender means which she affords to the relieving these necessities', and that in society 'his wants multiply every moment upon him'; the advantage of society was that it augmented man's power to satisfy his numberless and multiplying wants. (*Treatise of Human Nature*, Book III, Part II, Section II.)

authorized him to enlarge his powers by acquiring, in addition to his natural powers, command over the powers of others: property being, as the economists saw, not only command over things but also command over the powers of other men.

We may now summarize the logical chain that leads to the transfer of powers. The net transfer of powers in a free society is the result of the accumulation of the material means of labour in the hands of one set of people. This accumulation is the result of two factors: (a) the society's decision to set up a right of unlimited individual appropriation, and (b) the natural inequality of individual capacities. Of these two factors, I assume that (b) is inherent in any society short of a genetically managed one. Factor (a) I find to be the result of the society's double value judgment: (i) that individual freedom is preferable to authoritative allocation of work and reward, and (ii) that the chief purpose of man is an endless battle against scarcity in relation to infinite desire. Assumption (ii) can be restated as, or reduced to, the assumption that unlimited desire is natural and rational.

Putting the logical chain in the reverse order, and compressing it, we get: the acceptance, by the most active part of society, of the belief that unlimited desire is natural and rational *leads to* the establishment of the right of unlimited appropriation, which *leads to* the concentration of ownership of the material means of labour, which *leads to* the continual net transfer of powers.

In giving first place to the acceptance of the assumption about unlimited desire I do not mean to say that this change in ideas was the sole moving force. I do not enter into the general question of the primacy of ideas or material conditions. It is enough to argue that the acceptance of the assumption about unlimited desire was a necessary condition of the establishment of the right of unlimited appropriation. Without attempting here to assign weights and relations to all the forces which led to the emergence of the capitalist market society, it is enough to point out that a widespread acceptance of the assumption about unlimited desire was needed to justify the institutions of that society, particularly to justify the right of unlimited appropriation. The right of unlimited appropriation was needed as an incentive to increased productivity. An incentive to increased productivity was needed to make possible the increase of wealth (and power) which a new enterprising class saw in prospect for themselves. And to get *any substantial* increase in productivity then, it was necessary to recast the institutions in a way that could only be justified by postulating *infinite* desire. In short, the assumption of the rationality of infinite desire may be said both to have produced the capitalist market society and to have been produced by that society.

The point of drawing attention to the assumption of scarcity in relation to infinite desire, or of the rationality of unlimited desire, is that this assumption is in the twentieth century beginning to appear not to be permanently valid. It is beginning to appear that this assumption will not be needed to make a free society operate, and even that it will have to be dropped to allow our society to operate.

If this can be established, it offers some hope. For the root difficulty of our justifying theory is, I have argued, that the transfer of powers which is produced by the assumption about unlimited desire contradicts the moral principle implicit in the value judgment ((i) above) that individual freedom is preferable to authoritative allocation of work and reward.

The moral principle implicit in that value judgment is the principle that all individuals should be equally able to use and develop their natural capacities. The transfer of powers contradicts that principle because it denies the greater part of men equal access to the means of using and developing their natural capacities.

VI

The chief new factor which seems to make the assumption about unlimited desire dispensable is the prospect now present in people's minds that scarcity can be ended once and for all by the technological conquests of nature that are now so rapidly advancing. The exploitation of new sources of energy and new methods of productive control of energy – automation and all that – seem capable of ending the need for incessant compulsory labour. Whether they will in fact do this, and whether they are capable of doing this within the framework of market institutions, are questions on which expert opinion is divided. But the vision of a society in which a fraction of the present compulsory labour can produce plenty for all is a vision not likely now to be extinguished by the disclaimers of experts. For the vision has taken shape at a time when two-thirds of the world is already in revolt against the market morality and searching for new ways of establishing human dignity, which they had already tended to identify with the ending of compulsory labour. This shift in value judgments in the other two-thirds of the world would not necessarily in itself have any great effect on Western liberal-democratic societies, were it not for the fact that the latter must compete in technological advance with the most advanced of the non-Western nations. The Western nations can therefore not afford to slow down their rate of technological change, and so can scarcely avoid re-ducing the need for work. The claims of leisure, of non-work in the sense of non-compulsive-labour, will thus increase at the expense of the claims of incessant productive work.

Against this it may be argued that there is another possible outcome of the technological revolution in the West, namely, that desires will multiply as fast as technological advance can meet them, so that society as a whole will have reason to work as hard as ever. This seems the more probable outcome to those who discount the compulsive transfer of powers. They point out that scarcity and plenty are relative to levels of desire, and that one can only properly speak of ending scarcity in rela-tion to the present or some other finite level of desire. They then dismiss the possibility of ending scarcity, by postulating infinite desire as an innate quality of rational man.

But to make this assumption is, as I have argued, to mistake for an innate characteristic of man what was a historical novelty brought in by the needs of the capitalist market society. It was needed to justify the right of unlimited appropriation, which was needed as an incentive to increased productivity. To get any substantial increase in productivity, then, as I have said, it was necessary to recast the institutions in a way that could only be justified by postulating infinite desire. To establish and justify a society which would give more men more opportunity to enjoy and to develop their powers it was necessary to postulate a degree of desire for material satisfactions which soon led to a society in which the enjoyment and development of men's powers was submerged under the aim of satisfying their supposed infinite desire for utilities.

I am suggesting that we have now reached, or have now in prospect, a level of productivity which makes it no longer necessary to maintain this perverse, artificial and temporary concept of man. I am arguing that we are reaching a level of productivity at which the maximization of human powers, in the ethical sense, rather than of utilities or of powers in the descriptive sense, can take over as the criterion of the good society, and that in the present world climate it will have to be an egalitarian maximi-zation of powers.

We saw that the notion of maximization of powers went with the con-cept of the essence of man as an exerter and developer of his uniquely human capacities. In any general moral or political theory based on this concept, what had to be maximized was *each* man's ability to realize his essence. What had to be asserted was the *equal* right of every man to make the best of himself. The conditions for this had never existed in any class-divided society before the market society. Nor did they exist in the market society once the right and the incentive of unlimited appropriation had taken effect, for this produced a new form of transfer of powers. The unequal properties acquired in market operations became means by which some men increased their powers by acquiring the powers of others. The earlier moral idea of maximizing each man's human powers gave way to the market idea of allowing and encouraging each to try to maximize his power by engrossing some of the powers of others.

This kind of maximization of powers cannot serve as the criterion of a democratic society: it has no better standing than the maximization of utilities, of which it is only an ideological inversion (in the sense that it substitutes for the postulate of infinite desire for utilities a postulate of infinite desire for power over others).

I am suggesting that just as we can now do without the concept of man as an infinite desirer of utilities, so we can do without the concept of man as an infinite desirer of power over others, and can instal, with some hope of its realization, the concept of man as exerter and developer of *his own* powers.

But to say that we now can do without the concepts which have prevailed for the last two or three hundred years, and that we can instal finally the more humane concept that was never possible till now, is not to say that we are likely to do so. The hitherto prevalent concepts may no longer be needed to spur our societies on economically, but they are deeply ingrained. The prospect of abundance makes it *possible* for us to drop the old assumptions, but does anything make it *necessary* for us to do so? I suggest that certain new social facts of the second half of the twentieth century do make it necessary.

One new fact is that the West no longer dominates the whole world. Another new fact is that the West no longer expects to impose its pattern of society on the whole world. It cannot do so militarily because of another new social fact, the development of nuclear weaponry. Since it cannot impose its pattern on the rest of the world, the most it can do is compete with the rest of the world. It can compete economically, but with present rates of growth the odds are that the West's comparative advantage will diminish. It can compete in political and civil liberties, in which the West is well ahead so far, but again the odds are that its comparative advantage will diminish: in the scale of political and civil liberties, the communist nations have nowhere to go but up, while the demands of the warfare state can very easily push the Western nations down.

The West will therefore, I think, be reduced to competing morally. It will, that is to say, have to compete in the quality of life it makes possible for its citizens. And in these egalitarian decades, the quality of life is to be measured in terms of the maximization of *each* person's powers.

The notion of moral competition between West and East is somewhat strange. For whose favour, it may be asked, are they competing? An obvious partial answer is, for the esteem of the third world, the recently independent underdeveloped countries of Africa and Asia who have rejected liberal-democratic market values and institutions without embracing communist values and institutions. The third world is very numerous; it has arrived in the consciousness of the West; its poverty is already a burden on the conscience of the West. Yet both West and East are so confident of their technical and cultural superiority to the third world that their behaviour is unlikely to be determined by the notion of competing for its favour.

The question, for whose favour are West and East competing, is wrongly posed. The competition is not between West and East for the favour of any third party: it is between the leaders, the holders of political power, in both East and West, for the support of their own people. I do not mean that Western voters are likely suddenly to switch to communism, or the communist nations to liberal-democracy; there is no evidence, and I think little likelihood, of such shifts. What is more probable is that the people in the West will demand a levelling up, that is to say, an end to the transfer of powers, and the people in the East a levelling up in civil and political liberties. Both are becoming technically possible.

And unless the leaders in the West are prepared to make or accept the fundamental change in the liberal-democratic justifying theory which is now possible, the West stands to lose. For the communist nations can take over, and are taking over, the technological advances in productivity which were created in the capitalist world: capitalism is no longer the sole source of productive power. And as they take over those advances, they will become more able to offer a kind of human freedom which the market society has to deny. In the measure that they reach abundance they will be able to move unimpeded to the realization of their vision, a society free of compulsive labour and therefore providing a fully human life for all. We shall not be able to move to this without the fundamental change in our theory which the prospective conquest of scarcity makes possible. If we do not now resolve the contradiction that has been built into our Western theory, the contradiction between equal freedom to realize one's human powers and freedom of unlimited appropriation of others' powers, or between the maximization of powers in the ethical sense and the maximization of powers in the descriptive market sense, we are unlikely to be able to compete.

5 Truth and Politics

Hannah Arendt

I

The subject of these reflections is a commonplace. No one ever doubted that truth and politics are on rather bad terms with each other, and no one, as far as I know, ever counted truthfulness among the political virtues. Lies have always been regarded as necessary and justifiable tools not only of the politician's or the demagogue's but also of the statesman's trade. Why is that so? And what does it mean for the nature and the dignity of the political realm on one side, for the nature and the dignity of truth and truthfulness on the other? Is it in the very essence of truth to be impotent and in the very essence of power to be deceitful? And what kind of reality does truth still possess if it is powerless in the public realm which more than any other sphere of human life guarantees reality of existence to natal and mortal men, that is, to beings who know they have appeared out of non-being and will, after a short while, again disappear into it? Finally, is not impotent truth just as despicable as power that gives no heed to truth? These are uncomfortable questions, but they arise necessarily out of our current convictions in this matter.

What lends our commonplace its high plausibility can still be summed up in the old Latin adage: *fiat justitia, pereat mundus* – should justice be done if the world's survival is at stake? Obviously, this is a rhetorical question, and the only great thinker who ever dared to go against its grain and to reply: Yes, for it would not be worth while to live in a world utterly deprived of justice, was Immanuel Kant. But isn't this answer absurd? Doesn't the care for existence clearly precede everything else, every virtue and every principle? Is it not obvious that they become mere chimeras if the world, where alone they can be manifest, is in jeopardy? Wasn't the seventeenth century entirely right when it almost unanimously declared that every commonwealth was duty-bound to recognize no 'higher law than the safety of [its] own realm?'[1] For surely,

---

[1] I quote from Spinoza's *Political Treatise* because it is noteworthy that even Spinoza, for whom the *libertas philosophandi* was the true goal of all government, should have taken so radical a position. For is not 'leisure the mother of philosophy; and Commonwealth the mother of peace and leisure'? And does it not follow that the Commonwealth will act in the interest of philosophy when it suppresses a truth which undermines peace?

every principle that transcends sheer existence can be put in the place of justice, and if we put truth in its place – *fiat veritas pereat mundus* – the old saying sounds even more plausible. If we understand political action in terms of the means-ends category we may even come to the only seemingly paradoxical conclusion that lying can very well serve to establish or safeguard the conditions for the search of truth – as Hobbes, whose relentless logic never fails to carry arguments into those extremes where their absurdity becomes manifest, pointed out long ago.[2] And lies, since they are often used as substitutes for more violent means, are liable to be considered as relatively harmless tools in the arsenal of political action.

Reconsidering the old Latin argument, it will therefore come as something of a surprise that of all transcending principles the sacrifice of truth for the survival of the world must cause the greatest difficulty. For while we may refuse even to ask ourselves whether it would still be worth living in a world deprived of such notions as justice or freedom, the same, curiously enough, is not possible with respect to the seemingly so much less political idea of truth. What is at stake is survival, the perseverance in existence (*in suo esse perseverare*), and no human world, destined to outlive the short life-span of mortals within it, will ever be able to survive without men willing to do what Herodotus was the first to undertake consciously, namely, λέγειν τὰ ἐόντα, to *say* what is. No permanence, no perseverance in existence can even be conceived of without men willing to testify to what is and appears to them because it is.

The story of the conflict between truth and politics is an old and complicated one, and nothing would be gained by simplification or mere denunciation. Throughout history the truth-seekers and truth-tellers have been aware of the risk of their business; so long as they did not interfere with the course of the world they were covered with ridicule, and he who forced his fellow-citizens to take him seriously by trying to set them free from falsehood and illusion was in danger of his life: 'If they could lay hands on [such a] man . . . , they would kill him' – as Plato says in the last sentence of the Cave Allegory. The Platonic conflict between truth-teller and citizens cannot be explained by the Latin saying, or any of the later theories that, implicitly or explicitly, justify lying among other transgressions if the survival of the city is at stake. No enemy is mentioned in Plato's story; the many live peacefully in their cave among themselves, mere spectators of images, involved in

[2] In the *Leviathan* (chapter 46) Hobbes explains that 'disobedience may lawfully be punished in them, that against the laws teach even true philosophy'.

no action and hence threatened by nobody. This community has no reason whatsoever to regard truth and truth-tellers as their worst enemies, and Plato offers no explanation for their perverse love of deception and falsehood. If we could confront him with one of his later colleagues in political philosophy, namely, with Hobbes, who held that only 'such truth as opposeth no man's profit, nor pleasure, is to all men welcome' – an obvious statement which, however, he thought important enough to end his *Leviathan* with – he might have agreed on profit and pleasure but not on the assertion that there existed any kind of truth welcome to all men. Hobbes, but not Plato, consoled himself with the existence of indifferent truth, with 'subjects' in which 'men care not', with mathematical truth for instance, 'the doctrine of lines and figures' that 'crosses no man's ambition, profit or lust. For I doubt not, but if it had been a thing contrary to any man's right of dominion, or to the interest of men that have dominion, that the three angles of a triangle should be equal to two angles of a square; that doctrine should have been, if not disputed, yet by the burning of all books of geometry, suppressed, as far as he whom it concerned was able.'[3]

To be sure, there is a decisive difference between Hobbes' mathematical axiom and the true standard for human conduct which Plato's philosopher is supposed to bring back from his journey unto the sky of ideas, although Plato, who believed that mathematical truth opened the eyes of the mind to all truths, was not aware of it. Hobbes' example strikes us as relatively harmless; we are inclined to assume that the human mind will always be able to reproduce such axiomatic statements as that the 'three angles of a triangle should be equal to two angles of a square', and we conclude that 'the burning of all books of geometry' would not be radically effective. The danger would be considerably greater with respect to scientific statements; had history taken a different turn, the whole modern scientific development from Galileo to Einstein might not have come to pass. And certainly, the most vulnerable of this kind of truth would be those highly differentiated and always unique thought trains, of which Plato's doctrine of ideas is an eminent example, where men, since times immemorial, have tried to think rationally beyond the limits of human knowledge.

The modern age, which believes that truth is neither given nor disclosed to but produced by the human mind, has assigned, since Leibniz, mathematical, scientific, and philosophical truth to the common species of rational truth as distinguished from factual truth. I shall use this distinction for convenience's sake with-

---

[3] *Leviathan*, chapter 11.

out discussing its intrinsic legitimacy. Wanting to find out what injury political power is capable of inflicting upon truth, we look into these matters for political rather than philosophical reasons, hence may afford to disregard the question of what truth is, and be content to take the word in the common understanding of men. And if we now think of factual truths, of such modest verities as the role of a man by the name of Trotsky during the Russian Revolution who appears in none of Soviet Russian history books, we become at once aware of how much more vulnerable they are than all the kinds of rational truth taken together. Moreover, since facts and events, the invariable outcome of men living and acting together, constitute the very texture of the political realm, it is of course factual truth we are most concerned with here. Dominion, to speak Hobbes' language, when it attacks rational truth oversteps as it were its own domain, while it gives battle on its own ground when it falsifies or lies away facts. The chances of factual truth to survive the onslaught of power are very slim indeed; it is always in danger of being manoeuvred out of the world not only for a time but potentially for ever. Facts and events are infinitely more fragile things than axioms, discoveries, theories, even the most wildly speculative ones, produced by the human mind; they occur in the field of the ever-changing affairs of men in whose flux there is nothing more permanent than the admittedly relative permanence of the human mind. Once they are lost, no rational effort will ever bring them back. Perhaps the chances that Euclidean mathematics or Einstein's theory of relativity – let alone Plato's philosophy – would have been reproduced in time had their authors been prevented from handing them down to posterity are not so very good either; yet they are infinitely better than the chances that a fact of importance, forgotten or, more likely, lied away, will one day be rediscovered.

II

Although the politically most relevant truths are factual, the conflict between truth and politics was first discovered and articulated with respect to rational truth. The opposite of a rationally true statement is either error and ignorance as in the sciences, or illusion and opinion as in philosophy. Deliberate falsehood, the plain lie, plays its role only in the domain of factual statements, and it seems significant and rather odd that in the long debate of this antagonism of truth and politics from

Plato to Hobbes no one apparently ever believed that organized lying, as we know it today, could be an adequate weapon against truth. In Plato, the truth-teller is in danger of his life, and in Hobbes, where he has become an author, he is threatened with the burning of his books; mere mendacity is not an issue. It is the sophist and the ignoramus but not the liar who occupy Plato's thought, and where he distinguishes between error and lie, that is, between 'involuntary and voluntary ψεῦδος', he is, characteristically, much harsher on people 'wallowing in swinish ignorance' than on liars.[4] Is this because organized lying, dominating the public realm, as distinguished from the private liar who tries his luck on his own hook, was still unknown? Or has this something to do with the striking fact that, with the exception of Zoroastrianism, none of the major religions included lying as such in its catalogue of grave sins? Only with the rise of Puritan morality, which coincided with the rise of organized science whose progress had to be assured on the firm ground of absolute veracity and reliability of every scientist, were lies considered to be serious offences.

However that may be, historically the conflict between truth and politics arose out of two diametrically opposed ways of life, the life of the philosopher as interpreted first by Parmenides and then by Plato, and the way of life of the citizen; the philosopher opposed to the citizens' ever-changing opinions about human affairs, which themselves were in a state of constant flux, the truth about those things that in their very nature were everlasting and from which therefore principles could be derived to stabilize human affairs. Hence the opposite to truth was mere opinion, which was equated with illusion, and it was this degrading of opinion that gave the conflict its political poignancy; for opinion, and

---

[4] I hope no one will tell me anymore that Plato was the inventor of the 'noble lie'. This belief rested on a misreading of a crucial passage (414C) in the *Republic*, where Plato speaks of one of his myths – a 'Phoenician tale' – as a ψεῦδος. Since the same Greek word signifies 'fiction', 'error', and 'lie' according to context – if Plato wants to distinguish between error and lie, the Greek language forces him to speak of 'involuntary' and 'voluntary' ψεῦδος – the text can be rendered with Cornford as 'bold flight of invention' or be read with Eric Voegelin (*Order and History. Plato and Aristotle*, p. 106, Louisiana State University, 1957) as satirical in intention; under no circumstances can it be understood as a recommendation of lying as we understand it. Plato, of course, was permissive about occasional lies to deceive the enemy or insane people – *Republic*, 382; they are 'useful. . . in the way of medicine . . . to be handled by no one but a physician', and the physician in the Polis is the ruler (388). But, contrary to the Cave Allegory, no principle is involved in these passages.

not truth, belongs indeed among the indispensable prerequisites of all power. 'All governments rest on opinion' (Madison), and not even the most autocratic ruler or tyrant could ever rise to power, let alone keep it, without the support of those who are like-minded. By the same token, every claim in the sphere of human affairs to an absolute truth, whose validity needs no support from the side of opinion, strikes at the very roots of all politics and all governments. This antagonism between truth and opinion was further elaborated by Plato (especially in the *Gorgias*) as the antagonism between communicating in the form of 'dialogue', which is the adequate speech for philosophic truth, and in the form of 'rhetoric' by which the demagogue, as we would say today, persuades the multitude.

Traces of this original conflict can still be found in the earlier stages of the modern age though hardly in the world we live in. In Hobbes, for instance, we still read of an opposition of two 'contrary faculties': 'solid reasoning' and 'powerful eloquence', 'the former being grounded upon principles of truth, the other upon opinions . . . and the passions and interests of men, which are different and mutable'.[5] More than a century later, in the age of Enlightenment, these traces have almost but not quite disappeared, and where the ancient antagonism still survived, the emphasis had shifted. In terms of pre-modern philosophy, Lessing's magnificent *Sage jeder, was ihm Wahrheit dünkt, und die Wahrheit selbst sei Gott empfohlen* ('Let each man say what seems to him true, and let's leave truth itself safely in God's hands') would have plainly signified: Man is not capable of truth, all his truths, alas, are δόξαι, mere opinions; whereas for Lessing it meant, on the contrary: Let us thank God that we don't know *the* truth. Even where the note of jubilation, the insight that for men, living in company, the inexhaustible richness of human discourse is infinitely more significant and meaningful than any One Truth could ever be, is absent, the awareness of the frailty of human reason has prevailed since the eighteenth century without complaint or lamentation. We can find it in Kant's grandiose *Critique of Pure Reason*, where reason is led to recognize its own limitations, as we hear it in the words of Madison who more than once stressed that 'the reason of man, like man himself, is timid and cautious when left alone, and acquires firmness and confidence in proportion to the number with which it is associated'.[6] Considerations of this kind, much rather than notions about the individual's right to self-expression, played a decisive part in

---

[5] *Leviathan*, Conclusion.
[6] This and the following quotations from Madison in *The Federalist*, No. 49.

the finally more or less successful struggle to obtain freedom of thought for the spoken and the printed word.[7]

In our context, the question of numbers mentioned by Madison is of special importance. The shift from rational truth to opinion implies a shift from man in the singular to men in the plural, and this means a shift from a domain where nothing counts except the 'solid reasoning' of one mind to a realm where 'strength of opinion' is determined by the individual's reliance upon 'the number which he supposes to have entertained the same opinions' – a number, incidentally, which is not necessarily the number of one's contemporaries. Madison still distinguishes this life in the plural, which is the life of the citizen, from the life of the philosopher for whom such considerations 'ought to be disregarded'; but this distinction has no practical consequence, for 'a nation of philosophers is as little to be expected as the philosophical race of kings wished for by Plato'. We may note in passing that the very notion of a 'nation of philosophers' would have been a contradiction in terms for Plato whose whole political philosophy, including its outspoken tyrannical traits, rests on the conviction that truth can be neither gained nor communicated among the many.

In the world we live in, the last traces of this ancient antagonism between the philosopher's truth and the opinions on the market-place have disappeared. Neither the truth of revealed religion, which the political thinkers of the seventeenth century still treated as a major nuisance, nor the truth of the philosopher, disclosed to man in solitude, interfere any longer with the affairs of the world. As to the former, the separation of Church and State has given us peace, and as to the latter, it has ceased long ago to claim dominion – unless one takes the modern ideologies philosophically seriously, which is difficult indeed since their adherents openly proclaim them to be political weapons and consider the whole question of truth and truthfulness to be irrelevant. Thinking in terms of the tradition, one may be entitled to conclude from this state of affairs that the old conflict has finally been settled, and that especially its original cause, the clash of rational truth and opinion, has disappeared.

This, however, strangely enough, is not the case, for the clash of factual truth and politics, which we witness today on such a large scale, bears, in some respects at least, very similar traits. For while probably

[7] It would be interesting to compare in this respect two outstanding champions of freedom of thought and speech, Spinoza's position in the seventeenth century and Kant's arguments at the end of the eighteenth. For Spinoza, see chapter 20, of the *Theologico-Political Treatise;* for Kant, the late writings, especially 'What is Enlightenment?'.

no former time tolerated so many deviating opinions on religious or philosophical matters, factual truth, if it happens to oppose a given group's profit or pleasure, is greeted today with greater hostility than ever before. To be sure, state secrets have always existed; every government must classify certain information, withhold it from public notice, and who reveals authentic secrets has always been treated as a traitor. With this I am not concerned here. The facts I have in mind are publicly known, and yet the same public that knows them can successfully and often spontaneously prohibit their public discussion and treat them as though they were what they are not, namely, secrets. That their assertion then should prove as dangerous as for instance preaching atheism or some other heresy in former times seems a curious phenomenon, and its significance is enhanced when we find it also in countries that are ruled tyrannically by an ideological government.[8] What seems even more disturbing is that to the extent that unwelcome factual truths are tolerated in free countries they frequently are consciously or unconsciously transformed into opinions – as though the fact of Germany's support of Hitler, or of France's collapse before the German armies in 1940, or of Vatican policies during World War II, were not matters of historical record but of opinion. Since such factual truth concerns issues of immediate political relevance, there is more at stake here than the perhaps inevitable tension between two ways of life within the framework of a common and commonly recognized reality. What is at stake here is this common and factual reality itself, and this is indeed a political problem of the first order. And since factual truth, though so much less open to argument than philosophical truth, and so obviously within the grasp of everybody, seems liable to suffer a similar fate when exposed on the market-place, namely, to be countered not by lies and deliberate falsehoods but by opinion, it may be worth while to reopen the old and apparently obsolete issue of truth versus opinion.

For, seen from the viewpoint of the truth-teller, the tendency to transform fact into opinion, to blur the dividing line between them, is no less perplexing than the truth-teller's older predicament, so vividly expressed in the Cave allegory, where the philosopher, upon his return from his solitary journey to the sky of everlasting ideas, tries to communicate his truth to the multitude with the result that it disappears in the diversity of views, which to him are illusions, and is brought down to

[8] Even in Hitler's Germany and Stalin's Russia it was more dangerous to spread the news about deportation, concentration and extermination camps – regular governmental procedures which were not only 'legal' but had routine character and could not possibly be regarded as authentic state secrets – than to hold different opinions on racism and communism.

the uncertain level of opinion; so that now, back in the Cave, truth itself appears in the guise of the δοκεῖ μοι, 'it seems to me', the very δόξα he had hoped to leave behind once and for all. But the reporter of factual truth is even worse off. He does not return from any journey into regions beyond the realm of human affairs, and he cannot console himself with the thought that he has become a stranger in this world. Similarly, we have no right to console ourselves with the notion that his truth, if truth it should be, is not of this world. If his simple factual statements are not accepted, a truth seen and witnessed with eyes of the body and not the eyes of the mind, the suspicion arises that it may be in the nature of the political realm to deny or pervert truth of every kind, as though men were unable to come to terms with its unyielding, blatant, unpersuasive stubbornness. If this were the case, things would look even more desperate than Plato assumed, for Plato's truth, found and actualized in solitude, transcends by definition the realm of the many, the world of human affairs. (One can understand that the philosopher in his isolation yields to the temptation to use his truth as a standard to be imposed upon human affairs, that is, to equate the transcendence inherent in philosophic truth with the altogether different kind of 'transcendence' by which yardsticks and measurements are separated from the multitude of objects they are to measure; and one can equally well understand that the multitude will resist these standards, since they are actually derived from a sphere that is foreign to the realm of human affairs and can be justified only by a confusion.) Philosophic truth, when it enters the market-place, changes its nature and becomes opinion, because a veritable μετάβασις εἰς ἄλλο γένος, a shifting not merely from one kind of reasoning to another, but from one way of human existence to another, has taken place.

Factual truth, on the contrary, is always related to others; it concerns events and circumstances in which many are involved, it is established by witnesses and depends upon testimony, it exists only to the extent that it is being spoken about even if it occurs in the domain of privacy. It is political by nature. Facts and opinions, though they must be kept apart, are not antagonistic to each other, they belong to the same realm. Facts inform opinions, and various opinions, inspired by different interests and passions, can differ widely and still be legitimate so long as they respect factual truth. Freedom of opinion is a farce unless factual information is guaranteed and the facts themselves are not in dispute. In other words, factual truth informs political thought just as rational truth informs philosophical speculation.

But do facts independent of opinion and interpretation exist at all? Have not generations of historians and philosophers of history demonstrated the impossibility of ascertaining facts without interpretation, since they must be first picked out of a chaos of sheer happenings (and the principles of choice are surely not factual data) and then be fitted into a story which can be told only in a certain perspective that has nothing to do with the original occurrence? No doubt these and many more perplexities inherent in the historical sciences are real, but they are no argument against the existence of factual matter, nor can they serve as a justification for blurring the dividing lines between fact, opinion, and interpretation, or as an excuse for the historian to manipulate facts as he pleases. Even if we admit that every generation has the right to write its own history, we admit no more than that it has the right to rearrange the facts in accordance with its own perspective; we don't admit the right to touch the factual matter itself. To illustrate this point, and as an excuse for not pursuing this issue any further: During the twenties, so a story goes, Clemenceau, shortly before his death, found himself engaged in a debate with a representative of the Weimar Republic on the question of guilt for the outbreak of World War I. 'What in your opinion,' Clemenceau was asked, 'will future historians think of this troublesome and controversial issue?' Whereupon Clemenceau replied: 'This I don't know. But I know for certain that they will not say that Belgium invaded Germany.' We are concerned here with this kind of brutally elementary data whose indestructibility has been taken for granted even by the most extreme and most sophisticated believers in historicism.

It is true, considerably more than the occasional whims of historians would be needed to eliminate from the record the fact that in the night of August 4, 1914, German troops crossed the frontier of Belgium; it would require no less than a power monopoly over the entire civilized world. But such a power monopoly is far from being inconceivable, and it is not difficult to imagine what the fate of factual truth would be if power interests, national or social, had the last say in these matters. Which brings us back to our suspicion that it may be in the nature of the political realm to be at war with truth in all its forms, and hence to the question why a commitment even to factual truth is felt to be an anti-political attitude.

III

When I said that factual, as opposed to rational, truth is not antagonistic to opinion, I stated a half truth. All truths, the various kinds of rational as well as factual truth, are opposed to opinion in their mode of asserting validity. Truth carries with itself an element of coercion, and the frequently tyrannical tendencies, so deplorably obvious among professional truth-tellers, may be caused less by a failing of character than by the strain of habitually living under a kind of compulsion. Statements such as: 'The three angles of a triangle are equal to two angles of a square'; 'The earth moves around the sun'; 'It is better to suffer wrong than to do wrong'; 'In August 1914 Germany invaded Belgium'; are very different in the way they are arrived at, but once perceived as true and pronounced as such they have in common that they are beyond agreement, dispute, opinion, or consent. For those who accept them, they are not changed by the number or lack of number that entertain the same proposition; persuasion or dissuasion is useless, for the content of the statement is not of a persuasive but of a coercive nature. For all of them is true what Le Mercier de la Rivière once remarked about mathematical truth: *'Euclide est un véritable despote; et les vérités géométriques qu'il nous a transmises sont des lois véritablement despotiques.'* Much in the same vein, Grotius – when he wished to limit the power of the absolute prince – had insisted about a hundred years earlier that 'even God cannot cause two times two should not make four'. He invoked the compelling force of truth against political power, he was not interested in the implied limitation of divine omnipotence. These two remarks show how truth looks in the purely political perspective, from the viewpoint of power; and the question is whether power could and should be checked, not only by a constitution and a Bill of Rights, or by a multiplicity of powers as in the system of checks and balances where *le pouvoir arrête le pouvoir*, that is, by factors that arise out of and belong to the political realm proper, but by something which arises from without, has its source outside the political realm, and is as independent of the wishes and desires of the citizens as is the will of the worst tyrant.

Seen from the viewpoint of politics, truth has a despotic character. It therefore is hated by tyrants who rightly fear the competition of a coercive force they cannot monopolize, and it enjoys a rather precarious status in governments that rest on consent and abhor coercion. Facts are beyond agreement and consent, and all talk about them, all exchange of opinion based on correct information will contribute nothing to their establishment. Unwelcome opinion can be argued with, rejected, or compromised upon, but unwelcome facts possess an infuriating stubbornness that nothing can move except plain lies. The trouble is that factual like all other truth peremptorily claims to be acknowledged and precludes debate, and debate constitutes the very essence of political life. The modes of thought and communication that deal with truth, if seen from the political perspective, are necessarily domineering; they don't take into account other people's opinions, which is the hallmark of all strictly political thinking.

Political thought is representative. I form an opinion by considering a given issue from different viewpoints, by making present to my mind the standpoints of those who are absent, that is, I represent them. This process of representation does not blindly adopt the actual views of those who stand somewhere else and hence look upon the world from a different perspective; this is a question neither of empathy, as though I tried to be or to feel like somebody else, nor of counting noses and joining a majority, but of being and thinking in my own identity where actually I am not. The more people's standpoints I have present in my mind while pondering a given issue and the better I can imagine how I would feel and think if I were in their place, the stronger will be my capacity for representative thinking and the more valid my final conclusions, my opinion. (It is this capacity for an 'enlarged mentality' that enables men to judge; as such, it was discovered by Kant – in the first part of his *Critique of Judgment* – who, however, did not recognize the political and moral implications of his discovery.) The very process of opinion-formation is determined by those in whose places somebody thinks and uses his own mind, and the only condition for this exertion of imagination is disinterestedness, the liberation from one's own private interests. Hence, even if I shun all company or am completely isolated while forming an opinion, I am not simply together only with myself in the solitude of philosophic thought; I remain in this world of mutual interdependence where I can make myself the representative of everybody else. To be sure, I can refuse to do this and form an opinion that takes only my own interest, or the interests of the group to which I belong, into account; nothing indeed is more common, even among highly sophisticated people, than this blind obstinacy which becomes manifest in lack of imagination and failure to judge. But the very quality of an opinion as of a judgment depends upon its degree of impartiality.

No opinion is self-evident. In matters of opinion, but not in matters of truth, our thinking is truly discursive, running, as it were, from place to place, from one part of the world to the other through all kinds of conflicting views, until it finally ascends from all these particularities to some impartial generality. Compared with this process, in which a particular issue is forced into the open that it may show itself from all sides, in every possible perspective, until it is flooded and made transparent by the full light of human comprehension, statements of truth possess a peculiar opaqueness. Rational truth enlightens human understanding and factual truth must inform opinions, but these truths, though they are never obscure, are not transparent either, and it is in their very nature to withstand further elucidation as it is in the nature of light to withstand enlightenment. Nowhere, moreover, is this opacity more patent and more irritating than where we are confronted with facts and factual truth, for facts have no conclusive reason whatsoever for being what they are; they could always have been otherwise, and this annoying contingency is literally unlimited. It is because of their haphazardness that pre-modern philosophy refused to take seriously the realm of human affairs, which is permeated by factuality, or to believe that any meaningful truth could ever be discovered in the 'melancholy haphazard' sequence of events (Kant) which constitutes the course of this world. Nor has any modern philosophy of history ever been able to make its peace with the intractable, unreasonable stubbornness of sheer factuality; they have conjured up all kinds of necessity, from the dialectical necessity of a world spirit or of material conditions to the necessities of an allegedly unchangeable and known human nature, in order to cleanse the only realm where men are truly free from the last vestiges of that apparently arbitrary 'it might have been otherwise' which is the price of freedom. It is true that in retrospect, that is, in historical perspective, every sequence of events looks as though it could not have happened otherwise; but this is an optical or rather an existential illusion: nothing could ever happen if reality did not kill by definition all potentialities originally inherent in any given situation.

In other words, factual truth is no more self-evident than opinion, and this may be among the reasons why opinion-holders find it relatively easy to discredit it as just another opinion. Factual evidence, moreover, is established through testimony by eye-witnesses – notoriously unreliable – by records, documents, and monuments, all of which can be suspected of forgery. In case of dispute, only other witnesses but no third and higher instance can be invoked, and settlement is usually arrived at by way of majority, that is, in the same way as the settlement of opinion disputes, a wholly unsatisfactory procedure, since nothing can prevent a majority of witnesses from being false witnesses; on the contrary, under certain circumstances the feeling of belonging to a majority may even encourage false testimony. To the extent, in other words, that factual truth is exposed to the hostility of opinion-holders, it is at least as, and perhaps more, vulnerable than rational philosophical truth.

I mentioned before that in some respects the factual truth-teller is worse off than Plato's philosopher, that his truth has no transcendent origin and possesses not even the relatively transcendent qualities of such political principles as freedom, justice, honour, or courage, all of which may inspire, and then become manifest in, human action. We shall now see that this disadvantage has more serious consequences than we thought before, namely, consequences which concern not only the person of the truth-teller but, more importantly, the chances for his truth to survive. Inspiration of, and manifestation in, human action may not be able to compete with the compelling evidence of truth, but it can compete, as we shall see, with the persuasiveness inherent in opinion. I took the Socratic proposition, It is better to suffer wrong than to do wrong, as example of a philosophic statement which concerns human conduct and hence has political implications. My reason was partly that this sentence has become the beginning of Western ethical thought, and partly that, as far as I know, it has remained the only ethical proposition which can be derived directly from the specifically philosophic experience. (Kant's Categorical Imperative, the only competitor in the field, could be stripped of its Hebrew-Christian ingredients which account for its formulation as an imperative instead of a simple proposition. Its underlying principle is the axiom of non-contradiction – the thief contradicts himself because he wants to keep the stolen goods as his property – and this axiom owes its validity to the same conditions of thought which Socrates was the first to discover.)

The Platonic dialogues tell us time and again how paradoxical the Socratic statement, a proposition and not an imperative, sounded, how easily it stood refuted in the market-place where opinion stands against opinion – is it not rather obvious that one is better off doing wrong than suffering it? – and how unable Socrates was to prove and demonstrate it to the satisfaction not only of his adversaries but also of his friends and disciples.[9] Everything that can be said in its defence we find in the various Platonic dialogues. The chief argument states that for man *being one* it is better to be at odds with the whole world than to be at odds

[9] The decisive passage for Socrates' admitted inability to convince, by mere force of argument, his friends and disciples is *Republic*, 367. See also *Crito*, 49d, 'I know that there are and always will be few people who think like this, and consequently between those who do think so and those who do not there can be no agreement on principle.'

with and contradicted by himself,[10] an argument which is compelling indeed for the philosopher whose thinking is characterized as a silent dialogue with himself,[11] and whose existence therefore depends upon a constantly articulated intercourse with himself, a splitting-into-two of the one he nevertheless *is*; for a basic contradiction between the two partners who carry on the thinking dialogue would destroy the very conditions of philosophizing. In other words: Insofar as man carries with himself a partner from whom he can never win release, he will be better off not to live together with a murderer or a liar; or: since thought is the silent dialogue carried out between me and myself, I must be careful to keep the integrity of this partner intact, for otherwise I shall surely lose the capacity for thought altogether.

To the philosopher, or rather to man insofar as he is a thinking being, this ethical proposition about doing and suffering wrong is no less compelling than mathematical truth; but to man insofar as he is a citizen, an acting being concerned with the world and the public welfare rather than with his own well-being – as for instance his 'immortal soul' whose 'health' should have precedence before the needs of a perishable body – the Socratic statement is not true at all. The disastrous consequences for a community which in all earnest would begin to follow ethical precepts that are derived from man in the singular – be they Socratic, or Platonic, or Christian – have been frequently pointed out. Long before Machiavelli recommended the protection of the political realm against the undiluted principles of the Christian faith – those who refuse to resist evil permit the wicked 'to do as much evil as they please' – Aristotle warned against giving philosophers any say in political matters: men who for professional reasons must be so unconcerned with 'what is good for themselves' cannot very well be trusted with what is good for others, least of all with the 'common good', the down-to-earth interests of the community.[12]

Since philosophic truth concerns man in his singularity it is unpolitical by nature. If the philosopher nevertheless wishes his truth to prevail over and above the opinions of the multitude, he will suffer defeat,

---

[10] See *Gorgias* where Socrates tells Callicles, his opponent, that he will 'not be in agreement with himself but that throughout his life, he will contradict himself'. He then adds: 'I would much rather that the whole world be not in agreement with me and talk against me than that I, *who am one*, should be in discord with myself and talk in self-contradiction' (482).

[11] For a definition of thought as the silent dialogue between me and myself, see especially *Theaetetus* 189–190, and *Sophist* 263–264.

[12] *Nicomachean Ethics*, Book Six, esp. 1140 b9 and 1141 b4.

and he is likely to conclude from this defeat that truth is impotent – a truism which is just as meaningful as if the mathematician, unable to square the circle, should deplore the fact that a circle is not a square. He then may be tempted, like Plato, to win the ear of some philosophically inclined tyrant, and in the fortunately highly unlikely case of success, he might erect one of those tyrannies of 'truth' which we know chiefly from the various political utopias and which of course, politically speaking, are as tyrannical as other forms of despotism. In the slightly less unlikely event, on the other hand, that his truth should prevail without the help of violence, simply because men happen to concur in it, he would have won a Pyrrhic victory. For truth would then owe its prevalence not to its own compelling quality but to the agreement of many who might change their minds tomorrow and agree on something else; what had been philosophic truth would have become mere opinion.

Since however philosophic truth carries with itself an element of coercion, it may tempt the statesman under certain conditions no less than the power of opinion is tempting the philosopher. Thus, in the Declaration of Independence, Jefferson declared certain 'truths to be self-evident' because he wished to put the basic consent between the men of the Revolution beyond dispute and argument; like mathematical axioms, they should express 'beliefs of men [which] depend not on their own will, but follow involuntarily the evidence proposed to their minds'.[13] But by saying: '*We hold* these truths to be self-evident', he conceded, albeit without becoming aware of it, that the statement: 'All men are created equal', is not self-evident but stands in need of agreement and consent, that equality, insofar as it is political, is an opinion and not 'the truth'. To be sure, there exist philosophic or religious statements that correspond to this opinion – such as that all men are equal before God, or before death, or insofar as they all belong to the same species of *animal rationale*; but none of them was ever of any political or practical consequence because the equalizer – God, or death, or nature – transcended and remained outside the realm where human intercourse takes place. Such 'truths' are not between men but above them, and nothing of the sort lies behind the modern or ancient, especially Greek, consent to equality. That all men are created equal is neither self-evident nor can it be proved. We hold this opinion because freedom is possible only among equals, and we believe that the joys and gratifications of free company are to be preferred to the doubtful pleasures of holding dominion. To be sure, such preferences are politically of the greatest importance, and there are few things by which men are so profoundly dis-

---

[13] See Jefferson's 'Draft Preamble to the Virginia Bill establishing religious Freedom'.

tinguished from each other as by such choices. Their human quality, one is tempted to say, and certainly the quality of every kind of intercourse with them, depends upon them. Still, these are matters of opinion and not of truth – as Jefferson, much against his will, was forced to admit. Their validity depends upon free agreement and consent, they are arrived at by discursive, representative thinking, and they are communicated by means of persuasion and dissuasion.

The Socratic proposition, It is better to suffer wrong than to do wrong, is not an opinion but claims to be truth, and though one may doubt that it ever had a direct political consequence, its impact upon practical conduct as an ethical precept is undeniable; only religious commandments, which are absolutely binding for the community of believers, can claim greater recognition. Does this fact not stand in clear contradiction to the generally accepted impotence of philosophic truth? And since we know from the Platonic dialogues how unpersuasive Socrates' statement remained for friend and foe alike whenever he tried to prove it, we must ask ourselves how it could ever have obtained its high degree of validation. Obviously, this has been due to a rather unusual kind of persuasion; Socrates decided to stake his life on this truth, to set an example, not when he appeared before the Athenian Tribunal but when he refused to escape the death sentence. And this teaching by example is indeed the only form of 'persuasion' philosophic truth is capable of without perversion or distortion; by the same token, philosophic truth can become 'practical' and inspire action without violating the rules of the political realm only when it manages to become manifest in the guise of an example. It is the only chance for an ethical principle to be verified. Thus, in order to verify, for example, the notion of courage, we may recall the example of Achilles, or to verify the notion of goodness, we are inclined to think of Jesus of Nazareth or of St. Francis; these examples teach or persuade by inspiration, so that whenever we try to perform a deed of courage or of goodness, it is as though we imitated someone else – the *imitatio Christi* or whatever the case might be. It has often been remarked that 'a lively sense of filial duty is more effectually impressed on the mind of a son or daughter by reading *King Lear*, than by all the dry volumes of ethics and divinity that ever were written',[14] and that 'general precepts learned at the feet either of priests or philosophers, or even drawn from one's own resources, are never so efficacious as an example of virtue or holiness',[15] and the reason, as Kant explains, is that we always need 'intuitions . . . to verify the reality of our concepts. . . . If they are pure concepts of the under-

---

[14] Jefferson in a letter to W. Smith of November 13, 1787.
[15] Kant, *Critique of Judgment*, paragraph 32.

standing [such as the concept of the triangle] the intuitions go by the name of schemata', such as the ideal triangle, perceived only by the eyes of the mind and yet indispensable to recognize all real triangles; if however the concepts are practical, relating to conduct, the 'intuitions are called *examples*'.[16] And unlike the schemata which our mind produces of its own accord by means of imagination, these examples derive from history and poetry through which an altogether different 'field of imagination is laid open to our use' (Jefferson).

To be sure, this transformation of a theoretical or speculative statement into exemplary truth of which only moral philosophy is capable is a borderline experience for the philosopher; by setting an example and 'persuading' the multitude in the only way open to him, he has begun to act; and today when hardly any philosophic statement, no matter how daring, will be taken seriously enough to endanger the philosopher's life, even this rare chance of having a philosophic truth politically validated has disappeared. In our context, however, the point is that such a possibility exists at all for the teller of rational truth, for it does not exist under any circumstances for the factual truth-teller, who in this as in other respects is so much worse off. Not only do factual statements contain no principles upon which men could act and which thus could become manifest in the world; their very content defies this kind of verification. A factual truth-teller, in the unlikely case that he wished to stake his life on a particular fact, would achieve a kind of miscarriage: what would become manifest in his act would be his courage or, perhaps, his stubbornness, but neither the truth of what he has to say nor even his own truthfulness. For why shouldn't a liar stick to his lies with great courage, especially in politics where he might be motivated by patriotism or some other kind of legitimate group partiality?

IV

The hallmark of factual truth is that its opposite is neither error nor illusion nor opinion, none of which reflects upon personal truthfulness, but the deliberate falsehood or lie. Error of course is possible and even common with respect to factual truth, in which case it is in no way different from scientific or rational truth. But the point is that with respect to facts there exists another alternative in addition to mere error, and this alternative, the deliberate falsehood, no longer belongs to the same species of propositions which truly or mistakenly intend no more than

[16] Kant, *Critique of Judgment*, paragraph 59.

what is, or how something that is appears to me. A factual state-
̲̲̲̲ – Germany invaded Belgium in August 1914 – acquires political
implications only by being put into an interpretative context. But the
opposite proposition which Clemenceau, still unacquainted with the
art of re-writing history, thought absurd needs no context to be of political significance: it clearly is an attempt at changing the record, and as
such it is a form of *action*. And the same is true when the liar, lacking the
power to make his falsehoods stick, does not insist on the gospel truth
of his statement but pretends that this is his 'opinion' to which he claims
his constitutional rights. This is frequently done by subversive groups,
and the resulting confusion can be considerable in a politically immature
public. The blurring of the dividing line between factual truth and
opinion belongs among the many forms lying can assume, all of which
are forms of action.

While the liar is a man of action, the truth-teller, whether he tells
rational or factual truth, most emphatically is not. If the factual truth-
teller wants to play a political role and therefore to be persuasive, he will,
more often than not, go to considerable lengths to explain why his
particular truth serves the best interests of some group. And just as the
philosopher wins a Pyrrhic victory when his truth becomes a dominant
opinion among opinion-holders; the factual truth-teller, when he enters
the political realm and identifies himself with some partial interest and
power formation, compromises on the only quality which could have
made his truths appear plausible, namely, his personal truthfulness,
guaranteed by impartiality, integrity, and independence. There is hardly
a political figure more likely to arouse justified suspicion than the professional truth-teller who has discovered some happy coincidence between truth and interest. The liar, on the contrary, needs no such
doubtful accommodations to appear on the political scene; he has the
great advantage that he always is, so to speak, already in the midst of it.
He is an actor by nature; he says what is not because he wants things to
be different from what they are, that is, he wants to change the world.
He takes advantage of the undeniable affinity of our capacity for action,
for changing reality, with this mysterious faculty of ours that enables us
to *say*, The sun shines, when it is raining cats and dogs. If we were as
conditioned in our behaviour as some philosophies have wished us to
be we would never be able to accomplish this little miracle. In other
words, our ability to lie – but not necessarily our ability to tell the truth
– belongs among the few obvious, demonstrable data that confirm
human freedom. That we can change the circumstances under which we
live at all rests on our relative freedom from them, and it is this freedom
that is abused and perverted through mendacity. If it is the almost irre-

sistible temptation of the professional historian to fall into the trap of necessity and to deny implicitly freedom of action, it is the almost equally irresistible temptation of the professional politician to overestimate the possibilities of this freedom and to condone implicitly the lying denial or distortion of facts.

To be sure, as far as action is concerned, organized lying is a marginal phenomenon, but the trouble is that its opposite, the mere telling of facts, leads to no action whatsoever. It even tends, under normal circumstances, to accept things as they are[17]. Truthfulness has never been counted among the political virtues because it has indeed little to contribute to that change of world and circumstances which is among the most legitimate political activities. Only where a community has embarked upon organized lying on principle, and not only with respect to particulars, can truthfulness as such, unsupported by the distorting forces of power and interest, become a political factor of the first order. Where everybody lies about everything of importance, the truth-teller, whether he knows it or not, has begun to act, he too has engaged himself in political business; for in the unlikely event that he survives, he has started to change the world.

In this situation, however, he will soon find himself again at an annoying disadvantage. I mentioned before the contingent character of facts, which always could have been otherwise and therefore possess by themselves no trace of self-evidence or plausibility for the human mind. Since the liar is free to fashion his 'facts' until they fit the profit and pleasure, or even the mere expectation, of his audience, the chances are that he will be more persuasive than the truth-teller. He usually will indeed have plausibility on his side; his exposition will sound more logical, as it were, since the element of unexpectedness, one of the outstanding characteristics of all events, has mercifully disappeared. It is not only rational truth that, in the Hegelian phrase, stands common sense on its head; reality quite frequently offends the soundness of common-sense reasoning no less than it offends profit and pleasure.

We must now turn our attention to the relatively recent phenomenon of mass manipulation of fact and opinion as it has become evident in the re-writing of history, in image-making, and in actual government policy. The traditional political lie, so prominent in the history of diplomacy and statecraft, used to concern either true secrets, data that had never appeared in public, or intentions which anyhow do not possess the same

---

[17] This, of course, is not to deny that the disclosure of facts may be legitimately used by political organizations or that, under certain circumstances, factual matters brought to public attention will considerably encourage and strengthen the claims of ethnic and social groups.

degree of reality as accomplished facts; like everything that goes on merely inside ourselves, intentions are only potentialities, and what was intended to be a lie can always turn out to be true in the end. In contrast, the modern lies deal efficiently with things that are no secrets at all but known to practically everybody.

This is obvious in the case of re-writing contemporary history under the eyes of those who witnessed it, but it is equally true in 'image making' of all sorts where again every known and established fact can be denied or neglected if it is likely to hurt the image; for an 'image', unlike an old-fashioned portrait, is not supposed to flatter reality but to offer a full-fledged substitute for it. And this substitute, because of modern techniques and the mass media, is of course much more in the public eye than the original had ever been. We are finally confronted with highly respected statesmen who, like de Gaulle and Adenauer, have been able to base their basic policies on such evident non-facts as that France belongs among the victors of the last war and hence is one of the great powers, or that the majority of the German people were opposed to Hitler.[18] All these lies, whether their authors know it or not, harbour an element of violence; organized lying always intends to destroy whatever it has decided to negate, although only totalitarian governments have consciously adapted lying as the first step to murder. When Trotsky learned that he had never played a role in the Russian Revolution he must have known that his death warrant had been signed. Clearly, it is easier to eliminate a public figure from the record of history if, at the same time, he can be eliminated from the world of the living. In other words, the difference between the traditional and the modern lie more often than not will amount to the difference between hiding and destroying.

Moreover, the traditional lie concerned only particulars and was never meant to deceive literally everybody; it was directed at the enemy and meant to deceive only him. These two limitations restricted the injury inflicted upon truth to such an extent that it may appear almost harmless to us in retrospect. Since facts always occur in a context, a particular lie – that is, a falsehood that makes no attempt at changing the whole context – tears, as it were, a hole in the fabric of factuality. As every historian knows, one can spot a lie by noticing incongruities,

---

[18] For France, see the excellent article 'De Gaulle: Pose and Policy', in *Foreign Affairs*, July 1965. For Adenauer, see his *Memoirs 1945–53*, Chicago, 1966, p. 89, where he puts into the minds of the occupation powers what he has repeated many times since, namely, 'that the barbarism of National Socialism had affected only a relatively small percentage of the country'.

holes or junctures of patched up places. So long as the texture as a whole is kept intact, the lie will eventually show up as if of its own accord. The second limitation concerns those who are engaged in the business of deception. They used to belong to the restricted circle of statesmen and diplomats who among themselves still knew and could preserve the truth. They were not likely to fall victims to their own falsehoods, they could deceive others without deceiving themselves. Both of these mitigating circumstances of the old art of lying are conspicuously absent from the manipulation of facts which confronts us today.

What then is the significance of these limitations, and why are we justified in calling them mitigating circumstances? Why has self-deception become an indispensable tool in the trade of image-making, and why should it be worse, for the world as well as for the liar himself, to be deceived by his own lies than it would be if he merely deceived others? What better moral excuse could a liar offer than that his aversion to lying was so great that he had first to convince himself before he could lie to others? And, finally and perhaps most disturbingly, if the modern political lies are so big that they require a complete rearrangement of the whole factual texture, the making of another reality, as it were, into which they will fit without seam, crack, or fissure, exactly as the facts fitted into their own original context, what prevents these new stories, images, and non-facts from becoming an adequate substitute for reality and factuality?

An old medieval anecdote illustrates nicely and succinctly how difficult it can be to lie to others without lying to oneself. It is the story of what happened one night in a town on whose watch-tower a sentry was on duty day and night to warn the people of the approach of the enemy. The sentry was a man given to practical jokes, and when he gave the danger signal he just wanted to give the townsfolk a nice little scare. His success was overwhelming: everybody rushed to the walls – and he himself was the last to run to protect the town from a non-existent enemy. The tale suggests to what an extent our common sense for reality is dependent upon sharing the world with our fellow men, and what strength of character is required to stick to anything, truth or lie, which is unshared by anybody else. In other words, the more successful a liar is the more likely it is that he will fall prey to his own fabrications. The self-deceived joker, on the other hand, who proves to be in the same boat as his victims will appear vastly superior in trustworthiness to the cold-blooded liar who permits himself to enjoy his prank from without. Only self-deception is likely to create a semblance of truthfulness, and the only persuasive factor which in a debate about facts sometimes has a chance to prevail against pleasure, fear, and profit is personal appearance.

Current moral prejudice tends to be rather harsh on cold-blooded lying, whereas the frequently highly developed arts of self-deception are usually regarded with great tolerance and permissiveness. Among the few examples in literature that can be quoted against this current evaluation is the famous scene in the monastery at the beginning of the *Brothers Karamazov* where the father, an inveterate liar, asks the Staretz: 'And what must I do to gain salvation?', and the Staretz replies: '*Above all, never lie to yourself.*' Dostoevski adds no explanation or elaboration. Arguments in support of a statement: It is better to lie to others than to deceive yourself, would have to point out that the cold-blooded liar remains aware of the distinction between truth and falsehood, and that the truth he is hiding from others has not yet been manoeuvred out of the world altogether; it has found its last refuge in him. The injury done to reality is neither complete nor final, and, by the same token, the injury done to the liar himself is not final or complete either. He lied but he is not yet a liar. Both he and the world he deceived are not beyond 'salvation' – to put it into the language of the Staretz.

Unknown to former times, such completeness and potential finality are the dangers that arise out of the modern manipulation of facts. Even in the free world where the government has not monopolized the power to decide and tell what factually is or is not, gigantic interest organizations have generalized a kind of *raison d'état* mentality that was formerly restricted to the handling of foreign affairs and, in its worst excesses, limited to situations of clear and present danger. National propaganda on the governmental level, on the other side, has learnt more than a few tricks from business practices and Madison Avenue methods. Images made for domestic consumption, as distinguished from lies directed at a foreign adversary, can become a reality for everybody, first of all for the image-makers themselves who, while still in the act of preparing their 'products', are already overwhelmed by the mere thought of their victims' potential number. No doubt, the originators of the lying image who 'inspire' the hidden persuaders still know that they want to deceive an enemy on the social or the national level, but the result is that a whole group of people and even whole nations may take their bearings from a web of deceptions to which their leaders wished to subject their opponents.

What then happens follows almost automatically. The main effort of the deceived group and the deceivers themselves is likely to be directed toward keeping the propaganda image intact, and this image is less threatened by the enemy and by real hostile interests than by those who, inside the group itself, have managed to escape its spell and insist on talking about facts or events that do not fit the image. Contemporary history is full of examples when factual truth-tellers were felt to be more dangerous and even more hostile than the real opponent. These arguments against self-deception must not be confused with protests of 'idealists', whatever their merit, against lying on principle and against the age-old arts of deceiving the enemy. Politically, the point of the matter is that the modern arts of self-deception are liable to transform an outside matter into an inside issue, so that an international or inter-group conflict boomerangs back on to the scene of domestic politics. The self-deceptions practised on both sides in the period of the Cold War are too numerous to enumerate, they obviously are a case in point. Conservative critics of mass democracy have frequently outlined the dangers this form of government brings to international affairs – without, to be sure, mentioning the dangers peculiar to monarchies or oligarchies. The strength of their arguments lies in the undeniable fact that under fully democratic conditions deception without self-deception is well-nigh impossible.

In our present system of global communication between a great number of independent nations, no power is even conceivably great enough to make its 'image' fool-proof. Under these conditions, images have a relatively short life-expectancy; they are likely to explode, not only when the chips are down and reality makes its reappearance in public, but even before, when fragments of facts constantly disturb and throw off-gear the propaganda war between conflicting images. However, this is not the only, and even less the most significant, way in which reality takes its revenge on those who dare defy it. The life-expectancy of these images is not likely to be significantly increased even under conditions of a world government, or some other modern version of the *Pax Romana*. This is best illustrated by the relatively closed systems of totalitarian governments and one-party dictatorships, which are of course by far the most effective in shielding ideologies and images against the impact of reality and truth.[19] Their trouble is that they con-

[19] An amusing illustration of the difficulties besetting the re-writers of history has been published in Merle Fainsod's publication of the Smolensk Archive (*Smolensk under Soviet Rule*, Cambridge, 1958, p. 374). 'In a memorandum dated February 19, 1935 . . . a whole series of questions' was raised. 'What should be done with speeches by Zinoviev, Kamenev, Rykov, Bukharin, et al. at Party Congresses, plenums of the Central Committee, in the Cominterns, the Congress of Soviets, etc.? What of anthologies in Marxism . . . written or edited jointly by Lenin, Zinoviev, . . . and others? What of Lenin's writings edited by Kamenev? . . . What should be done in cases where Trotsky . . . had written an article in an issue of the *Communist International*? Should the whole number be confiscated?' These are indeed puzzling questions; unfortunately, the Archive contains no replies.

stantly must change the falsehoods they offer as substitute for the real story; changing circumstances require the substitution of one history book for another, the exchange of pages in the encyclopedias and reference books, the disappearance of certain names and the appearance of others, unknown or little known before. And though this utter lack of stability gives no indication of what the truth might be, it is an indication, and even an all-important one, of the lying character of all public utterances concerning the factual world. It has frequently been noticed that the surest result of brain-washing in the long run is a peculiar kind of cynicism, the absolute refusal to believe in the truth of anything, no matter how well it may be established. In other words, the result of a consistent and total substitution of lies for factual truth is not that the lie now will be accepted as truth, and truth be defamed as lie, but that the sense by which we take our bearings in the real world – and the category of truth versus falsehood is among the mental means to this end – is being destroyed.

And for this trouble there is no remedy. It is but the other side of the disturbing contingency of all factual reality. Since everything that actually happened in the realm of human affairs could just as well have been otherwise, the possibilities for lying are boundless, and it is this boundlessness that makes for self-defeat. Only the occasional liar will find it possible to stick to a particular falsehood with unwavering consistency; those who adjust images and stories to ever-changing circumstances will find themselves floating in the wide-open horizon of potentiality, staggering from one possibility to the next, unable to hold on to their own fabrication. Far from achieving an adequate substitute for reality and factuality, they have transformed facts and events back into the potentiality out of which they originally appeared, and the surest sign of their factuality is precisely this stubborn thereness whose inherent contingency ultimately defies all attempts at conclusive explanation. The images, on the contrary, can always be explained and made plausible – this gives them their momentary advantage over factual truth – but they can never compete in stability with that which simply is because it happens to be thus and not otherwise. This is the reason why consistent lying, metaphorically speaking, pulls the ground from under our feet and provides no other ground on which to stand. This experience of a trembling, wobbling motion of everything we rely on for our sense of direction and reality is among the outstanding and most common experiences of men under totalitarian rule.

Hence, the undeniable affinity of lying with action, with changing the world, in short, with politics, is limited by the very nature of the things that are open to man's faculty for action. The convinced image-maker is in error when he believes that he may anticipate changes by lying about factual matters everybody wishes to eliminate anyhow. The erection of Potemkin's villages, so dear to the politicians and propagandists of underdeveloped countries, never leads to the establishment of the real thing but only to a proliferation and perfection of make-believe. Not the past, and all factual truth concerns of course the past, and the present insofar as it is the outcome of the past, but the future is open to action; if this past and present are treated as parts of the future – that is, changed back into their former potentiality – the political realm is deprived not only of its main stabilizing force but of the starting-point from which to change and begin something new. What then begins is the constant shifting and shuffling in utter sterility which is so characteristic of many new nations that had the bad luck of being born in an age of propaganda.

That facts are not secure in the hands of power is obvious, but the point here is that power by its very nature can never produce a substitute for the secure stability of factual reality which, because it is past, has grown into a dimension outside our reach. Facts assert themselves by being stubborn, and their fragility I mentioned before is oddly combined with great resiliency – the same irreversibility that is the hallmark of all human action. The stubbornness of facts is in this respect superior to power; they are less transitory than power formations, which arise when men get together but disappear as soon as the original purpose is achieved or lost. Its transitory character makes power a highly unreliable instrument for permanence of any kind, and this means that not only truth and facts, but also untruth and non-facts are not secure in its hands. The political attitude to facts must indeed tread the very narrow path between the danger of taking them as the results of some necessary development which men could never prevent and about which they therefore can do nothing, and the danger of denying them, of trying to manipulate them out of the world.

V

In conclusion, I shall return to the questions I raised at the beginning of these reflections. Truth, though powerless and always defeated in a head-on clash with the powers-that-be, possesses a strength of its own: whatever those in power may contrive, they are unable to discover or invent a viable substitute for it. Persuasion and violence can defeat truth, but they cannot replace it. And this applies to rational or religious truth as it applies, more obviously, to factual truth. To look upon politics from the perspective of truth, as I have done here, means to take one's stand outside the political realm. This standpoint is the standpoint of the truthteller, who forfeits his position, and with it the validity of what he has to say, if he tries to interfere directly with human affairs and to speak the language of persuasion or violence. It is to this position and its significance for the political realm that we must now turn our attention.

The standpoint outside the political realm, outside the community to which we belong and the company of our peers, is clearly characterized by one of the various modes of being alone. Outstanding among the existential modes of truth-telling are the solitude of the philosopher, the isolation of the scientist and the artist, the impartiality of the historian and judge, and the independence of the fact-finder, the witness, or the reporter. (This impartiality differs from that of the qualified, representative opinion, mentioned before, insofar as it is not acquired inside the political realm but inherent in the position of outsider required for these occupations.) These modes of being alone differ in many respects, but they have in common that so long as the occupation lasts, no political commitment, no adherence to a cause is possible. They are of course common to all men, they are modes of human existence as such; only when one of them is adopted as a way of life, which even then is never lived in complete solitude or isolation or independence, is it likely to conflict with the demands of the political.

It is only natural that we become aware of the non-political and, potentially, even anti-political nature of truth – *Fiat veritas, pereat mundus* – only in case of conflict, and I have insisted up to now on this side of the matter. But this cannot possibly tell the whole story. It leaves out of account certain public institutions, established and supported by the powers-that-be, in which, contrary to all political rules, truth and truthfulness have always been the highest criteria of speech and endeavour. To these belong notably the judiciary, which either as a branch of government or as direct administration of justice is carefully protected against social and political power, and all institutions of higher learning to which the state entrusts the education of its future citizens. To the extent that Academe remembers its ancient origins, it must know that it was founded by the most determined and most influential opponent of the polis. To be sure, Plato's dreams did not come true; Academe never became a counter-society, and nowhere do we hear of even an attempt from the side of the universities at seizing power. But what Plato had never dreamt of did come true: the political realm recognized that it needed an institution outside the power struggle in addition to the impartiality required in the administration of justice; for whether these places of education and higher learning are in private or in public hands is of no great importance, their very existence as well as their integrity depend upon the good will of the government anyhow. Very unwelcome truths have emerged from the universities, and very unwelcome judgments have been handed down from the bench, time and again, and these like other refuges of truth have remained exposed to all the dangers arising from social and political power. Yet, the chances of truth to prevail in public are of course greatly improved by the mere existence of such places and the organization of independent, supposedly disinterested scholars associated with them. And it can hardly be denied that, at least in constitutionally ruled countries, the political realm has recognized, even in case of conflict, that it has a stake in the existence of men and institutions over which it has no power.

This authentically political significance of Academe is today easily overlooked because of the prominence of its professional schools and the evolution of its natural-science divisions where pure research has yielded so many unexpected and decisive results of vital necessity to the country at large. No one can possibly gainsay the social and technical usefulness of the universities, but this importance is not political. The historical sciences and the humanities which are supposed to find out, stand guard over, and interpret factual truth and human documents are politically of greater relevance. Factual truth-telling comprehends much more than the daily information, supplied by reporters, publicists and journalists, without whom we should never find our bearings in an ever-changing world and, in the most literal sense, would never know where we are. This, to be sure, is of the most immediate political importance, but if the press should ever really become the 'fourth branch of government', it would have to be protected against governmental power and social pressure even more carefully than the judiciary. For this most important political function of sheer information is done from outside the political realm strictly speaking; no action and no decision are, or should be, involved.

Reality is different from, and more than, the totality of facts and events which anyhow is unascertainable. Who says what is – λέγει τὰ ἐόντα – always tells a story, and in this story the particular facts lose their contingency and acquire some humanly comprehensible meaning. It is perfectly true that 'all sorrows can be borne if you put them into a story or tell a story about them' – as Isak Dinesen said, who was not only one of the great story-tellers of our time but, almost unique in this respect, also knew what she was doing. She could have added that joy and bliss too become bearable and meaningful for men only when they can talk about them and tell them as a story. To the extent that the factual truth-teller is also a story-teller, he brings about that 'reconciliation with reality' which Hegel, the philospher of history *par excellence*, understood as the ultimate goal of all philosophic thought and which indeed has been the secret motor of all historiography that transcends mere learnedness. The transformation of the given raw material of sheer happenings, which the historian, like the fiction writer (a good novel is by no means a simple concoction or figment of pure fantasy), must perform is closely akin to the poet's transformation of moods or movements of the heart, the transfiguration of grief into lamentation or of jubilation into praise. We may see, with Aristotle, in the poet's political function the operation of a Catharsis, a cleansing or purging of all emotions that could prevent men from acting. The political function of the story-teller, historian or novelist, is to teach acceptance of things as they are. Out of this acceptance, which also can be called truthfulness, arises the faculty of judgment – that, again in Isak Dinesen's words, 'at the end we shall be privileged to view, and review, it – and that is what is named the day of judgment'.

No doubt all these politically relevant functions are performed from without the political realm. They require non-commitment and impartiality, freedom from interest in thought and judgment. Disinterested pursuit of truth has a long history; its origin, characteristically, precedes all our theoretical and scientific traditions, including our tradition of philosophic and political thought. I think it can be traced to the moment when Homer chose to sing the deeds of the Trojans no less than those of the Achaeans, and to praise the glory of Hector, the foe and the defeated man, no less than the glory of Achilles, the hero of his kinfolk. This had happened nowhere before; no other civilization, no matter how splendid, had been able to look with equal eyes upon friend and foe, upon success and defeat which, since Homer, have not been recognized as ultimate standards of men's judgment, even though they are ultimates for their lives' destinies. Homeric impartiality echoes throughout Greek history, and it inspired the first great factual truth-teller who became the father of history: Herodotus tells us even in the first sentences of his stories that he set out to prevent the 'great and wondrous deeds of the Greeks *and* the barbarians from losing their due meed of glory'. This is the root of all so-called objectivity, this curious passion, unknown outside Western civilization, for intellectual integrity at almost any price. Without it, no science would ever have come into being.

Since I have dealt here with politics from the perspective of truth, hence from a viewpoint outside the political realm, I have failed to mention even in passing the greatness and the dignity of what goes on inside it. I have spoken as though it were no more than a battlefield of partial, conflicting interests where nothing counts but pleasure and profit, partisanship, and the lust for dominion. In short, I have dealt with politics as though I, too, believed that all public affairs are ruled by interest and power, that there would be no political realm at all if we were not bound to take care of life's necessities. The reason for this deformation is that factual truth clashes with the political only on this lowest level of human affairs, just as Plato's philosophic truth clashed with the political on the considerably higher level of opinion and agreement. In this perspective, we remain unaware of the actual content of political life, of the joy and the gratification that arise out of being in company with our peers, of acting together and appearing in public, of inserting ourselves into the world by word and deed, thus acquiring and sustaining our personal identity and beginning something entirely new.

However, what I meant to show here is that this whole sphere, its greatness notwithstanding, is limited, that it does not encompass the whole of man's and the world's existence. It is limited by those things which men cannot change at will. And it is only by respecting its own borders that this realm, where we are free to act and to change, can remain intact and keep its own integrity and its own promises. Conceptually, we may call truth what we cannot change; metaphorically, it is the ground on which we stand and the sky that stretches above us.

6 Alienation and Anomie[1]

Steven Lukes

Both Marx and Durkheim were profound critics of industrial society in nineteenth-century Europe. What is striking is the markedly different bases of their criticisms of the ills of their societies, which can best be brought out by a careful consideration of the different assumptions and implications that belong to the two concepts of alienation and anomie, which they respectively employed.[2] These concepts were elaborated by the two thinkers in their earliest writings and remain implicit as basic and integral elements in their developed social theories. Thus a study of the differing perspectives which they manifest should be fruitful. I shall argue: first, that they are both socio-psychological concepts, embodying hypotheses about specific relationships between social conditions and individual psychological states; second, that they differ precisely in the sorts of hypotheses they embody; and third, that this difference derives in part from a fundamental divergence in the views of human nature they presuppose. Fourthly, I shall examine the nature of that divergence, and in particular the extent to which the dispute is an empirical one. I shall conclude by asking to what extent such approaches to the analysis of society remain relevant and important today.

First, however, I need to make the negative point that contemporary uses of the notions of alienation and anomie, while claiming to derive from Marx and Durkheim, are not for our purposes a useful starting-point. 'Alienation' in particular has achieved considerable and widespread contemporary currency, but it has become debased in consequence. Its evident resonance for 'neo-marxist' thinkers, in both the West and the East, for existentialist philosophers and theologians, for psychiatrists and industrial sociologists, for *déraciné* artists and intellectuals and student rebels, has meant that it has been widely extended and altered in the interests of a number of contemporary preoccupations;

[1] My thanks are especially due to Dr S. Avineri, Professor Sir I. Berlin and Mr J. P. Plamenatz for their kind and helpful comments on an earlier draft of this article.
[2] For other discussions of these concepts, treating them together but in ways rather different both from one another and from that adopted here, see J. Horton, 'The Dehumanisation of Anomie and Alienation', *British Journal of Sociology*, XV, 4, December 1964, and E. H. Mizruchi, 'Alienation and Anomie', in I. L. Horowitz (ed.), *The New Sociology: Essays in Social Science and Social Theory* (New York, 1964).

as a result the core of Marx's concept has been lost.[3] 'Anomie' has been less widely used, but it too has achieved a new life, within American social science. In particular, Robert Merton's paper 'Social Structure and Anomie'[4] (published 1938) has led to an extensive literature of conceptual refinement and empirical research, chiefly concerned with 'deviance' in all its forms.[5] But here too, much of the original meaning of the concept has been lost: in particular, most writers have followed Merton in discarding Durkheim's theory of human nature.

Furthermore, modern versions of these concepts vary widely in the range of their empirical reference. In the work of sociologists they are often taken as synonymous or else one is taken to be a sub-type of the other. Thus Nettler, Seeman and Scott in recent attempts to develop typologies of alienation count anomie as a variant, while Srole[6] counts alienation as a variant of anomie. Worse, there has been endless dispute in the case of both concepts about whether they are to be taken as sociological or psychological or as socio-psychological and, if the last, in what sense. Thus Merton defines 'the sociological concept of anomie' as 'a breakdown in the cultural structure, occurring particularly when there is an acute disjunction between the cultural norms and goals and the socially structured capacities of members of the group to act in accord with them',[7] and Robin Williams observes that 'Anomie as a

---

[3] Robert Nisbet writes: 'The hypothesis of alienation has reached an extraordinary degree of importance. It has become nearly as prevalent as the doctrine of enlightened self-interest was two generations ago' (*The Quest for Community*, New York, 1953, p. 15). There is even an 'alienation reader' (E. and M. Josephson, *Man Alone*, New York, 1962).
[4] R. K. Merton, *Social Theory and Social Structure* (Glencoe, revised edition, 1957), ch. IV.
[5] According to a recent article on the subject (H. McClosky and J. H. Schaar, 'Psychological Dimensions of Anomy', *American Sociological Review*, 30, 1965) there have been since Merton's paper first appeared about 35 papers on 'anomy'. 'In addition, the concept has been used in a large number of books and essays and applied to discussions of an astonishing variety of topics, ranging from delinquency among the young to apathy among the old, and including along the way such matters as political participation, status aspirations, the behaviour of men in prisons, narcotics addiction, urbanization, race relations, social change, and suicide'. *Art. cit.* p. 14.
[6] G. Nettler, 'A Measure of Alienation', *American Sociological Review*, 22, 1957. M. Seeman, 'On the Meaning of Alienation', *American Sociological Review*, 24, 1959. M. B. Scott, 'The Social Sources of Alienation', *Inquiry*, 6, 1963. L. Srole, 'Social Integration and Certain Corollaries', *American Sociological Review*, 21, 1956.
[7] *Op. cit.*, ch. V, p. 162.

social condition has to be defined independently of the psychological states thought to accompany normlessness and normative conflict'; while, for example, Riesman, MacIver, Lasswell and Srole[8] take it to refer to a state of mind. Similarly, 'alienation' is sometimes taken to refer to an objective social condition, which is to be identified independently of people's feelings and beliefs, as in the work of Lukacs and those who follow him: men live within 'reified' and 'fetishist' social forms and the task is precisely to make them *conscious* of their history, which is 'in part the product, evidently unconscious until now, of the activity of men themselves, and in part the succession of the processes in which the forms of this activity, the relations of man with himself (with nature and with other men) are transformed';[9] on the other hand, very many writers take alienation to be a state of mind (e.g. existentialist writers, theologians, psychiatrists, American sociologists). One writer even takes alienation to be synonymous with frustration of any kind, arguing that it 'lies in every direction of human experience where basic emotional desire is frustrated.'[10]

Concepts can embody hypotheses and, in the case of these two concepts, when the focus is sociological there is frequently assumed to be a psychological correlate, and vice versa. Thus, e.g., Merton classifies the psychological states resulting from sociological anomie, while others make assumptions about the social causes of psychological anomie; similarly, Marxist sociologists make assumptions about the psychological effects of alienated social forms, while, e.g., Eric Fromm sees the psychological state of alienation as a function of market society.

A basic unclarity thus exists about the range of reference of each of these concepts and, even where the concepts are clearly used to embody hypotheses about relationships between social conditions and mental states, the very diversity of such hypotheses makes an analytical comparison of the concepts in their modern forms unmanageable in a short space. Where 'alienation' can mean anything from 'bureaucratic rules which stifle initiative and deprive individuals of all communication among themselves and of all information about the institutions in which

[8] R. Williams, *American Society* (New York, 1951), p. 537.
D. Riesman, *The Lonely Crowd* (New Haven, 1950), pp. 287.
R. MacIver, *The Ramparts We Guard* (New York, 1950), pp. 84–5. H. Lasswell, 'The Threat to Privacy' in R. MacIver (ed.), *Conflict of Loyalties* (New York: 1952), and Srole, *Loc. cit.*, p. 712.
[9] G. Lukacs, *Histoire de Classe et Conscience de Classe* (Paris, 1960), p. 230.
[10] L. Feuer, 'What is Alienation? The Career of a Concept', *New Politics*, 1962, p. 132.

they are situated'[11] to 'a mode of experience in which the person experiences himself as an alien',[12] and where 'anomie' can extend from the malintegration of the cultural and social structure to 'the state of mind of one who has been pulled up by his moral roots',[13] then the time has come either to abandon the concepts or return to their origins for guidance.

I

(A) Marx distinguishes four aspects of alienated labour: (1) 'the relationship of the worker to the *product of labour* as an alien object which dominates him'. Thus, 'the more the worker expends himself in work the more powerful becomes the world of objects which he creates in face of himself, the poorer he becomes in his inner life, and the less he belongs to himself'; (2) 'the relationship of labour to the *act of production*', with the result that 'the work is *external* to the worker, that it is not part of his nature; and that, consequently, he does not fulfil himself in his work but denies himself, has a feeling of misery rather than wellbeing, does not develop freely his mental and physical energies but is physically exhausted and mentally debased. The worker, therefore, feels himself at home only during his leisure time, whereas at work he feels homeless. His work is not voluntary but imposed, *forced labour*. It is not the satisfaction of a need, but only a *means* for satisfying other needs'; (3) The alienation of man from himself as a 'species-being', from 'his own active function, his life-activity', which is 'free, conscious activity'. Man is thus alienated from 'his own body, external nature, his mental life and his *human* life'; (4) The alienation of man 'from other *men*. When man confronts himself he also confronts other men . . . in the relationship of alienated labour every man regards other men according to the standards and relationships in which he finds himself placed as a worker.' Social relations 'are not relations between individual and individual, but between worker and capitalist, between farmer and landlord, etc.' Further, men's lives are divided up into different spheres of activity, where conflicting standards apply: 'The nature of alienation implies that each sphere applies a different and contradictory norm, that morality does not apply the same norm as political economy, etc., because each of them

[11] C. Lefort in 'Marxisme et Sociologie', *Les Cahiers du Centre d'Etudes Socialistes*, 34–5, 1963, p. 24.
[12] E. Fromm, *The Sane Society* (New York, 1955), p. 120.
[13] MacIver, *The Ramparts We Guard*, p. 84.

is a particular alienation of man; each is concentrated upon a specific area of alienated activity and is itself alienated from the other.'

'Alienation' thus refers to the relationship of the individual to elements of his social and natural environment and to his state of mind, or relationship with himself. Marx contends that 'the division of labour . . . impoverishes the worker and makes him into a machine', that 'the division of labour offers us the first example of how . . . man's own deed becomes an alien power opposed to him, which enslaves him instead of being controlled by him. For as soon as labour is distributed, each man has a particular exclusive sphere of activity, which is forced upon him and from which he cannot escape.' In conditions where men must work for the increase of wealth, labour is 'harmful and deleterious'; the division of labour, which develops in such conditions, causes the worker to become 'even more completely dependent . . . upon a particular, extremely one-sided mechanical kind of labour'. All the aspects of alienation are seen to derive from the worker's role in production: his view of his work, his products, the institutions of his society, other men and himself. In general, the capitalist economic system 'perfects the worker and degrades the man'. Thus Marx's socio-psychological hypothesis concerning alienation is that it increases in proportion to the growing division of labour under capitalism, where men are forced to confine themselves to performing specialized functions within a system they neither understand nor control.

(B) Durkheim uses 'anomie' in *The Division of Labour* to characterize the pathological state of the economy, 'this sphere of collective life (which) is, in large part, freed from the moderating action of regulation', where 'latent or active, the state of war is necessarily chronic' and 'each individual finds himself in a state of war with every other'. In *Suicide* it is used to characterize the pathological mental state of the individual who is insufficiently regulated by society and suffers from 'the malady of infinite aspiration': 'unregulated emotions are adjusted neither to one another nor to the conditions they are supposed to meet: they must therefore conflict with one another most painfully'. It is accompanied by 'weariness', 'disillusionment', 'disturbance, agitation and discontent', 'anger' and 'irritated disgust with life'. In extreme cases this condition leads a man to commit suicide, or homicide. It is aggravated by sudden crises, both economic disasters and 'the abrupt growth of power and wealth': with increased prosperity, for instance, anomie '. . . is heightened by passions being less disciplined, precisely when they need more discipline'. Anomie is the peculiar disease of modern industrial man, 'sanctified' both by orthodox economists and by extreme socialists. Industry, 'instead of being still regarded as a means to an end transcending itself, has become the supreme end of individuals and societies alike'. Anomie is accepted as normal, indeed 'a mark of moral distinction', and 'it is everlastingly repeated that it is man's nature to be eternally dissatisfied, constantly to advance, without relief or rest, toward an indefinite goal'. Religion, governmental power over the economy and occupational groups have lost their moral force. Thus 'appetites have become freed of any limiting authority' and 'from top to bottom of the ladder, greed is aroused without knowing where to find ultimate foothold. Nothing can calm it, since its goal is far beyond all it can attain'. The lives of 'a host of individuals are passed in the industrial and commercial sphere', where 'the greater part of their existence is passed divorced from any moral influence . . . the manufacturer, the merchant, the workman, the employee, in carrying on his occupation, is aware of no influence set about him to check his egoism'.[14]

'Anomie', like 'alienation', thus also refers first to the relationship of the individual to elements of his social environment and second to his state of mind. Durkheim initially thought that the division of labour itself has a 'natural' tendency to provide the necessary regulative force, that it produces solidarity because 'it creates among men an entire system of rights and duties which link them together in a durable way', for 'functions, when they are sufficiently in contact with one another, tend to stabilize and regulate themselves'. Anomie is prevalent because of the rapid growth of the market and big industry, for since 'these changes have been accomplished with extreme rapidity, the interests in conflict have not yet had time to be equilibrated'; also there is the harmful existence of 'the still very great inequality in the external conditions of the struggle'. Later he came to believe that it was primarily due to the lack of occupational groups which would regulate economic life by establishing 'occupational ethics and law in the different economic occupations': anomie 'springs from the lack of collective forces at certain points in society; that is, of groups established for the regulation of social life'. Both explanations are consistent with Durkheim's sociopsychological hypothesis concerning anomie, which is that it is a function of the rapid growth of the economy in industrial society which has occurred without a corresponding growth in the forces which could regulate it.

[14] Durkheim, *Professional Ethics and Civic Morals*, tr. C. Brookfield (London, 1957), p. 12. This quotation, incidentally, confirms that, despite Durkheim's attempt to distinguish 'anomie' from 'egoism' in *Suicide*, they are not in the end conceptually distinct. See B. D. Johnson, 'Durkheim's One Cause of Suicide', *American Sociological Review*, 30, 6, 1965, pp. 882–6.

II

Alienation and anomie have in common the formal characteristic that they each have a multiple reference to: (1) social phenomena (states of society, its institutions, rules and norms); (2) individual states of mind (beliefs, desires, attitudes, etc.); (3) a hypothesized empirical relationship between (1) and (2); and (4) a presupposed picture of the 'natural' relationship between (1) and (2). Thus, whereas Marx sees capitalism as a compulsive social system, which narrows men's thoughts, places obstacles in the way of their desires and denies the realization of 'a world of productive impulses and faculties', Durkheim sees it as a state of moral anarchy in the economic sphere, where men's thoughts and desires are insufficiently controlled and where the individual is not 'in harmony with his condition'. We will later notice the extent to which (3) is related to (4) in the two cases. Let us here concentrate on (3), and in particular on the difference between the hypotheses in question.

Compare what the two thinkers have to say about the division of labour. For Marx it is *in itself* the major contributing factor in alienation, in all its forms, and not just for the worker but for all men. All men are alienated under the division of labour (for, as he says, 'capital and labour are two sides of one and the same relation' and 'all human servitude is involved in the relation of the worker to production, and all the types of servitude are only modifications or consequences of this relation'). Men have to enter into 'definite relations that are indispensable and independent of their wills', they are forced to play determined roles within the economic system, and, in society as a whole, they are dehumanized by social relations which take on 'an independent existence' and which determine not only what they do, but the very structure of their thought, their images of themselves, their products, their activities and other men. Alienated man is dehumanized by being conditioned and constrained to see himself, his products, his activities and other men in economic, political, religious and other categories – in terms which deny his and their human possibilities.

Durkheim sees the division of labour as being (when properly regulated) the source of solidarity in modern industrial society: the prevalence of anomie is due to a lag in the growth of the relevant rules and institutions. Interdependence of functions (plus occupational groups) should lead to growing solidarity and a sense of community, although the division of labour in advanced societies is also (ideally) accompanied by the growth of the importance of the individual personality and the development of values such as justice and equality. For Durkheim the economic functions of the division of labour are 'trivial in comparison with the moral effect it produces'. By means of it 'the individual becomes aware of his dependence upon society; from it come the forces which keep him in check and restrain him'. When educating a child, it is 'necessary to get him to like the idea of circumscribed tasks and limited horizons', for in modern society 'man is destined to fulfil a special function in the social organism, and, consequently, he must learn in advance how to play this role'. The division of labour does not normally degrade the individual 'by making him into a machine': it merely requires that in performing his special function 'he feels he is serving something'. Moreover, 'if a person has grown accustomed to vast horizons, total views, broad generalities, he cannot be confined, without impatience, within the strict limits of a special task'.

By now it should be apparent that alienation, in Marx's thinking, is, *in part*, what characterizes precisely those states of the individual and conditions of society which Durkheim sees as the solution to anomie: namely, where men are socially determined and constrained, when they must conform to social rules which are independent of their wills and are conditioned to think and act within the confines of specialized roles. Whereas anomic man is, for Durkheim, the unregulated man who needs rules to live by, limits to his desires, 'circumscribed tasks' to perform and 'limited horizons' for his thoughts, alienated man is, for Marx, a man in the grip of a system, who 'cannot escape' from a 'particular, exclusive sphere of activity which is forced upon him'.[15]

Whence does this difference derive? In part, obviously, from the fact that Marx and Durkheim wrote at different periods about different stages of industrial society. Also it is clear that Marx was concerned chiefly to describe the alienated worker, while Durkheim saw economic anomie as primarily characterizing employers. But there is also a theoretical difference that is striking and important: these concepts offer opposite and incompatible analyses of the relation of the individual to society.

Compare Marx's statements that 'it is above all necessary to avoid postulating "society" once again as an abstraction confronting the individual' and that communism creates the basis for 'rendering it impossible that anything should exist independently of individuals' with

---

[15] But Durkheim obviously did not want to see men treated as commodities or as appendages to machines. (See *Division of Labour*, pp. 371–3), and Marx had much to say, especially in Vol. III of *Capital*, about avarice and unregulated desires prevalent under capitalism (see also his account of 'raw communism' in the 1844 manuscripts).

Durkheim's that society is 'a reality from which everything that matters to us flows', that it 'transcends the individual's consciousness' and that it 'has all the characteristics of a moral authority that imposes respect'. Marx begins from the position that the independent or 'reified' and determining character of social relationships and norms is precisely what characterizes human 'pre-history' and will be abolished by the revolutionary transition to a 'truly-human' society, whereas Durkheim assumes the 'normality' of social regulation, the lack of which leads to the morbid, self-destructive state of 'non-social' or Hobbesian anarchy evident in unregulated capitalism. Social constraint is for Marx a denial and for Durkheim a condition of human freedom and self-realization.

III

It is my contention that one can only make sense of the empirical relationships postulated between social conditions and individual mental states which are held to constitute alienation and anomie by taking into account what Marx and Durkheim see as the 'natural' (or 'human' or 'normal' or 'healthy') condition of the individual in society. Alienation and anomie do not identify themselves, as it were, independently of the theories from which they derive: witness the diversity of contemporary uses of the terms, discussed above. They are, in fact, only identifiable if one knows what it would be *not* to be alienated or anomic, that is, if one applies a standard specifying 'natural' states of institutions, rules and norms and individual mental states. Moreover, this standard must be external. That is, neither the individual mental states nor the social conditions studied can provide that standard, for they themselves are to be evaluated for their degree of alienation and anomie.

Thus despite recent attempts to divest these concepts of their non-empirical presuppositions,[16] they are in their original form an inextricable fusion of fact and value, so that one cannot eliminate the latter while remaining faithful to the original concepts.

The standard specifying the 'natural' condition of the individual in society involves, in each case, a theory of human nature. Marx's view of man is of a being with a wide range of creative potentialities, or

[16] See e.g. B. F. Dohrenwend, 'Egosim, Altruism, Anomie and Fatalism: A Conceptual Analysis of Durkheim's Types', *American Sociological Review*, 24, 1959, p. 467, where anomie is described as 'ambiguous . . . indistinct . . . and infused with value judgments about what is "good" and "bad" ', and e.g., Seeman, *op. cit.*

'species powers' whose 'self-realization exists as an inner necessity, a need'. In the truly human society there will be 'a new manifestation of *human* powers and a new enrichment of the human being', when 'man appropriates his manifold being in an all-inclusive way, and thus is a whole man'. Man needs to develop all his faculties in a context where neither the natural nor the social environment are constraining: 'objects then confirm his individuality . . . the wealth of subjective human sensibility . . . is cultivated or created' and 'the practical relations of everyday life offer to man none but perfectly intelligible and reasonable relations with regard to his fellow men and to nature'. With the end of the division of labour, there will be an end to 'the exclusive concentration of artistic talent in particular individuals and its suppression in the broad mass'. The 'detail worker of today', with 'nothing more to perform than a partial social function', will be superseded by 'an individual with an all-round development, one for whom various social functions are alternative modes of activity'[17] Furthermore, with the end of the social determination of 'abstract' individual roles, man's relationship with man and with woman will become fully human, that is, fully reciprocal and imbued with respect for the uniqueness of the individual. As Marx says, 'the relation of man to woman is the most *natural* relation of human being to human being. . . . It also shows how far man's needs have become human needs, and consequently how far the other person, as a person, has become one of his needs, and to what extent he is in his individual existence at the same time a social being.' Thus Marx assumes that the full realization of human powers and 'the return of man himself as a *social*, i.e. really human, being' can only take place in a world in which man is free to apply himself to whatever activity he chooses and where his activities and his way of seeing himself and other men are not dictated by a system within which he and they play specified roles.

Durkheim saw human nature as essentially in need of limits and discipline. His view of man is of a being with potentially limitless and insatiable desires, who needs to be controlled by society. He writes:

[17] Cf. the famous passage from the *German Ideology* in which Marx writes of 'communist society, where no one has one exclusive sphere of activity but each can become accomplished in any branch he wishes' and where it is 'possible for me to hunt in the morning, fish in the afternoon, rear cattle in the evening, criticize after dinner, just as I have a mind, without ever becoming hunter, fisherman, shepherd or critic'. See also *Capital* (Moscow, 1959), I, pp. 483–4 and Engels, *Anti-Dühring* (Moscow, 1959), pp. 403 and 409. On the other hand, Marx seems to have changed his attitude at the end of his life to a concern with leisure in the 'realm of freedom'.

To limit man, to place obstacles in the path of his free development, is this not to prevent him from fulfilling himself? But . . .
this limitation is a condition of our happiness and moral health.
Man, in fact, is made for life in a determinate, limited environment. . . .

'Health' for man in society is a state where 'a regulative force' plays 'the
same role for moral needs which the organism plays for physical needs',
which makes men 'contented with their lot, while stimulating them
moderately to improve it' and results in that 'calm, active happiness . . .
which characterizes health for societies as well as for individuals'.
Durkheim's picture of a healthy society in modern Europe is of a society
that is organized and meritocratic, with equality of opportunity and
personal liberty, where men are attached to intermediary groups by
stable loyalties rather than being atomized units caught in an endemic
conflict, and where they fulfil determinate functions in an organized
system of work, where they conform in their mental horizons, their
desires and ambitions to what their role in society demands and where
there are clear-cut rules defining limits to desire and ambition in all
spheres of life. There should be 'rules telling each of the workers his
rights and duties, not vaguely in general terms but in precise detail'
and 'each in his sphere vaguely realizes the extreme limit set to his ambitions and aspires to nothing beyond . . . he respects regulations and is
docile to collective authority, that is, has a wholesome moral constitution'. Man must be governed by 'a conscience superior to his own, the
superiority of which he feels': men cannot assign themselves the 'law
of justice' but 'must receive it from an authority which they respect and
to which they yield spontaneously'. Society alone 'as a whole or through
the agency of one of its organs, can play this moderating role'. It alone
can 'stipulate law' and 'set the point beyond which the passions must
not go'; and it alone 'can estimate the reward to be prospectively offered
to every class of human functionary, in the name of the common
interest'.

IV

The doctrines of Marx and Durkheim about human nature are representative of a long and distinguished tradition of such doctrines in the
history of political and social theory. The difference between them is
also representative of that tradition (and parallel differences can be
traced back to the Middle Ages). Doctrines of this general type can be
seen to underlie, for example, the work of Hobbes, Rousseau, the Uto-

pian Socialists and Freud; and it is evident that, in large measure, Durkheim sides with Hobbes and Freud where Marx sides with Rousseau and the Utopians. For the former, man is a bundle of desires, which need to be regulated, tamed, repressed, manipulated and given direction for the sake of social order, whereas, for the latter, man is still an angel, rational and good, who requires a rational and good society in which to develop his essential nature – a 'form of association in which each, while uniting himself with all, may still obey himself alone. . . .'[18] For the former, coercion, external authority, and restraint are necessary and desirable for social order and individual happiness; for the latter, they are an offence against reason and an attack upon freedom.

I want here to ask two difficult questions. First, how is one to understand Marx's and Durkheim's theories of human nature, and, in particular, what is their logical and epistemological status? And, second, how is one to account for their divergence?

(A) Statements about human nature can be construed in many different ways. They commonly include such terms as 'need', 'real self', 'real will', 'basic desires', 'human potentialities', 'human powers', 'normal', 'healthy', and so on. Statements of this sort might be taken to refer to: (1) man as existing before or apart from society, (2) man considered analytically, with those factors due to the influence of society abstracted, (3) man considered in an *a priori* manner, i.e. according to some *a priori* definition, (4) man considered from the point of view of features which seem to be common to men in all known societies, (5) man considered from the point of view of features which are held to characterize him in certain specifiable social conditions as opposed to others.[19]

My suggestion is that very often, and in particular in the cases I am discussing, the last is the most accurate way to read statements about human nature. It is, in general, not absurd to take statements about human needs, 'real' wants, potentialities and so on as asserting that individuals in situation S are unable to experience satisfactions that situation S_1 is held to make possible for them and which they would experience and value highly. Now, it is, in my view, not necessary that such statements refer to actual *discontents* of individuals in situation S: both Marx and Durkheim, for example, were clear that individuals could acquiesce in and even value highly their alienated or anomic con-

---

18 J.-J. Rousseau, *The Social Contract*, tr. G. D. H. Cole (London, 1913), p. 12.
19 These possibilities are distinguished for analytical purposes. Clearly, in most actual cases they are combined. Rousseau, for instance, combines (1) and (2), while Pareto combines (2) and (4). I shall in the end argue that Marx and Durkheim combine (4) and (5).

dition. What is required is that, once they are in S_1, they experience satisfactions unavailable in S.

Thus far it is evidently an empirical matter. It is an empirical and testable question (1) whether the satisfactions in question are precluded in S; (2) whether they would be available in S_1, and (3) whether they would be actually experienced by individuals in S_1 and would be important and valuable to them. (1) can in principle be investigated directly. To take easy examples, it is not difficult to show that work on the assembly line precludes work-satisfaction or that the life of the highly ambitious businessman precludes a mental condition of harmonious contentment. (2) and (3) can be investigated indirectly or directly. To do so indirectly would involve looking at evidence available in S and, indeed, in other societies, which provides a strong presumption in their favour. Thus Marx can write of what happens when 'communist artisans form associations'. When 'French socialist workers meet together', he writes, 'society, association, entertainment which also has society as its aim, is sufficient for them: the brotherhood of man is no empty phrase but a reality, and the nobility of man shines forth upon us from their toil-worn bodies'. And he writes in *The Holy Family* that one 'must be acquainted with the studiousness, the craving for knowledge, the moral energy and the unceasing urge for development of the French and English workers to be able to form an idea of the *human* nobleness of that movement'. Durkheim can appeal to countless examples of cohesive social groups – primitive tribes, medieval guilds, rural Catholic communities, the Jews, and to the evidence of, e.g., differential suicide rates. He compares, for instance, the poor with the rich and argues that 'everything that enforces subordination attenuates the effects of (anomie). At least the horizon of the lower classes is limited by those above them, and for this same reason their desires are more modest. Those who have only empty space above them are almost inevitably lost in it. . . .' *Direct* investigation of (2) and (3) can be pursued only by social experiment. Thus the final test for Marx's theory of human nature is the communist revolution; and that for Durkheim's is the institution of a kind of centralized guild-socialism.

We have analysed statements about human nature as empirical statements (in this case, hypothetical predictions) about the condition of man in S_1. But our analysis is as yet incomplete, for they also involve the affirmation that this condition is privileged – that it is evaluated as preferable to all other conditions. How is one to analyse this evaluation: is it also empirical, that is, a ranking in accordance with what men actually want, or is it non-empirical – a mere exhortation to look at the world in one way rather than another?

If it is empirical, the question arises: by *whom* is the condition of man in S_1 said to be preferred – which men's wants are relevant here? If one believes, as Marx and Durkheim did, that man is largely conditioned by social circumstances, that new needs are generated by the historical process, that his very picture of himself and others is a function of his situation, then the problem becomes even more acute, for no one is in a position genuinely to compare and evaluate alternatives, like Mill's wise man deciding between higher and lower pleasures. An appeal to men in S_1 is self-defeating, for it carries the presumption that their evaluations are privileged, which is what is at issue. An appeal to men in S will not do either, for they would not ordinarily have the necessary evidence, and, again, why should their judgments be privileged? Worse still, what criteria are appropriate? If men in S_1 are satisfied, fulfilled, contented in certain ways, what is privileged about judgments which value these states rather than others?

Both Marx and Durkheim *thought* that they had found solid empirical ground upon which to base statements about human nature. They both had a picture of history as a process of the progressive emergence of the individual and both thought that man's potentiality for individual autonomy and for genuine community with others (both of which they envisaged differently) was frustrated by existing social forms. They thought that they had found conclusive evidence for their respective views of human nature in present and past societies: they assumed that, despite the continual generation of new needs throughout history, men's fundamental aspirations, more or less hidden, and the conditions of their ultimate happiness had always been and would continue to be the same. They were both impressed by the growth of industrialism and by the possibilities it had opened up for human fulfilment[20] and they believed that men were, despite the present, and temporary, obstacles, increasingly becoming (and would continue to become) what they had it in them to be; one could identify *this* by looking at their miseries and sufferings, as well as at their strivings and aspirations towards 'human' or 'healthy' forms of life, and at historical examples of societies or institutions in which alienation or anomie were less severe or even absent. Yet this evidence about men's wants is itself selected

[20] As Marx says, 'The history of *industry* and industry as it *objectively* exists is an *open* book of the *human faculties*' (*Early Writings*, ed. T. B. Bottomore, London, 1963, p. 162); and, as Durkheim says, 'society is, or tends to be, essentially industrial' (*Division of Labour*, ed. G. Simpson, Glencoe, 1933, p. 3) and what characterizes its morality is 'that there is something more human, and therefore more rational' about modern, organized societies (*ibid.*, p. 407).

and interpreted, and that requires a prior perspective, providing criteria of selection and interpretation.

It would seem, therefore, that statements about human nature, such as those examined here, are partly empirical and partly not. One can often get a long way with support of the empirical part, for evidence of all kinds is relevant to the question of what men's lives would be like in alternative circumstances. The hypothetical prediction about S_1 may be verifiable; at least one would know how to verify it, and one could in principle point to evidence which strongly supports it. The claim, however, that life in S_1 is to be judged superior, though it may rest on an appeal to evidence about men's wants, is ultimately non-empirical, for that evidence has been selected and interpreted in the light of the claim. Which men's wants and which of their wants has already been decided. Moreover, the claim of superiority does not follow logically from the evidence: one must add the premise that certain wants and satisfactions are more 'human' or 'healthy' than others. In the end what is required is a perspective and an initial set of evaluations.

(B) It is precisely here that Marx and Durkheim differed radically. Marx wrote that the 'socialist perspective' attributed importance to 'the wealth of human needs, and consequently also to a *new mode of production* and to a new *object* of production' as well as to a 'new manifestation of human powers and a new enrichment of the human being'. He began from an image of man in society, where a morality of duty would be unnecessary because irrelevant, an image in which *aesthetic* criteria were of predominant importance in assessing the quality of man's relationship with the natural and social world.[21]

Yet where Marx wrote in the *Theses on Feurbach* from 'the standpoint of . . . human society', Durkheim argued in the *Rules of Sociological Method* that it was 'no longer a matter of pursuing desperately an objective that retreats as one advances but of working with steady perseverance to maintain the normal state, of re-establishing it if it is threatened,

---

[21] This image is, I would argue, ultimately Romantic in origin. Compare the following from Schiller's *Briefe ueber die aesthetische Erziehung des Menschen*: '. . . enjoyment is separated from labour, the means from the end, exertion from recompense. Eternally *fettered* only to a single little fragment of the whole, man fashions himself only as a fragment; ever hearing only the monotonous whirl of the wheel which he turns, he never displays the full harmony of his being . . .' (*Sixth letter*). For Schiller, and, I believe, for Marx it is 'the aesthetic formative impulse' which 'establishes . . . a joyous empire . . . wherein it releases man from all the fetters of circumstance, and frees him, both physically and morally, from all that can be called constraint' (*ibid.*, *Twenty-Seventh Letter*).

and of rediscovering its conditions if they have changed'. He was haunted by the idea of man and society in disintegration. Here he appealed to the remedy of moral rules, defining and prescribing duties in all spheres of life, especially where men's anarchic and unstable desires had the greatest scope. This is a moral vision, for, as he said, 'the need for order, harmony and social solidarity is generally considered moral'.[22]

Where Marx valued a life in which in community with others 'the individual' has the means of 'cultivating his gifts in all directions', and where the relations between men are no longer defined by externally imposed categories and roles – by class and occupation – and men freely come together in freely-chosen activities and participate in controlling the conditions of their social life, Durkheim held that 'we must contract our horizon, choose a definite task and immerse ourselves in it completely, instead of trying to make ourselves a sort of creative masterpiece', and hoped to see men performing useful functions in a rationally organized society, in accordance with clearly defined roles, firmly attached to relevant groups and under the protective discipline of rules of conduct at home, at work and in politics. They both sought liberty, equality, democracy and community, but the content which they gave these notions was utterly different.

V

What is the relevance of these concepts today? This question needs to be subdivided into three more specific questions, which follow the lines of the preceding argument. First, how valid is the empirical hypothesis which each embodies? To what extent do they succeed in identifying and adequately explaining phenomena in modern industrial societies? Second, how plausible is the theory of human nature which each presupposes? What does the evidence from past and present societies, from

[22] *Division of Labour*, p. 63. Whereas Marx's model of disalienated work is artistic creation, Durkheim writes that 'art is a game. Morality, on the contrary, is life in earnest' and 'the distance separating art and morality' is 'the very distance that separates play from work' (*Moral Education*, New York, 1961, p. 273). This is the protestant ethic transposed into Kantian terms: 'the categorical imperative is assuming the following form: Make yourself usefully fulfil a determinate function' (*Division of Labour*, p. 43). As to self-realization, Durkheim writes, 'As for a simultaneous growth of all the faculties, it is only possible for a given being to a very limited degree' (*Division of Labour*, p. 237, amended translation, S. L.).

sociology and psychology, suggest about the plausibility of their respective hypothetical predictions, and about the nature of the changes which men and institutions would have to undergo to attain the conditions they predict and advocate? And third, how desirable is the ideal, how attractive is the vision to which each ultimately appeals? How today is one to evaluate these ideals: what degree of approximation to either, or both (or neither), are we to think desirable?

These questions are challenging and far-reaching. Here I shall raise them and offer tentative suggestions as to how one might begin to answer them.

I   One problem in answering the first question is to know at what level of generality it is being posed. How *specifically* is one to read Marx's account of alienation and Durkheim's of anomie? Marx and Durkheim identified certain features of their own societies and offered explanations of them. But they may also be seen to have identified features characteristic of a number of societies including their own; indeed, one may even see them, to some extent, as having identified features which may be said to characterize any conceivable society. Is it a specific type of technology, or form of organization, or structure of the economy, or is it the existence of classes or of private property, or the accumulation of capital, or the division of labour, or industrial society, or the human condition which is the crucial determinant of alienation? Is it the lack of a specific type of industrial organization (technical or administrative?), or the absence of appropriate occupational groups, or an economy geared to the pursuit of profit, or the cultural imperatives of a 'success ethic', or the fact of social mobility, or the erosion of a traditionally stable framework of authority, or social change, or industrial society, or the human condition, that is the major factor leading to anomie? Alienation and anomie are phenomena which have particular aspects, unique to particular forms of society or institution, other aspects which are more general and still others which are universal. We may attempt to identify new forms of these phenomena, using these concepts and the hypotheses they embody in the attempt to describe and explain them. They are in this sense concepts of 'the middle range'. They allow for specific new hypotheses to account for particular new forms, or they may account for them by means of the existing, more general hypotheses. In general, the contemporary forms of alienation and anomie are best approached on the understanding that their causes are multiple and to be sought at different levels of abstraction. A systematic investigation of alienation and anomie would range from the most particular to the most universal in the search for causes.

Marx and Durkheim attributed, as we have seen, certain types of mental condition (specified positively, in terms of what occurs, and negatively, in terms of what is precluded) to certain types of social condition. Marx pointed to meaninglessness of work and a sense of powerlessness to affect the conditions of one's life, dissociation from the products of one's labour, the sense of playing a role in an impersonal system which one does not understand or control, the seeing of oneself and others within socially-imposed and artificial categories, the denial of human possibilities for a fully creative, spontaneous, egalitarian and reciprocal communal life. He attributed these, in particular, to the form taken by the division of labour under capitalism and, more generally, to the fact of class society. Durkheim pointed to greed, competitiveness, status-seeking, the sense of having rights without duties, the concentration on consumption and pleasure, the lack of a sense of community with others, of a feeling of limits to one's desires and aspirations, and of the experience of fulfilling a useful function and serving a purpose higher than one's own self-interest, and the denial of human possibilities for an ordered and balanced life, where everyone knows his station and its duties. He attributed these, in particular, to the industrial revolution and the failure of society to provide appropriate groups to adjust to it, and, more generally, to social disorganization.

We are familiar with countless examples of these phenomena, though in many cases not all the features isolated by the concepts are necessarily present. Let me give just two examples.

Alienation is found today in perhaps its most acute form among workers in assembly-line industries, such as the motor-car industry, where, as Blauner writes in his sensitive study of workers' alienation, 'the combination of technological, organizational and economic factors has resulted in the simultaneous intensification of all the dimensions of alienation'. Here, in the extreme situation, 'a depersonalized worker, estranged from himself and larger collectives, goes through the motions of work in the regimented milieu of the conveyor-belt for the sole purpose of earning his bread', 'his work has become almost completely compartmentalized from other areas of his life, so that there is little meaning left in it beyond the instrumental purpose', and it is 'unfree and unfulfilling and exemplifies the bureaucratic combination of the highly rational organization and the restricted specialist. In relation to the two giant bureaucracies which dominate his life, he is relatively powerless, atomized, depersonalized, and anonymous'.[23]

Likewise, anomie is noticeably evident and acute among 'the Unattached', well described by Mary Morse, especially those in 'Seagate'

[23] R. Blauner, *Alienation and Freedom: The Factory Worker and his Industry* (Chicago and London, 1964), pp. 182 and 122.

– the drifting, purposeless and unstable teenagers, who felt no connection with or obligation to family, work, school or youth organization, the children of *nouveau riche* parents, suffering from 'a sense of boredom, failure and restlessness' and refusing 'to accept limitations, whether their own or external'. Often there was 'a failure to achieve unrealistic or unattainable goals they had set for themselves or had had set for them'; also there was 'a general inability to postpone immediate pleasure for the sake of future gain', there was 'a craving for adventure', and 'leisure-time interests were short-spanned, constantly changing and interspersed liberally with periods of boredom and apathy'. Finally, they showed 'pronounced hostility towards adults', adult discipline was quite ineffective and, in general, 'all adults in authority were classed as "them" – those who were opposed to and against "us"' [24]

These are merely two instances, but they illustrate the general point made above. The causes of alienation and anomie must be sought at different levels of abstraction. At the most specific level, all sorts of special factors may be of primary importance. In a case of alienation, it may be the technical or organizational character of an industry or the structure of a bureaucracy; in a case of anomie, it may be a combination of personal affluence and a breakdown, rejection or conflict of norms of authority at home, at school and at work. But clearly, too, the nature of the wider society is of crucial importance. The extent and nature of social stratification, the structure of the economy, the character of the political system, the pace of industrialization, the degree of pluralism, the nature of the predominant social values – all these will affect the nature and distribution of alienation and anomie. Again, one can plausibly argue that *some* degree of alienation and of anomie is inseparable from life in an industrial society, characterized as it is, on the one hand, by the ramifying growth of organization and bureaucracy in all spheres of life, by economic centralization and by the increasing remoteness and technical character of politics; and, on the other, by built-in and permanent social changes, by the impermanence of existing status hierarchies and the increasing role given to personal ambition and career mobility. And at the most general level, they may each be seen to relate to the most universal features of social structure and social change. In this sense, some alienation must exist wherever there are reified social relations, socially-given roles and norms; while some anomie must exist wherever hierarchies disintegrate and social control is weakened.

II   What about the plausibility of Marx's and Durkheim's theories of human nature? They each had definite views about men's needs, which

[24] M. Morse, *The Unattached* (Penguin Books, London, 1965), pp. 75–6 and 28–9.

they believed to be historically generated and empirically ascertainable. How plausible today is the picture of mutually co-operative individuals, each realizing a wide range of creative potentialities, in the absence of specific role-expectations, lasting distinctions between whole categories of men and externally imposed discipline, in conditions of inner and social harmony, where all participate in planning and controlling their environment? What, on the other hand, is the plausibility of the view of human happiness, in which men are socialized into specific roles, regulated, and to some extent repressed, by systems of rules and group norms (albeit based on justice, equality of opportunity and respect for the individual), serving the purposes of society by fulfilling organized functions – all of which they accept and respect as constituting a stable framework for their lives?

These questions confront all those who hold versions of these ideals today. One cannot begin to appraise either, or compare them with one another, until one has come to some view about the likelihood of either being realized. What evidence is there that if the social conditions are constituted in the way Marx and Durkheim wanted, men would experience and would value highly the satisfactions of which they speak? Here one would, for example, need to examine all the accumulated evidence throughout history of experiments in community-living and in workers' control, of communes, collective farms and kibbutzim, on the one hand; and of experience in 'human relations' and personnel management, of professionalism and of life in organizations, on the other. There is a vast amount of such evidence available, but it has never been systematically reviewed in this light.

Let us look at two examples in this connection. In the opinion of Friedmann the Israeli kibbutz represents 'an original and successful application, on a limited scale, of communist principles', nearer to 'the ethical ideal defined by the philosophy of Marx and Engels (for instance, with regard to the role of money, the distinction between manual and intellectual labour, family life)' than life in Moscow or on a kolkhoz. 'The kibbutz movement,' he writes, 'despite its limitations and its difficulties, constitutes the fullest and most successful "utopian" revolutionary experiment, the one which approximates most closely to the forms of life which communism has assigned itself as an aim. It is in the kibbutzim that I have met men of ample culture, and even creators, artists, writers, technicians, among whom the contradiction between intellectual and manual work, denounced by Marx, is truly eliminated in their daily life.' Friedmann goes on, of course, to qualify and elaborate this: in particular, he outlines the perpetual confrontation between the kibbutzim and the wider society, devoted to economic growth and 'imbued with models of abundance, where, with the development of the private sector, there is proclaimed a sort of material and moral New Economic Plan'.[25] He examines the attempts of the kibbutzim to reduce to a minimum the tensions and frustrations of community life and asks the crucial questions: whether the kibbutz will be able to adapt to the economic and technical demands of an industrial society, while retaining its essential values; and whether the wider society will evolve in a direction that is compatible or incompatible with these values.

Let us take a second example, which relates to the plausibility of Durkheim's ideal, the overcoming of anomie. Perhaps the best instance is the evidence accumulated and interpreted by the theorists of modern managerialism, concerned to remedy 'the acquisitiveness of a sick society'[26] and treating the factory, the corporation and the large organization as 'a social system'. Particularly relevant are the writings of the 'organicists', whose aim is to promote 'the values of social stability, cohesion and integration'[27] and to achieve, within the 'formal organization' (the 'explicitly stated system of control introduced by the company') the 'creation and distribution of satisfactions' among the members of the system.[28] Selznick, who typifies the attempt to explore communal values within large corporations and administrative organizations, argues that the organization requires 'stability' in its lines of authority, subtle patterns of informal relationships, 'continuity' in its policies and 'homogeneity' in its outlook.[29] Another writer describes its reification and normative significance for those who participate in it in the following terms – terms of which Durkheim might well have approved: 'One might almost say that the organization has a character, an individuality, which makes the name real. The scientist will not accept any such reification or personalizing of an organization. But participants in these organizations are subject to no such scientific scruples, and generations of men have felt and thought about the organizations they belonged to as something real in themselves.'[30] For

[25] G. Friedmann, *Fin du Peuple Juif?* (Paris, Gallimard, 1965), pp. 95, 99, 96.
[26] E. Mayo, *The Human Problems of an Industrial Civilisation* (New York, Macmillan, 1933), pp. 152–3.
[27] I am particularly indebted in the discussion of this example to the pages on this subject in S. S. Wolin, *Politics and Vision* (London, Allen and Unwin, 1961), pp. 407–14.
[28] F. J. Roethlisberger and W. J. Dickson, *Management and the Worker* (Cambridge, Mass., Harvard University Press, 1939), p. 551.
[29] Wolin, *op. cit.*, p. 412.
[30] E. W. Bakke, *Bonds of Organization*, quoted in Wolin, *op. cit.*, p. 506.

Selznick, social order and individual satisfaction are reconciled when 'the aspirations of individuals are so stimulated and controlled, and so ordered in their mutual relations, as to produce the desired balance of forces'.[31]

I have merely suggested two areas in which one might look for evidence that is relevant to the plausibility of the hypothetical predictions which partially constitute Marx's and Durkheim's theories of human nature. Clearly there is much else that is relevant in, for instance, the work of industrial sociologists, social psychologists, in community studies and the writings of organization theorists. It is also important to look at what evidence there is about the prevalence of existing tendencies in modern societies which favour or hinder the sorts of changes which would be necessary in order to approach these ideals. Here it would be necessary to look, for example, at the changes in the nature of occupations brought about by automation – the replacement of the detail worker by the more educated and responsible technician; at the effects of economic planning on small-scale decision-making; at the effects of the growth of organizations on status aspirations; at contemporary trends in consumption patterns. All this, and much else, is relevant to an assessment of the costs of approaching either ideal in our societies. Without these detailed inquiries, it is hardly possible to state firm conclusions, but it would appear that Durkheim's ideal is much nearer to and easier of realization in the industrial societies of both West and East than is that of Marx.

III   Finally, how is one to evaluate these ideals? To do so involves a commitment to values and an assessment of costs. Either may be seen to conflict with other values or may not be considered to be worth the cost of its realization. Both sociological evidence and conceptual inquiry are relevant in the attempt to decide these matters, but in the end what is required is an ultimate and personal commitment (for which good, or bad, reasons may, none the less, be advanced). One may, of course, hold, as both Marx and Durkheim in different ways did, that one's values are, as it were, embedded in the facts, but this is itself a committed position (for which, again, good, or bad, reasons may be advanced).

This is no place to argue about these matters at the length they require. Let it be sufficient to say that these two quite opposite and incompatible ideals represent in a clear-cut form two major currents of critical and normative thinking about society, to be found throughout

---

[31] P. Selznick, *Leadership in Administration*, quoted in Wolin, p. 413.

the whole tradition of political and social theory in the West and still very much in evidence.

It is becoming increasingly common for that tradition to be attacked, by the advocates of a 'scientific' social and political theory, as being rudimentary and speculative, and lacking in scientific detachment. It is all rather like Sir James Frazer's view of primitive religion as 'bastard science'. What is required, it is argued, is the abandonment of concepts which are internally related to theories of the good life and the good society. Evaluation of this sort should be kept strictly apart from the process of scientific inquiry.

Yet the desire for scientific rigour is not in itself incompatible with the sort of inquiry which is concerned precisely to put to the task of empirical analysis concepts which have the type of relation I have outlined to theories of human nature and thereby to prior evaluative perspectives. This type of inquiry is exactly what has primarily characterized social and political theory in the past (under which heading I include the writings of the classical and many modern sociologists). The case for eliminating it necessarily involves advocating the abandonment of the application of models of alternative and preferred forms of life to the critical analysis of actual forms. That case has yet to be made convincing.

7 The Lawful Government[1]

R M Hare

When I was an undergraduate at Balliol before the war, there was another undergraduate there, slightly my senior, who later became a distinguished philosopher; but what was remarkable about him then was that he was a Jacobite. That is to say, he maintained, both in private and on occasion by public demonstration, that the rightful king of England was not George the Sixth (so-called) but a certain Bavarian prince, called, so far as I remember (appropriately) Rupert, and the nearest heir to the Stuart kings.

Shortly after that, when the war began, another acquaintance of mine, a Scottish Nationalist, refused military service on the unusual ground that the Act of Union was not legally binding upon the people of Scotland, since the Scottish Parliament at the time when it was passed was under constraint; and that therefore the present regime had no power to declare war on behalf of Scotland or to require her people to bear arms. He was brought before the courts, whose authority he did not acknowledge, and sent to prison.

These cases are of philosophical interest; for they are only extreme examples of a problem which recurs continually: How does a *de facto* government turn into a *de jure* government? Revolutions are constantly occurring, and the legality of governments is constantly being called in question. Although in this country I have had to go rather far back and give some somewhat bizarre examples, we have only to consider the cases of Iraq, or China, or Russia, or France to see that it is a very real and practical problem, how the fiats of a group of people who have seized power from the previous government by brute force, contrary to the laws of the previous government, come to be regarded as – even in some sense to *be* – laws binding upon the people of a territory. What decides who *are* the lawful government of the Congo or Viet Nam?

I am no lawyer, and shall probably merely succeed in displaying my

[1] This lecture is reprinted in the form in which it was delivered some years ago, and must not be taken as necessarily expressing my present views. In particular, I have not incorporated any discussion of Professor Hart's *The Concept of Law*, which appeared after the lecture was written. I must, however, thank him, and also Professor Alf Ross, for much helpful comment, doubly kind in that they both dissent from many things that I say.

ignorance of the law in discussing this problem; but nevertheless, since it *is* a philosophical problem and not merely a legal one, I make no apology for attempting a treatment of it, especially since it is a problem which has very close affinities with certain well-known problems in moral philosophy with which I have had a good deal to do.

It is a feature of nearly all attempts to solve this problem that they proceed by looking for a *criterion* of lawfulness in governments. This seems a very natural procedure; for, it might be said, what else could we be after? The problem is that we use this expression 'The lawful government'; it evidently has a meaning; and what else would do as an explanation of its meaning than a statement of the criterion, or the conditions, for calling a government lawful? That this approach to the problem has been thought to be the only one just shows how fatally attractive is the attitude to philosophical analysis which may be called, in the most general sense, *descriptivism*. A descriptivist is a person who thinks that to explain the meaning of any predicate is to give the criteria or conditions which have to be satisfied by a subject before this predicate is correctly predicated of it. I need not now rehearse the many mistakes that have been caused in other branches of philosophy (especially moral philosophy) by this assumption; we shall see that in the philosophy of law it has been just as damaging. If you want an example to show that descriptivism won't do, I will give perhaps the most hackneyed one: in order to understand the meaning of 'I promise' it is not sufficient or necessary to know what criteria or conditions have to be fulfilled by me before I can properly say 'I promise'.

Let us then, bearing this general point in mind, consider some of the stock solutions to the problem of the meaning of the expression 'lawful government'. First and most obvious we have what may be called the 'Might is Right' solution. This name is a bit unfair, as we shall see; but it will do. According to this view, the criterion of lawfulness is this: if a group of people (called the government) is able to enforce its will upon the people of a territory, then it is the lawful government of that territory, and its enactments are binding laws. Anybody who breaks these laws is then a criminal (or tortfeasor, etc.). And that is all there is to be said. This solution solves the problem by denying that there is any real difference between *de facto* and *de jure* governments. It is by far the simplest solution.

The phrase 'Might is Right' is, however, as I said, unfair. For 'Right' is naturally taken to mean 'morally right'; and this introduces a red herring, which puts this view at an unfair disadvantage. Of course it is most implausible (to put it no stronger) to suggest that whatever a government *can* do, it is morally right for it to do. So a proponent of this view might justly protest that we ought to leave morals out of it; he is not talking about morals, but about laws. Whatever may be the moral issues involved, and whether the laws made by the government are morally good or bad, the question whether they are *legally* binding is simply the question whether the government has the power to secure general obedience to them. On this view (which is very plausible) we say that Mr Kosygin's regime, and not the descendants of the Tsar (if any), is the lawful government of Russia simply because its writ runs in Russia and theirs does not.

But there are well-known objections to this view. If a group of brigands seizes power in, say, Panama, and makes a lot of regulations for the conduct of the people of Panama, does it by that fact alone become the lawful government of Panama? If this were so, then a number of questions which manifestly do trouble us would not do so. The citizens of Panama, and foreign governments, ask themselves questions like 'Is this the lawful government of Panama?' and hesitate about the answer to it. But if the writ of the brigands runs, what further question can there be of this nature, according to the theory which we are considering? Suppose that I am a Panamanian supporter of the previous regime; is it logically absurd for me to say 'Yes, I know that these brigands have the power to put in prison or to shoot anybody who breaks their regulations; but nevertheless the whole procedure is quite unlawful'? Suppose that people who think like this band together, and perhaps enlist the assistance of a foreign power, and overthrow the brigands. They will then no doubt declare that the acts of the brigands were illegal. But, on the 'Might is Right' theory, this would be a manifest falsehood; for, during the five years, say, that the brigands enjoyed power, their writ *did* run in Panama; and therefore, on the theory, their enactments *were* binding laws. The theory, by denying a distinction which we require to make, that between power and legal authority, makes nonsense of the whole conception 'legally binding'. It may of course be that the conception *is* nonsense – or at any rate is nonsense when applied in unsettled circumstances like those we have been describing. But it would be hasty to draw this pessimistic conclusion before we have examined some other solutions. If we say that it is altogether nonsense, we shall be up against the objection that people seem to use it quite satisfactorily and to make themselves understood; but if we say that it is nonsense under unsettled conditions, but sense under normal conditions, we shall have on our hands a very difficult demarcation problem – not perhaps an insoluble one, but one which, in view of the examples with which I started, one does not want to have to face if one hasn't got to.

We might try to modify the 'Might is Right' theory in order to get over these objections. An attractive modification is to say that it isn't enough for a group of people to have the power to enforce their will; there must be something which is recognisable as a *legal system*. So if we find a brigand leader shooting people who don't do what he says, that isn't enough to make his commands laws; there have to be enactments couched in a universal form, with recognisable and consistent procedures for making and enforcing them, including a legislature, courts of law with judges, etc. Where there is such a system, we say that those enactments are legally binding which are used in making decisions, giving verdicts, etc., by the courts. But this is still a recognisable version of the 'Might is Right' theory, because all these conditions are not sufficient, even on the revised version of the theory, unless the system does command the power to enforce its enactments. One could have all the rest of the conditions (some people making enactments and others condemning and sentencing people they called criminals, and so on); but if the 'criminals' always went scot free, because the courts had no power to enforce their sentences, then, on this theory, there would not be a legal system, and the so-called 'laws' would not be binding.

Now here we must carefully distinguish between two questions: the question 'Is there a legal system in such and such a territory?' and the question 'Are the enactments of the system legally binding on the inhabitants of the territory?'. I think that most people would be prepared to agree that, if all the conditions which I have just listed are fulfilled in a territory, there is a legal system in that territory. But the cases of the Jacobite and the Scottish Nationalist with which I started ought to make us see that it is possible, without contradiction, to admit that there is a legal system in this sense, but to deny that its enactments are legally binding. The Scottish Nationalist was put in prison; but was his contention that the court did not have authority over him empirically refuted by pointing to all these judges sitting up in big chairs wearing wigs, and all the policemen and warders and hangmen doing what the judges say? He would surely reply 'Yes, I agree that a very exact travesty of the forms of law is being put on; but that doesn't make the procedures any more lawful; for all these judges, etc., are appointed by a government which owes its power to an act of unlawful force perpetrated upon the lawful Scottish parliament in 1707.' Whether or not we agree about the historical facts upon which he is relying, we surely cannot deny that a similar argument brought forward by a French Royalist or a Russian Tsarist would have considerable weight against the theory which we are discussing. The mere existence of a legal system, as described, does not constitute its legality, in the sense of 'lawfulness'.

I conclude that even this modification of the 'Might is Right' theory will not save it. Force does not become law by disguising itself in the trappings of law. But since I am more interested in the general defect of all descriptivist theories of law, I will now go on to mention other examples of such theories. We may consider next the theory often known as 'popular sovereignty'. According to this, a government is lawful if it enjoys the support of the people of a territory. If there is a revolution in a territory, then the revolutionary group becomes the lawful government if and when, and only if and when, the people of the territory acknowledge it as the government – which acknowledgment they give, either in words, or more commonly by acquiescing in or more positively supporting the acts of the group.

It is not all that easy to distinguish this theory from the modified form of the 'Might is Right' theory which I have just been discussing. There is nevertheless a crucial difference; for it is not an analytic truth, but a contingent fact, that it is impossible for a government to survive for long without popular support. An up-to-date tyrant, equipped with the latest military and psychological machinery, might continue indefinitely to *impose his will* on the inhabitants, in the sense that they obeyed his regulations; yet such a person would not be said to enjoy their support. He would, indeed, have to lead the operators of the machinery 'like men by their opinion' (as Hume put it[2]); but that does not affect my point. So, in such a situation, the modified 'Might is Right' theory would call the tyrant the lawful government, but the 'Popular Sovereignty' theory would not. And this difference is very important.

Next we must consider two descriptivist theories which, though like the two we have just considered in that they too seek to explain the meaning of 'lawful government' by giving a criterion for its application, differ from them in that the criterion offered is of a more elusive character. I will call these the 'Hereditary' theory and the 'Natural Law' theory. The hereditary theory is now old-fashioned, but was once almost universally accepted. According to it, a lawful government is one consisting of a legitimate ruler (or, in exceptional cases, rulers). A ruler is legitimate if he is the rightful heir of a legitimate ruler. Now there are certain well-known difficulties in this theory – theoretical difficulties which give rise to very real practical ones, and are in fact the main reason why this theory has lost its appeal. I mean difficulties about how we determine what are the rules of rightful succession, and – more serious – about how the *first* legitimate ruler became legitimate.

These indeterminacies in the theory are symptomatic of a deeper defect, as we shall see. They have often led to the hereditary theory

[2] *Essay IV.*

being backed up by an appeal to the natural law theory, which we must now consider. It might be suggested that questions of who is the legitimate ruler, and what are the laws of rightful succession, since they cannot without circularity be determined by the ordinary laws of the territory, might be determined by appeal to a natural law above all actual human laws. And such appeals were often made (e.g. by Sir Robert Filmer to whom Locke replied).

Without entering into the details of this question, I should like to point out the main distinctions between what may be called 'empirical' descriptivist theories of law (like the first two we considered) and what may be called 'non-empirical' descriptivist theories (like the last two). Empirical theories give a tolerably determinate criterion of lawfulness in governments; we can at any rate make a decent show of determining whether the criterion is satisfied by a given government. The cost of this determinacy is that the theories are easily shown to be absurd; it is obvious that we use the expression 'lawful government' in a different way from that which these theories claim. This can be shown by pointing out that it is not self-contradictory to say that a certain government has the power to impose its will, but deny that it is the lawful government; and that it is not self-contradictory to say that a government has the support of the people but is not the lawful government. Such theories are *obviously* absurd, once one has had this pointed out, because the phrases to which they make the expression 'lawful government' equivalent have a more or less determinate meaning, and this is clearly not the same as that of the *definiendum*.

Non-empirical descriptivist theories, in a conscious or unconscious attempt to evade this kind of refutation, introduce into their *definientia* expressions whose meaning is sufficiently indeterminate for us not to be able to say with certainty whether or not they are equivalent to a given expression. This makes theories of this kind sufficiently slippery to elude the kind of refutation made popular by Moore, of which we have just given examples. But it lays these theories open to another charge, that of saying nothing definite at all. They claim to give a criterion of lawfulness, but leave it entirely unclear what falls under this criterion and what does not. Thus, suppose that, for example, there is a dispute about whether a certain kingdom can pass in the female line. Now there might, of course, be already in 'existence' a law of succession which determined this question. It would not determine it finally, for the reason (circularity) already alluded to, which will become even plainer as we proceed. But for the moment let us suppose that there is no such law. We may then find the two parties both appealing to the natural law. One of them, fingering the pages of Aristotle's *Politics*, may claim that woman is naturally unfitted to rule a kingdom, and that therefore the kingdom cannot be inherited in the female line; the other party may claim that woman is naturally the equal of man. How could such a dispute possibly be settled? Here, as to wider issues, we may apply the remark of the distinguished Danish jurist Alf Ross that 'like a harlot, natural law is at the disposal of everyone. The ideology does not exist that cannot be defended by an appeal to the law of nature' (*On Law and Justice*, p. 261).

I will now turn to an attempt to give a more satisfactory account than those which I have so far discussed. And in order to do so I shall import from moral philosophy a device which has proved of some assistance there. This is the distinction between so-called 'first-order' moral judgments and so-called 'inverted-commas' moral judgments. It would be out of place here to try to explain what is meant by a first-order moral judgment; this class includes most of the typical moral judgments that we make. I am concerned only with the relation between these and the 'inverted-commas' moral judgments. An inverted-commas moral judgment is true if and only if some first-order moral judgment is actually made by some determinate or at least roughly determinable set of people. For example, there is a use of the sentence 'We ought to call on the Joneses' such that it does not express a first-order moral judgment of our own, but only the judgment that our calling on the Joneses is required in order to conform to the moral judgments made by a certain set of people, viz, those known as 'polite society'.

This distinction is even more applicable to the field of law than it is to the field of morals – and has indeed been frequently made use of in other terms. There is a school of jurists who, in seeking to define 'lawful' by giving a *criterion* of lawfulness (the programme of all those theories which I am criticizing), think that they can achieve this object by treating all legal statements as if they were inverted-commas legal statements. This is the origin of the well-known theory that 'the law is what the courts will decide'. Now this theory might seem at first sight an adequate account of legal statements made by certain classes of people: for example, law dons instructing their pupils, solicitors advising their clients, and counsel giving counsel's opinion. It is, however, as has been pointed out in a justly famous article by Professor Hart,[3] an inadequate account of declarations of what is or is not the law made by judges giving their judgments in court. For the judges are then not *predicting* what the courts *will* or *would* decide; they are themselves deciding. It may be all right to interpret a solicitor's advice in an in-

---

[3] 'The Ascription of Responsibility and Rights', in *Logic and Language, First Series* (ed. A. G. N. Flew).

verted-commas way as a statement which is true if and only if the courts would make a certain first-order judgment if the case were put to them; but the inverted-commas judgment cannot be fully explained unless an explanation is forthcoming of the first-order judgment. Any attempt to explain *this* as an inverted-commas judgment lands us in circularity or in regress. I am ignoring, for the sake of simplicity, the complications introduced by the existence of higher and lower courts.

Professor Hart, in the article to which I have referred, called the judgments of courts 'ascriptive', to distinguish them from ordinary descriptive judgments such as the statements of solicitors may be. It may be all right to say that if a solicitor says that a certain piece of land is my property, he is (in a wide philosophical sense) describing it; for he is stating that the land possesses a certain relational characteristic, namely that if I claim in court to be protected in certain ways in the enjoyment of it, the protection will be forthcoming. But the court, in giving me this protection, is not *describing* the land in any sense; rather, it is *instructing* the police and all whom it may concern to preserve my enjoyment of the land.

Hart does not in this article (which is concerned chiefly with the notion of responsibility) pursue the question of how these ideas are to be applied to problem-situations such as are created by revolutions, *coups d'état* and the like. It seems to me, however, that we cannot stop just where Hart leaves the matter. He considers only what is the case where we have a settled régime, and where it is clear to all (*given*, we might almost say) what persons sitting in what places are properly referred to as 'the courts'. But in revolutions this ceases to be the case. And it seems to me that the fact that it ceases to be the case in revolutions reveals a gap in our account of what happens even in settled times. For, as the examples with which I started show, it is possible even in settled times for somebody without self-contradiction to challenge the lawfulness – or the authority or competence – of the 'courts' which (he admits) are generally *accepted* as lawful, or of the régime of which they are a part. And we have to think what we could say to such a person.

If a solicitor says that a certain piece of land is my property, it may be that he means that if I went before a lawfully constituted court, I should be protected in the enjoyment of this land. And the same will apply, *mutatis mutandis*, if a Scottish Nationalist goes to *his* solicitor and asks him whether Her Majesty's 'government' have lawful authority to require him to bear arms. But what happens if the Scottish Nationalist asks his solicitor what is the lawfully constituted court of supreme jurisdiction for Scotland? The solicitor will no doubt say that the House of Lords is; but what does he mean by this? Perhaps we can interpret it, as before, to mean that if the question is put, in due form, to the lawfully constituted court of supreme jurisdiction, it will say 'The House of Lords is the lawfully constituted court of supreme jurisdiction'. For short, 'The lawful supreme court will say "The House of Lords is the lawful supreme court" '. But this will obviously not satisfy the Scottish Nationalist. For if he does not acknowledge that the House of Lords is the lawful supreme court, it is no use telling him that the *House of Lords* will say 'The House of Lords is the lawful supreme court'. This would not be, in his eyes, the judgment of a lawful court at all (in a case concerning Scotland), let alone that of the lawful supreme court. He would only acknowledge as the lawful supreme court for Scotland some Scottish court, which perhaps does not at the present time exist. So anything that his solicitor could say to him is quite irrelevant to his question. The solicitor can only report or predict what other people have said or would say; he cannot make a first-order legal judgment. And of all the people who *can* make first-order legal judgments, we can ask '*Quo jure?*' – a question which cannot be answered, without circularity, by appealing to the same courts for a pronouncement upon their own competence or authority.

So, then, we are left in an apparently inescapable *impasse*. If we say that all legal statements are inverted-commas statements, we make their meaning altogether inexplicable, since inverted-commas statements of any kind cannot be interpreted unless we know the meaning of the corresponding first-order statements. But if we admit any first-order legal statements, the question arises, How do we know who is competent to pronounce them? And since the statement that somebody is competent is itself a legal statement, this question seems unanswerable without circularity.

The way out of this impasse, as it seems to me, is to recognize that *there is no reason to confine the notion of ascription to what is said by courts.* There are, that is to say, some uses of words like 'lawful', even by ordinary people and not judges, which have to be called 'ascriptive'. These ascriptive uses by ordinary people are in settled times not common; but their existence or at least possibility has to be acknowledged if we are to understand other uses of the terms which are parasitic upon them. In unsettled times they become quite common.

Let me first give examples of such uses in unsettled times. Let us suppose that there is a revolution in progress (for example a republican revolution against a monarchy), and that it is as yet uncertain which side will win. We may then find one side saying things like 'The King's government is the lawful government of this country', and the other side saying 'The King is a tyrant; the lawful government is one resting upon the will of the people.' Now it is most important to notice that, odd as it may at first sight seem, these two sets of people may *mean the same* by the word 'lawful'; indeed, they must mean the same, if these two utterances are to express a disagreement between them. The monarchists emphatically do not *mean* by 'lawful', 'set up by the rightful heir of a legitimate monarch'; and the republicans do not mean 'supported by the people'. Otherwise their utterances would be reduced to something near triviality. They are judgments of substance, and in substantial disagreement with each other. And they are not inverted-commas judgments; the parties are not saying that somebody else would or will judge in a certain way; they are themselves doing some judging. In fact, in a revolutionary situation like this, since any judge is, as it were, tainted by adherence to one side or the other, and since, therefore, legality cannot be established by appeal to judges, every man has to be his own judge, and ascribe to one government or the other the right to be called the lawful government. We may call this kind of ascriptive performance an *act of allegiance*. That is what, in a revolutionary situation, the declaration that a certain government is lawful amounts to. The revolution may be said to be over (*de facto*) when the bulk of the population (or of that part of it which is capable of influencing affairs) has come over to one side by implicitly or explicitly declaring its allegiance.

There is another kind of judgment of legality which we must notice which takes place at times of revolution – that made by foreign governments. They have in the end to recognize one side or the other as the lawful government of the territory. When they do this they are not describing the government – they are not saying that it possesses a certain feature named lawfulness. They are doing what they are said to be doing – performing an act of recognition, which is one kind of ascription. It would be inappropriate to say 'No, your statement that it is the lawful government is false; the government does not have the feature called lawfulness.'

Notice that it is not, at any rate normally, any Tom, Dick or Harry in the United States that has to decide whether Mao's government is the lawful government of China. The United States has a government acknowledged by its citizens as lawful; and its citizens cannot at one and the same time acknowledge it as lawful, and make for themselves independent judgments about what is the lawful government of China. For part of what they are doing in acknowledging as the lawful government of the U.S. the government of Johnson is to depute to Johnson and his government the task of recognizing or refusing to recognize foreign governments as lawful. So, as we should expect, the status of the citizens of the U.S. is different in this respect from the status of the citizens of China whose government is the object of the act of recognition. The citizens of China recognize (or, better, give their allegiance to) their government directly, having nobody else to depute the act to; the citizens of the U.S. recognize it, if they do, only indirectly, by acknowledging the U.S. government as the proper body to do it (or refuse to do it) on their behalf.

At this point I must warn you against a common misinterpretation. If I do not warn you, somebody may attribute to me the view that the following statement is analytic: 'Whatever government is given allegiance by the bulk of the people of a country is the lawful government.' At least, this commonly happens in the corresponding controversy in moral philosophy. This is not what I mean; indeed this view is a descriptivist view of just the sort I have been attacking, very similar to the one I called the popular sovereignty theory. It is an attempt to give an inverted-commas account of a first-order legal judgment, and, like all such attempts, is destined to prove abortive. Only in an inverted-commas sense could 'the lawful government' be the equivalent of 'the government to whom the bulk of the people gives allegiance'; for the latter expression means much the same as 'the government *called* "the lawful government" by the bulk of the people'. If this were what it meant, we should have an infinite regress on our hands, in that the *definiendum* recurs in the *definiens*, and thus the *definiens* can be infinitely expanded (without illuminating us in the least) by substituting the *definiens* for the occurrence of the *definiendum* inside itself. This absurdity is not what I am suggesting. What I am saying is that some statements of the form 'So and so is the lawful government' are themselves acts of allegiance, not that they are equivalent to statements that somebody has performed or would perform acts of allegiance.

Nevertheless, though my own theory is to be emphatically distinguished from the popular sovereignty theory, I may perhaps claim that it does restate correctly the truth which was incorrectly stated by that theory. In moral philosophy, similarly, my own view is often confused with the view called 'subjectivism'; I would claim, however, that my own view does state correctly a truth which subjectivism tries to state but lands in falsehood. But I won't digress into moral philosophy.

I must also utter another warning, because there is another objection that is sure to be made. It will be said that I have given a purely 'emotive' account of legal judgments, reducing them to mere shouts like 'Vive la république!' This is not my intention. I hope it is not now generally thought, as it used to be, that if an utterance is not descriptive, it must be a mere expression of feeling.

There is, however, a legitimate objection which might be made to what I have said so far – in fact several. The first is this: You have maintained, it might be said, that, in certain contexts (especially revolutionary ones), the expression 'The lawful government' is to be understood as the key phrase in an act of recognition or of allegiance; but this explains nothing until you tell us what these things called allegiance and recognition are that are being expressed. The second objection is that I have not said whether there are (as there are generally thought to be) any *reasons* which entitle us to give or withhold recognition or allegiance; surely, it may be said, if they are just acts that we can perform or not perform, why shouldn't we, on your theory, just toss a coin. Surely, though, argument is in place here: whether to give allegiance or recognition is a difficult question; you make it sound too easy. And of course somebody will go on from there to suggest that I have put the cart before the horse – the only sufficient and necessary reason for giving allegiance or recognition to a government is that it is the lawful government; first we have to establish the *fact* that it is the lawful government, and then, when we have established that, we can recognize it. The third objection is the following: it may be allowed that I have made out my case with regard to revolutionary situations; but it may be maintained that in settled conditions there is nothing to correspond to all this.

Let us consider these objections in turn. The first is: What is recognition or allegiance? I will answer simply, but in the knowledge that a lawyer would add a good deal of complications and refinements. First, recognition. A foreign power, in recognizing a government, is according to that government certain rights, especially rights over the citizens of the recognizing power; these rights then become enforcible through the courts of the recognizing power. Thus an act of recognition may be interpreted as an instruction, rather like an ordinary piece of legislation, to the courts of the recognizing power to treat the recognized power and its citizens in certain determined ways. The recognizing power also, in the act of recognition, declares its readiness to enter into diplomatic relations of the normal sort. There are no doubt other elements in recognition which an international lawyer would list. Allegiance is something different. In giving my allegiance to a certain government, I am committing myself to treat its regulations as laws binding upon myself; that is to say, I am submitting or subjecting myself to it. After I have made such an act of allegiance, or acknowledged it to be the lawful government, I can no longer complain if the government, in pursuance of its laws, puts me into prison (or rather, though I can complain, as any citizen can complain if he considers the laws unjust, I cannot make a certain kind of complaint, namely the kind of complaint that I might make if brigands kidnapped me and kept me confined against my will).

I do not think that I can at the moment give any clearer explanation than that.

The second objection is about what are the reasons for giving or withholding allegiance or recognition. The answer is that there are plenty of reasons, only they are not *legal* reasons. The position is a little similar (though there are important differences) to that in which a body of people form a club. There may be many reasons for forming a club – the desire to play cricket, or to undertake concerted action against one's employers, or many other reasons. To form a club is to incur certain obligations; but one does not form the club *because* one has the obligations. Similarly, to give one's allegiance to a government is to lay upon oneself certain obligations; but one does not, in asking whether one shall give one's allegiance, ask first whether one has the obligations, and, if one has, give the allegiance. The reasons for giving one's allegiance to a government are of many kinds. It may be the desire to have protection; or the desire to promote a state of society of which one approves; or the desire to have a government which supports a religion to which one adheres. Some of these reasons are moral ones, some prudential, some political, and some perhaps of other kinds. None of them is a legal reason.

The case with recognition is similar. There are many reasons for recognizing or refusing to recognize a foreign government, but none of them are legal reasons. It may be that recognition is refused because, since it does not control the territory, recognition would be pointless (it has not the power to discharge those obligations which are normally demanded in return for recognition). Or perhaps it is considered politically or even morally objectionable. Or perhaps it is merely that withholding recognition is thought to be a good move in power politics. But there is never, strictly speaking, a legal reason. For there to be a legal reason, the recognizing power would have to be able to say 'This government is the lawful government of the territory; therefore we hereby recognize it as the lawful government.' But this would be like saying 'You are my deputy, therefore I appoint you my deputy'; or 'This ship is called the *Queen Mary*, therefore I name her the *Queen Mary*.'

Put thus baldly, however, my thesis makes declarations of recognition and allegiance a bit too like legislation, and not like enough to judgments of the courts. It would be true to say that there cannot be legal reasons for enacting pieces of legislation (i.e. one cannot say 'This is the law, therefore I make it the law' – though natural-law jurists talk as if this were what one ought to do). So we require to qualify the doctrine. It is a matter of dispute among jurists to what extent judges *find in* an already existing law what they declare to be the law in difficult cases, and to what extent they actually *make* the law. It seems to me that the latter is at least sometimes the case. But it would be obviously wrong to maintain that it is always the case. Now acts of recognition in particular are or ought to be guided by principle and precedent in the same sort of way as judgments of the courts are in difficult cases. So it might be said that, although no specific legal reasons can be given for recognition, there is a body of legal precedent and principle which tells us when we ought to recognize a new government in a country which has had a revolution. In the case of allegiance, I do not think that there is any such body of legal precedent or principle – though there are obvious political and prudential and moral principles which might guide us. I do not think that these qualifications to my thesis make it altogether nebulous.

This second objection has been put to me in an even stronger form (privately) by Professor Hart. He says that 'it is the function of international law to provide legal reasons [for recognizing or not recognizing governments as lawful]: a government with general support and ordered control, after extinction of hopes of restoration of the displaced *de jure* government, may have a right to recognition'. This form of the objection raises the general question of the status of international law, into which I shall not have time to go. Briefly, the fundamental question seems to me to be, What makes international law the law? Not, certainly, the opinions of international lawyers; they cannot, any more than solicitors, determine what international law is to be; they can only try to say what it is. International law, it seems to me, has at any rate no stronger a position than the English common law, which depends on the accumulation of precedents. And the precedents in this case are past recognitions, etc., by sovereign states. So the situation remains as I described it.

The third objection is the most difficult to meet. This admits, for the sake of argument, that what I say about revolutionary situations is correct, but challenges me to produce anything going on in ordinary settled situations which could possibly be called 'acts of allegiance'. When faced with this objection, I am bound to admit that I do not know of any occasion in settled régimes in which anybody uses expressions like 'So-and-so is the lawful government of this country' as a declaration of allegiance. I can very well imagine, however, that such a form of words might be used if it were desired to have a test of allegiance or loyalty for candidates for office or army officers; and indeed there are forms of words in attestations, etc., which are reminiscent of this. It does not, however, particularly matter what people say; what we want to get at is something that they must all *think*, if they are loyal citizens. To be loyal to a certain régime is to acknowledge it as the source of binding laws, whether the acknowledgment is done verbally or not. If anybody does not acknowledge the government of his country as the source of laws binding upon himself, then he is, at least at heart, a rebel. And this, indeed, is all that can be said to the Scottish Nationalist and the Jacobite.

The view which I wish to contest may be caricatured as follows. If I am brought before the magistrates to be charged with a parking offence a friend may say to me 'Do you acknowledge the lawful authority of the court to try you?' According to the view which I am contesting, if I reply, 'Yes', all I am doing is to make a statement of fact to the effect that this court is set up in accordance with laws which higher courts in fact use in making their judgments; that its judgments, if they do not contain what the higher courts judge to be legal errors, will not be reversed by those higher courts simply because of the constitution of the magistrate's court. In short, I am saying that this court is acknowledged as having lawful authority by the courts of this country. But on my view I should be meaning more than this. *I* should be acknowledging the authority of the court over me. I should be doing something that a Scottish Nationalist, for example, might not do (though he might do all that, on the view of my opponents, I am doing). The Scottish Nationalist may readily make inverted-commas acknowledgments of lawfulness; but it may be that he will not, as I will, make first-order ones.

Of course I might only be using the expression in an inverted-commas way. Compare the following situation: I say to somebody in a letter that so-and-so is my agent; this might be mere statement of fact to the effect that I have appointed so-and-so as my agent; but it is much more likely to be taken as an act *committing* me to be bound by whatever so-and-so does in my name.

The non-descriptive, first-order character of such utterances comes out much more strongly when they are negated. If the Scottish Nationalist said 'I do not acknowledge the authority of this court to try me' or 'This court is not a lawfully-constituted court', he would clearly not be making a factual statement to the effect that the authority of this court would not be upheld by higher courts. He would be refusing to submit to the authority of the court.

The ordinary citizen, in settled times, does not need to go about performing acts of allegiance or acknowledgment of the lawful authority of courts or governments. It is taken for granted that as a loyal citizen he acknowledges their authority. And since he does this, it is left to them, acting as the special organs for declaring what the law is or what it is to be, to make laws (in the case of governments) and interpret and enforce them (in the case of the courts).

I have been speaking hitherto in a very loose way in characterizing *what* it is which is recognized, or to which allegiance is given, or which is acknowledged to be lawful. I have used expressions like 'the government' and 'the régime', and have treated the courts as if they were a part of these. I do not now wish to go into the complications of constitutional theory, and should only reveal my ignorance if I did. Nor do I wish to discuss at length the so-called problem of sovereignty. It is obvious that many difficult problems remain to be dealt with, with which I am not competent to deal. But may I end by restating my position in the barest possible outline? To acknowledge a government or régime as lawful is not, when this is a first-order judgment, to state any *facts* about it; in particular, it is not to state the fact that there are courts and that these *call* the government lawful, and use the laws made by it in their judgments. For we could acknowledge all this, and still call the monarch (supposing that he was a monarch) who made these laws a *pretender*; and

> Who pretender is, and who is king,
> God bless us all, that's *quite another thing*.

8 Responsibility, Blame and Punishment

John Plamenatz

I

Though men have often blamed and praised one another for being what they are and not only for acting as they do, and though they still do so, yet today, in many parts of the world, judges, teachers and others whose *office* it is to blame, to punish and to educate, do take it for granted that men deserve blame and punishment only for those of their actions for which they are responsible in the sense that, whether or not they actually chose to do them, they could have chosen not to do them. This is the principle on which these officers of blame and punishment act, or claim to act, when they carry out the duties of their office. And, no doubt too, the principle is widely accepted by other persons, especially in countries where such officers are important and influential. Though, even in these countries, the principle is often disregarded, it is widely recognized and seldom challenged.

It would seem that in primitive societies there is much less deliberate use of blame and punishment to achieve results. The student, contemplating a primitive society, may say that blame and punishment serve to discourage some kinds of behaviour and to encourage other kinds, to strengthen some feelings and attitudes and to weaken others. But of this the natives may be largely unaware. They blame and punish because, so they say, it is the *proper*, the *fitting*, thing to do; it is what everyone does on such occasions, and what everyone expects and approves. The propriety of what they do may be the reason they give for blaming or punishing, or it may be the reason which is much the most important to them. That being so, it seldom occurs to them to ask whether a man ought to be blamed or punished for doing what he cannot help doing, or for being as nature or circumstances beyond his control have made him.

But where there are professional judges and teachers, where there are persons whose *office* it is to uphold and inculcate principles by blaming and punishing (even though also in other ways), blame and punishment come to be looked upon as means to ends. Questions which to men in primitive societies are unintelligible come to be important. To justify blame and punishment it is no longer enough to say that they are *proper* on certain occasions, that they are what the occasions *call for*; and to establish their propriety it is no longer enough to appeal to custom. Where blame and punishment are recognized as means to ends, men enquire into the conditions of their effectiveness. They think it unreasonable to use them where they are ineffective. No doubt, older attitudes persist; but by those who look upon blame and punishment primarily as means, the older attitudes are called 'irrational'.

Everywhere blame and punishment attach to what is held to be wrong or evil or shameful. In simple illiterate communities, where men are blamed or punished not only for what they do but also for what they are or what has happened to them, certain qualities in them or misfortunes falling to their lot are held to be shameful. In such communities men are sometimes blamed for what others, who are close kin to them, do or are or suffer; and this even where there is no question of their having encouraged or made possible their kinsmen's behaviour or character or misfortune. But at least they are blamed for what is held to be wrong or shameful. In all communities, simple and sophisticated, men make a distinction (or, rather, behave as if they made one) between *blaming* and *punishing* offenders and their kin and merely taking action intended to prevent others doing what those who take the action do not want them to do. The distinction is made even where the preventive action consists of the making of threats or the putting them into effect. Men are blamed and punished only for breaking rules or for qualities and conditions held to be evil or shameful; and not for doing what the blamers and punishers do not want them to do, or for being what they do not want them to be.

We have seen that in some societies men are blamed or punished, not only for their own actions, but also for what others closely connected with them have done. Sometimes, too, they are blamed or punished for what they do unintentionally or without knowing that it is wrong. They may not understand the situation in which they act or may not know that there is a rule forbidding what they do; and yet they are not held blameless. A rule has been broken, a wrong done, and the wrong must be 'undone'; there is a need felt that matters should be as they were before the wrong was done. The wrong must be 'annulled', and the annulment 'requires' that the doer of the wrong or someone close to him should suffer. But in more sophisticated societies, though the feelings survive which find expression in the words *punishment annuls crime* (words not to be taken literally), the ignorant are accounted blameless, except when their ignorance is set down as negligence, and it is held that they ought to have noticed what they failed to notice or to have discovered what they failed to discover. And vicarious punishment is condemned.

Yet, even in these societies, there is a sphere in which the excusably ignorant are 'blamed' and 'punished'. At least, it is said that they are, for the treatment meted out to them is ordinarily called *blame* and *punishment*.

We speak of *blaming* and *punishing* children, even when it is clear to us that they do not understand the situations in which they act or the likely consequences of what they do, or do not know that what they do is wrong and there is no question of their being ignorant because they are negligent. We then 'blame' and 'punish' them, as Hegel saw, not for what they have done but in the hope of educating them. We 'blame' and 'punish' them to ensure that they eventually become the sort of persons who, should they act in these ways, would deserve blame and punishment. We cannot yet reason with them, for they are too young to understand the nature or to foresee the consequences of what they do. They understand something of what they do and foresee some of its consequences, but not enough to enable us to justify to them our treatment of them. Yet we do not merely tell them not to repeat what they have done, nor do we merely vent our displeasure, for we may feel none; we act in the hope of inducing in them a certain attitude to what they have done which will make it less likely that they will do it again. And if we do more than scold them, if we cause them further suffering, we do so, not so much in the hope that in the future fear of like suffering will deter them from like behaviour, as in the hope of strengthening this attitude in them. We do not 'blame' or 'punish' our childish victims in order to *reform* them, for they are as yet innocent; and we do so only to some extent in order to *deter* them. Our immediate purpose is to train them to 'feel' as they ought; and we may think it as important that they should have these feelings as that they should do or refrain from doing what these feelings encourage or discourage. They are still blameless but are already able to hurt others and themselves, and will soon be even more able; we therefore 'blame' and 'punish' them, and thus put an end to their innocence, by causing them to feel as they ought while they are as yet not old enough to be reasoned with.

And it may be that, if we did not thus early put an end to their innocence, we would find later, when they were old enough, that the appeal to reason was in vain. They might then, though not without the intelligence or the factual knowledge required to understand what was said to them, lack the feelings to be moved by it. For the appeal to the reason of a moral being is always also an appeal to the censor, the blamer and punisher, in him. It is always also an appeal to the feelings, though to feelings of which only rational beings, who control and persuade others and themselves, are capable. Certainly, if children were not already to some extent in use of their reason, we could not induce these feelings in them; but it may be also that, unless the feelings were induced in children before they had reason and experience enough to foresee the consequences to others and themselves of their behaviour, no pointing to these consequences later, when they were able to foresee them, would suffice to persuade them to behave well.

Those who look upon blame and punishment primarily as means to ends are concerned with them much more as deterrents than as instruments of reform. There is, especially in countries where these matters are the most discussed and studied, considerable evidence that the punishment of adults, and even of adolescents, serves as much to strengthen as to weaken the passions and attitudes which move them to do wrong. Blame and punishment may be effective, indeed indispensable, where it is a question of *forming* character not already formed; but their effectiveness as instruments for *reforming* character where it is already formed is much more open to doubt. The little child whose ability to reason is slight depends greatly on the adults who look after it, and is also often cherished by them; it is an object of love and a source of happiness, as well as a nuisance, to them, and it feels itself to be so; it cannot yet aspire to independence, self-centred and capricious though it is, and therefore does not resent dependence. It is imitative, avid of approval and upset by disapproval; it is amenable to discipline. It is blamed and punished, praised and rewarded, within a small circle of intimacy in which it is, and feels itself to be, precious as well as dependent. But the adult or adolescent, whether he is an habitual or a first offender, already has a character formed; he is blamed and punished, not in a small circle of intimates, but publicly by persons who perhaps never heard of him until he was brought before them for judgment. He may be an offender because he has become hostile or indifferent to others and has felt them to be so to him; and this hostility or indifference may become the deeper because he has been blamed and punished.

He may be, as the saying is, 'in revolt against society'; and if he is an habitual offender, he may break the rules, not because he has been moved to do what they forbid, perhaps without even knowing that they forbid it, but because they are rules to be broken. He asserts himself in breaking them; and when he breaks them with impunity, feels that he has won a victory. He has outwitted the enemy, the community of the law-abiding from which he feels himself estranged. Or, if he is not 'in revolt against society', he may care nothing for some of its important rules, and may pursue his interests regardless of them, except when it happens to be worth his while to behave as if he cared for them. The breaker of rules, whether he is 'in revolt against society' or is deliberately pursuing his aims by methods which are immoral or illegal, may be no less rational, no less consistent in his behaviour, no less realistic, than the habitually moral and law-abiding. His actions may be as well adapted to his goals, his goals as compatible with one another, his behaviour as much in keeping with his principles, and his estimates of what is possible in his circumstances just as accurate. Blame and punishment are not likely to reform him, to cause him to change his goals or his principles. He may run risks that the law-abiding do not run, but he also has opportunities which their principles prevent them taking; he has discounted the risks. Or he may even court them, as a man does who climbs a mountain which he knows to be dangerous. The authority of Hobbes notwithstanding, it is not a whit less rational to live dangerously than to seek security. If such a man is to be reformed, it must be by other means than those of which the judge and the gaoler dispose.

Such considerations as these make for scepticism about the reformative value of blame and punishment applied by public officers to adults and adolescents. Applied by parents or teachers to children in their care, they may be effective, indeed indispensable, instruments for the formation of character. But as instruments for the *reform* of persons whose ability to reason and to fend for themselves is already as great (or almost as great) as it will ever be, persons whose characters are already *formed*, they are lamentably inadequate. And sometimes they are worse than inadequate; they harden the hearts of those who suffer them, and are to be justified, if at all, only as deterrents.

Yet, even where official blame and punishment do less to reform offenders than to strengthen the attitudes which cause them to offend, we can justify them on other grounds than their being deterrents. They always do more than move would-be offenders to refrain from offence for fear of the consequences to themselves. They also affect the private judgments of men generally; they serve to maintain among the law-abiding respect for the rules whose breach exposes the breaker to official blame and punishment. Nor are they the less effective to this end because laws which run counter to widely accepted standards are often dead letters. Attitudes and actions support one another. Where no action is taken against those who do what is commonly held to be wrong, people's attitude to this behaviour is apt to change. Though in some spheres they may feel it incumbent upon themselves to take action, in others they leave action to those whose office it is to take it. But the effect on their attitudes is often much the same, whether it is they who fail to act or those whose office it is to take action on their behalf.

We are not affected by the blame and punishment of others as we are by our own. When others are punished, we are not exposed or humiliated. Even though we feel sympathy with the condemned man, we stand in his shoes in imagination only. We may come to understand how he felt when he committed his crime, and we may recognize, as never before, that we have it in us to do what he did. We may recognize in ourselves the passions which moved him to act. The sight or account of his trial and condemnation may affect us in ways which make it less likely that we shall do what he has done. But we have not been *deterred* from doing it – at least not in the sense of deterrence which we ordinarily have in mind when we speak of the *deterrent* effect of punishment. What we have witnessed of his trial and condemnation has not made us more afraid than we used to be of the consequences to ourselves of our acting as he did. Some feelings and dispositions in us have been strengthened and others weakened, and no doubt there are some among those that are stronger which are rightly named *fears*, but they are not fears of punishment. What we have 'witnessed', what we have observed or lived through in imagination, has not *deterred* but has *purged* us; it has relieved us of a burden. Or else, if we altogether lack sympathy for the condemned man, if we do not put ourselves in his shoes, if we are indignant, our indignation – even when it springs from our not daring to see how much we have in common with him – also serves to strengthen feelings and dispositions which make it less likely that we shall do what he did. In this second case, there is no purgation, or if there is, it is of a different kind; but also there is no *deterrence*, for that is not the proper word to describe the effects on this second observer of the trial and condemnation. Indeed, if we look carefully at the two cases, we must conclude, for all the differences between them, that the effects on both observers come closer to being reform than deterrence.

II

What do we mean when we say that a man is responsible for what he has done in the sense that he could have chosen or decided not to do it? Let us agree that, if we are to answer this question, we need not enquire whether or not there are causally undetermined choices; for that enquiry, whatever its result, would not help us. If we suppose that a man's choice was not causally determined, we are no nearer explaining the sense in which he could have chosen otherwise. A choice is a choice, whatever its causal antecedents, and it is that man's choice who made it.

Everyone agrees that the alternatives open to a man are limited by his situation and his character. If, then, we suppose that his choice was undetermined, it merely follows that, within certain limits, it was a matter of chance what choice he made; but this also follows if we suppose that one of the causes of his choice was undetermined. In either case, it could have happened that he chose otherwise than he in fact did choose. When we hold a man responsible for an action, when we say that he could have chosen otherwise, we cannot be saying merely that there was a chance that he might so choose. For chance can be measured; and if a man is to be held responsible for his actions because there was a chance that he might have chosen not to do them, ought we not to hold him the more responsible, the greater the chance – that is to say, the less predictable his behaviour?

What then do we mean when we say that a man is responsible for what he does when he could have chosen not to do it? We mean that, at the time that he acted, he was not beyond the reach of certain kinds of influence.

We mean that he could have chosen to act differently or not to act at all, for he may in fact have made no choice and yet his action have been avoidable. And when we say that he could have chosen to act differently, we mean that his condition, when he acted, was such that he was *persuadable*. We mean that, when he acted, he was amenable to influence by considerations of the kinds that men ordinarily put to themselves when they contemplate action or put to other men when they seek to persuade them to act or to refrain from action.

There are a variety of causes which put men more or less beyond the reach of these considerations; but, before we discuss them, we should notice that, on particular occasions when we are trying to estimate a man's responsibility for what he has done, we need not take all these causes into account, for some of them will not be relevant. One or other of these causes may affect some men more often or more strongly than others, and every man will be affected by them more strongly at some times than at others. It therefore makes sense to speak of degrees of responsibility, and of diminished responsibility. In practice, it is sometimes extraordinarily difficult, or even impossible, to establish whether or not, or to just what extent, these causes operate; or, in other words, to establish the degree of a man's responsibility. Yet, in principle, it does make sense to try to establish it. We know what kind of evidence to look for, though at times we may be hard put to it to find enough to enable us to make a confident judgment.

There are, no doubt, still differences of opinion as to what would constitute good evidence, but there is already a considerable measure of agreement, which is likely to increase as our understanding of human behaviour and of its causes and consequences grows. Moreover, much of the disagreement we now have is more apparent than real, either because it is merely verbal or because each of the supposedly incompatible views is true in its proper context. How we assess degrees of responsibility must always depend greatly on how we want to treat the persons whose responsibility we are assessing and how we want others to be affected by this treatment. It will also depend, if we belong to a profession whose office is to assess responsibility, on the rules of the profession. We must therefore expect the criteria which men use in assessing responsibility to differ from profession to profession, and to differ also with the purposes of the assessors. Assessors of responsibility, professional and unprofessional, may have an uncertain hold on the criteria they use; they may be more or less confused in their minds about the questions they are putting and also about how those questions should be answered. We should expect this confusion, especially at a time when standards are changing fast, and sociologists and psychologists are undermining old beliefs and putting forward hypotheses difficult to test and sometimes even to understand. But, even if there were no confusion of thought, we should still need to use different criteria of responsibility to suit our different purposes.

When a man has done what is wrong, and our purpose is to assess his responsibility for what he has done, we need answers to these questions: *Did he know what he was doing? Did he know that it was wrong? If he did not know, to what extent was his ignorance an effect of his own past actions, when he did know what he was doing? If he knew both what he was doing and that it was wrong, was he nevertheless in a condition which either made him incapable of acting on this knowledge or reduced his ability to do so?*

Every one of these apparently simple questions is in fact not simple. And in saying this I have not in mind the difficulties raised by ingenious philosophers, but the perplexities that face the practical man. How much must a man know of the situation in which he acts and of the likely consequences of his action in order to 'know what he is doing'? For, clearly, however much he knows, his knowledge is always limited. What is to be reckoned as part of the situation? What consequences are to be taken into account?

What is to be reckoned as part of the situation and what consequences are to be taken into account must vary with our purposes, with the behaviour we seek to control, with what we want to prevent (or to encourage), with the means at our disposal. When we hold a man responsible for what he has done – in the sense of responsibility we are now discussing – we make it clear that our intention is to influence him (and others who may be situated as he was when he did it) 'through his (or their) reason'. We want to ensure that when they are so situated in the future, he and they take certain considerations into account; that they take account of what will move them not to make the choice he made. If we wanted merely to prevent consequences of the kind produced by his action, we could perhaps do it more effectively in some other way which made it indifferent to us whether or not in producing these consequences men knew what they were doing. Our purpose is not (*pace* Bentham) merely to prevent harm; it is to deter from wrong-doing; it is to ensure, as far as possible, that men who act deliberately, who know what they are doing, refrain from doing wrong. And this is our purpose even when we hold that only those actions are wrong which ordinarily have harmful consequences.

The second question, *Did the man know his action was wrong?* can be understood in at least two ways. It may mean, *Did he know that what he did was forbidden?* Did he know that it was the sort of action for which a man is ordinarily punished or blamed when it is known that he did it? Or it can mean, *Is he a person who 'feels' about actions of this kind as men do who 'feel' that they are wrong?* These 'feelings' I need not describe. Whatever we take to be the correct description of them, we most of us recognize them in ourselves. We can therefore imagine a man who does not have them, who is 'morally insensitive'. This man would not know how other men felt about wrong actions. But he might know how they behaved towards anyone whom they accused of wrong-doing. In his eyes a wrong action would be merely an action of a kind which, if it were known about, would provoke this behaviour. He could then apply the word *wrong* to actions just as other people did who felt about them as he did not. And, of course, he could know that some action of his was the sort of action that provoked this behaviour. In that case, he would know, in one sense, that his action was wrong, and in another sense would not know.

A man who is 'morally sensitive' may not, at the time that he does something wrong, feel about his action as he ordinarily feels about actions of that kind. The passions moving him to do what is wrong may prevent his feeling that it is so, and may also blind him to some of his motives, to some aspects of the situation in which he acts, or to some of the likely consequences of his action. But, precisely because he is morally sensitive, we can cause him to 'feel' that his action was wrong by bringing vividly to his notice whatever his passions moved him not to see; and this 'feeling' (or combination of feelings and dispositions), when he comes to have it, may weaken his passions. If our bringing these things to his notice does not cause him to feel about his action as he ordinarily feels about wrong actions, we say that his passions have made him morally insensitive or have reduced his moral sensibility. We know from experience that men differ greatly in the extent to which this sensibility is reduced in them by this or that passion.

We often blame and punish men for their actions, even when they are not 'fully aware' of what they are doing. We blame and punish them for what they do when they are drunk. A drunken man is, almost by definition, a man who is not 'fully aware' of what he is doing; he is not a man who has merely taken much drink but one who has been affected by taking it. Though he knows what he is doing and knows that it is wrong, his 'knowledge' is seriously deficient. He has failed to 'take in' much that he would have taken in had he been sober; he holds mistaken beliefs, and he does not 'feel' as he would do if he were sober. At the time he acts, he is scarcely amenable to reason; there is almost nothing that can be said or done to him 'to bring him to his senses' – that is to say, to cause him to understand the situation and feel about it as he would do if he were sober. Thus, strictly speaking, in the sense of *responsibility* we are now discussing, he is hardly responsible for what he is doing; or, in other words, his responsibility is greatly diminished.

Yet we blame and may punish him for the harm he does in his drunkenness. For no one compelled him to get drunk; he took the drink voluntarily, knowing what it was and that it might make him drunk. Though he did not intend to get drunk, he is responsible for getting drunk; and he is responsible for it in exactly the same sense as he would, if sober, be responsible for hitting and hurting a man. But we have admitted that, being drunk, he is not responsible in this sense for what he does in his drunkenness. Why, then, should we blame and punish him for the harm he does in that condition? Why do we not blame and punish him for getting drunk and not for what he does when he is drunk?

Largely for reasons of economy. Our concern is not to prevent drunkenness but to prevent the harm men do when they are drunk. We blame and punish them for getting drunk, though they do no harm in that condition, only if they get drunk on occasions when their being so makes them unusually dangerous. For example, we punish them for being drunk when they drive a car, even though they do no harm to anyone. On most occasions when men get drunk, they do little harm, or they do the kind of harm which we do not seek to prevent by official blame and punishment. We can reduce the harm men do when they are drunk more effectively by punishing them for doing it than by punishing them for getting drunk, even though, in the sense of responsibility we are now discussing, they are often more responsible for getting drunk than for the harm they do when drunk.

But our drunkard may be a *dipsomaniac*. Whereas others can resist the temptation to drink on occasions when drunkenness is likely to make them dangerous, he cannot do so. Thus, though he is not less responsible than other men for the harm he does when he is drunk, he is less responsible than they are for getting drunk. He is not, in his drunkenness, less amenable to reason than they would be in the same condition; he is less amenable than they are only when he is sober and is tempted to drink. Punishment is not less likely to deter him than them from doing harm when drunk, but it is less likely to deter him from getting drunk; and that may be a reason for punishing him less severely or not at all.

The dipsomaniac, so it is said, *cannot resist* the temptation to drink. So, too, it is said of the kleptomaniac that he *cannot resist* the temptation to steal. Temptation can sometimes blind a man to some aspects of the situation in which he is tempted and to some of the consequences of what he is tempted to do. But it need not do so. He may understand as well as anyone the situation in which he finds himself and the probable consequences of his action. And he may *know*, in both the senses we have discussed, that what he is tempted to do is wrong. Indeed, the kleptomaniac is only tempted to do what he does because he knows that it is wrong; he is tempted to steal and not just to pick things up and put them in his pocket or bag. For if that were what tempted him, he could indulge himself in his own room. Nor, ordinarily, is he tempted to do what is merely forbidden, what most people call *wrong* and seek to prevent by subjecting whoever does it to unpleasant consequences. He feels, or has felt, as others feel about such actions as he is tempted to do. He is not tempted merely to provoke certain reactions, certain kinds of behaviour, in others; nor is he merely tempted to do what will bring suffering to him, though that may be part of his motive; he is no simple masochist but is tempted to do what he himself condemns as wrong.

The kleptomaniac has what is sometimes called an *irresistible impulse* to steal. But how, we may ask, does his situation differ from that of the man moved by jealousy to kill or wound? Let us suppose that the jealous man, like the kleptomaniac, understands what he is doing and the consequences of his action, and that he is, in general, no less given to such feelings as shame or fear of disapproval. He is ordinarily just as 'morally sensitive' as the kleptomaniac. Let us suppose, also, that he is no more responsible for his jealous disposition than the kleptomaniac for his impulse to steal. His disposition, like the other's mania, is not an effect of his past behaviour, or if it is, that behaviour happened long ago when he could not be expected to foresee its consequences. Or it is an effect of how others treated him when he was still too young to understand what they were doing. Why, this being so, should we hold the jealous man responsible for what he does, and not the kleptomaniac?

Jealousy, we may say, is a passion which the man unusually liable to it can guard against. He can avoid situations in which his jealousy is apt to get the better of him. Or, if he cannot avoid them, he can take precautions to ensure that he does not give way to his ruling passion; he can fortify his mind against it. He can argue himself beforehand into a more 'reasonable' frame of mind. We may also say that jealousy is weakened when the man subject to it recognizes it for what it is. Therefore, our jealous man, when not actually in situations which arouse his jealousy, can reflect upon this passion, its cost to others and himself, and by so doing can make it less likely that he will give way to it when next he feels it. If we blame and punish him, we make it more likely that he will guard against this passion either by avoiding situations which arouse it or by 'moral exercises' that weaken its hold on him; and we also make it more likely that others who suffer the torments of jealousy will do so too. But the kleptomaniac, if he really deserves the name, is much less able to guard against his impulse in these ways. Reflection upon his impulse and its consequences does not make it less likely that, when he is tempted to steal, he will not do so; or if it does, he is no genuine kleptomaniac. And it is much more difficult for him to avoid situations which arouse the impulse in him. He is not impelled to steal whenever he has an opportunity of doing so, and he cannot predict when the impulse will be upon him. Like other men, he must provide for his needs and go shopping.

A passion or impulse carries upon it no mark of irresistibility; we cannot by introspection see that it is irresistible. Nor can we say that the more intense it is, the less likely we are to resist it. This is not only because, in practice, we cannot measure the intensities of passions and impulses, given that every man's are private to himself and that no man can make exact comparisons between passions actually upon him and passions remembered. It is also because experience, defective though it is, does provide evidence that sometimes we give way to weak passions, and at other times do not give way to strong ones.

We can only watch behaviour and gather information about it, comparing, classifying, and counting instances; and on the strength of this information, we can make predictions. We can distinguish between people according to their behaviour, as intelligent or stupid, as mad or sane, as irritable or calm – and so on, making finer and finer distinctions, in innumerable ways. We learn from experience that people of one type can be induced by blame and punishment not to behave in certain ways, and that people of another cannot. We learn that some types can be *reformed* and others merely *deterred*. We learn, also, that there are types who, though they are aware of the consequences to themselves and others of certain kinds of actions, and feel about them as most men do who call them wrong, yet cannot be brought by blame and punishment to desist from them. They do not do wrong because they lack intelligence to weigh the consequences of doing it, nor yet because, having weighed them, they decide they have more to gain than to lose by doing it; they do wrong because, in certain situations, they are moved to do it in spite of being aware of the consequences and in spite of feeling about such behaviour as others feel, or else because the impulse to do it puts these consequences and this feeling out of their minds. They are the persons of whom we say that they have an *irresistible impulse* to do wrong.

A writer on morals or law could, no doubt, if he put his mind to it, describe a number of imaginary situations in which men do what is wrong, and could take into account how far they are responsible for getting into the situations and for what they do when they are in them. He could use the word *responsible* in the same sense in both cases, and could define it in terms of the likelihood that men, by being blamed and punished (or by other methods of persuasion which are appeals to take thought), would be brought so to think and feel about their actions as not to repeat them. He could, in these terms, give definite meanings to such expressions as an *irresistible impulse* and *diminished responsibility*. I have not even attempted to do this here, but I do not doubt it could be done. The task would not be easy, seeing how confused our thinking is in these regions and how much ordinary language reflects the confusions. Still, it could be done. The description of a series of imaginary or ideal situations would serve in part to *illustrate* how we already use the concept of responsibility and in part to *correct* our use of it. The correction would lie in making our use of it more consistent and better adapted to our purposes when we hold men responsible for what they do – among which purposes the most important is to control their behaviour.

Admittedly, it is one thing to describe ideal cases and quite another to get at the truth in real life. But, though the clearing away of confusions of thought is only preliminary to other and perhaps even more difficult tasks, it is important. Let me give an example. I tried earlier to distinguish two cases: the case of the jealous man whose jealousy is not an *irresistible* passion, and the case of the kleptomaniac whose impulse to steal is *irresistible*. My two cases were imaginary. I made a number of statements about an imaginary jealous man and what he could do or be induced to do to make it less likely that his passion would get the better of him; and I made other statements about the kleptomaniac and what he could not do or be induced to do to the same end. But there is nothing about jealousy, considered in itself, to explain why it should be less difficult for someone prone to it to guard against it than for someone prone to steal for the mere sake of stealing to guard against his impulse. There is nothing about this impulse to explain why blame and punishment should not serve to induce persons susceptible to it to resist it. Jealousy may sometimes be *irresistible* and stealing for stealing's sake sometimes be *resistible*.

And yet we seem readier to admit that the impulse to steal for stealing's sake is irresistible than that jealousy is so. This greater readiness is, I suggest, due in part to confusion of thought and in part to our greater familiarity with jealousy than with this impulse. We have often felt jealous, and we know that we have sometimes resisted the promptings of jealousy; we have taken ourselves to task on account of it, we have endeavoured to reason ourselves out of it and to weaken its hold on us. Jealousy is a passion that we are accustomed to deal with, both in others and ourselves; it is an old and a common enemy, whose disguises and perversities are known to us. We are in the habit of blaming one another and ourselves for giving way to it. Wherever we come across wrong-doing inspired by jealousy, we fall easily into the way of holding the wrong-doer responsible for it without troubling to enquire whether the conditions that would make him so actually hold. And we are the less disposed to enquire for being uncertain just what those conditions are. Though we do not assert, in a general way, that jealousy is never irresistible, our habit, when we come across it, is to behave towards its victim as if he could resist it. This being our habit, we seldom stop to enquire whether or not, in this or that particular case, jealousy is irresistible.

The impulse to steal for stealing's sake is much less familiar to us, and we are much less used to dealing with it. It may well be that we have been tempted to steal, but, if we have, it was in order to get what we needed and could not obtain as a gift or were unable or unwilling to pay for. The alleged kleptomaniac does for the sake of doing what is wrong, for the thrill of it, what most people who do it do for the sake of something else. He does not even, like the child stealing apples from a neighbour's orchard, do it to prove his courage by deliberately running a risk. His stealing strikes us as irrational because the motive that prompts it is unusual; and this inclines us to say that he is not responsible for it. But stealing for stealing's sake is no more irrational than anything else done because the rules forbid it, 'for the thrill of it' – than, for example, rudeness for the sheer pleasure of being rude, which to Proust, and to others, has seemed an aristocratic vice. Nor, of course, is it unintended; for the impulse is not to make a movement of which the maker is unconscious, nor yet to take something only for the pleasure of handling it; it is an impulse to steal, to do wrong, to take what the taker knows he ought not to take.

Criteria of responsibility could, I think, be clearly defined and consistently used; and we should expect such criteria to correspond closely to some current uses of the term. And yet the term is used loosely. So much so, indeed, that it has been suggested that the difference between actions for which we do, and actions for which we do not, hold one another responsible are to be looked for, not in our situations and mental conditions when we act, but in our customary reactions to behaviour. It has been suggested that we do not blame and punish men for what they do because they are responsible for doing it, but rather that we hold them responsible because we are accustomed to blame and punish them.

Those who make this suggestion need not, and ordinarily do not, deny that there are differences in the circumstances in which men act and in their mental conditions which make it reasonable or unreasonable for us to blame and punish them with a view to controlling their behaviour. They deny only that there is much correlation between these differences and our propensity to blame and to punish.

The sceptics who say this no doubt exaggerate, but just how much I do not know.

III

I would not venture to say whether in Britain we are too much or too little inclined to blame and to punish offenders; whether we err more often in holding them responsible for their actions when they are not so, or in holding them not responsible when they are. But I can see no reason why it should be worse to make the first mistake than the second. Yet there are people taking pride in their enlightenment who seem to take it for granted that it is. The less we punish and the more we seek to cure – so they seem to think – the better. To punish is to use the old method, the method that smacks of vindictiveness, the method that gives to those who use it a sense of superiority, often not justified. To seek a cure is to use the newer method, the gentler method, the method that gives those who use it the sense that they are helping their fellow men.

By all means, let us use the methods best suited to prevent the evils we wish to prevent; let us abandon the old punitive methods as soon as we find others more effective and not disproportionately expensive. But it is surely beside the point to speak of vindictiveness and superiority. Where punishment is the most effective method and the cheapest, does it matter what feelings accompany its use, so long as they do not lead to the abuse of it?

Besides, it may be that those whose business is to catch and punish offenders are, more than most men, aware of how much offenders have in common with the respectable, not excluding their captors and judges. Like all men who have to deal professionally with one person after another in quick succession, impartially and for a limited purpose, they must, if they are to be efficient, acquire a certain detachment; they must set themselves and their colleagues apart from the 'cases' they deal with, the persons they work *with* apart from the persons they work *on*. This detachment is not a sense of superiority; and it is as much needed by doctors and nurses as by judges and policemen, by those who seek to cure as by those who punish. The philosophy of the operator, the social engineer, the statistician, the long-headed calculator, the public official, the professional man who thinks of the persons he deals with in terms of the problems they present to him, is not the philosophy of the hard-hearted or vindictive. It is the philosophy of the busy, methodical man who has definite goals to reach and who takes account of the resources at his disposal. It is a limited philosophy, whose limits are sometimes unnoticed by the men most attracted to it; but, within limits, it is a good philosophy. It is the philosophy which moves us to put such questions as these: Do we know enough about the causes of crime to be able to remove them? Where we do not lack the knowledge, have we the resources? Given the present state of our knowledge, to what extent are punitive methods of preventing harmful behaviour still the least costly and the most efficient? How are the people who, from whatever cause, are the most inclined to this behaviour likely to be affected by the view that they are unfortunates to be helped or cured rather than wrong-doers to be punished? To what extent is a rapid shift from punitive to curative methods in dealing with offenders, especially young ones, likely to weaken the sense of duty in young people generally?

There is evidence that public and official punishment seldom reforms offenders; that old offenders discount it as one of the risks attached to their way of living, while first offenders are made resentful rather than penitent by it. There is perhaps also evidence that offenders treated in other ways, especially when they are first offenders, are more often reformed. Even where these other methods are more expensive than punishment, they may more than make up in efficiency for this greater cost, and so prove in the long run less expensive. But this may be so only while we confine our attention to their effects on the persons to whom they are applied. It is as instruments of reform that they are most likely to prove, in the long run, more efficient and cheaper than punishment. But how do they compare with punishment as deterrents? Do they deter from crime those who have not yet resorted to it? To some extent, no doubt; but presumably not to a great extent, for they are gentler methods than punishment and less shaming.

When we are dealing with physical illness, we find that one kind of treatment does not ordinarily reduce or increase the effectiveness of another, except when the second treatment is applied to the same patient at the same time or soon after the first. The medicines that Dr Smith gives to Jones to cure his lumbago do not make more or less effective the medicines given by Dr Brown to Robinson to cure the same ailment. But when we are dealing with human behaviour which we seek to prevent, one kind of treatment can make another less effective, even though the two are applied to different persons or to the same person at widely separate times. Punishment may now be less effective as a deterrent than it used to be because other methods are more widely used. And yet these other preventive methods may be less effective even than punishment has come to be. It may be that the more offenders are treated as unfortunates who need to be cured rather than punished, the less punishment is disgraceful to the punished, whether in their own eyes or in the eyes of their neighbours. But fear of disgrace has always been a large, and often the largest, element in the fear of punishment.

Fear of public disgrace is only one among several motives conducive to good behaviour. If, hitherto, in most places and at most times, it has been the strongest motive (and who knows whether in fact it has been?), it does not follow that it must be so always. To treat offenders in ways which weaken this fear as a motive for abstaining from offences is not necessarily to increase the number of offences. The less the temptation to offend, the smaller the need to provide motives for resisting temptation. And even though temptation should remain strong, we need not rely on fear of disgrace as the strongest motive for resisting it. The desire to attain goals incompatible with wrong-doing can be just as strong a motive for resisting temptation. And though the desire to attain these goals often weakens temptation, it by no means does so always. It is not obvious that wrong-doers are more strongly tempted than others to do wrong, nor yet that the others are more fearful of disgrace. Faithful husbands or wives are not always less attracted to other women or men than are unfaithful ones, nor always more concerned for their reputations, for they often have more than their reputations at stake.

It has been said that people are now less *responsible* than they used to be; that they are not to be relied upon, as they once were, to carry out their obligations. And one of the reasons given for their being less *responsible* in this sense is the much wider prevalence of the belief that people cannot help behaving as they do, and are therefore, when they behave badly, to be looked upon rather as unfortunates who need help than as evil-doers who deserve blame.

How far this is true, I do not know; nor do I know how we could find out. But, even if it were true, this might be due to other causes than the wider prevalence of the belief that persons who behave badly are more to be pitied than blamed. We are socially more mobile than our ancestors were, and this may have made us less sensitive to certain kinds of judgments and attitudes. We cannot expect, in large, intricate and quickly changing societies, the firm standards or the degree of harmony between private sentiments and imposed norms that we find in smaller and simpler societies, which sometimes change so slowly that change is imperceptible. In the past, most men lived in fewer neighbourhoods and moved in fewer circles, and died in social environments more like the ones they were born into; they did not, in the course of their lives, pass as often as we do from neighbourhood to neighbourhood and from circle to circle. Our social worlds change so much that what we come to know in old age could scarcely have been imagined by those who were old when we were young.

If we are less moved than our ancestors by *official* blame and punishment, by fear of *public* disgrace, or by shame on the occasions that used to call for it, it may not be because the belief has grown stronger in us that men are what circumstances make of them and cannot help behaving as they do. We may be as much given as ever our ancestors were to praising and blaming in the hope of controlling behaviour, and as much moved by fear of disgrace and by shame. We may differ from them chiefly in having more changing and more varied beliefs about right and wrong conduct. We may therefore be less in sympathy than they were with 'official' or with widely held beliefs about such conduct. We may be less to be relied upon to behave as others think we ought to behave, and yet have just as acute and discriminating a sense of duty; we may be just as morally sensitive. We may be more often without shame or fearless of disgrace on occasions when casual neighbours, or those whose profession is to judge, censure and educate, wish to see us ashamed or fearful; and yet we may be no less susceptible to shame and fear of disgrace in the circles in which we feel most at home and form our aspirations, or to which we look for assurance that we are as we should like to be. I do not say that it is so but only that it may be.

It is the *less educated* rather than the *well educated* (or should I say, the *much educated*?) who are said to be so much more irresponsible, so much less to be relied upon to carry out their obligations. Perhaps they are less to be relied upon than they used to be, and perhaps a main cause of their being so is the changed attitude to offences and offenders of those whose office it is to deal with them. I neither contest nor accept this hypothesis; for I am less concerned to argue for or against particular opinions than to consider possibilities.

It may be that certain beliefs about behaviour and the proper treatment of offenders, as they come to be more widely and strongly held in some sections of the community than in others, do least harm in the sections where they are the most strongly held. In support of this hypothesis, it might be said that the educated classes have traditionally been the leaders in society; they have been the prime holders of power and the innovators. They have been long accustomed to dealing with social problems and to speculating about them. Fear of official punishment and of the disgrace it brings has never, with them, been a particularly strong motive for not committing punishable offences. Not that they feel this kind of disgrace less when it comes to them; rather the contrary. But, having less need to commit punishable offences, they are less tempted to commit them; and, when they are tempted, have strong motives other than fear of punishment and of the disgrace it brings for resisting the temptation. These motives are connected with their social roles as they see them. They are brought up to believe that it is their business to think for society, to concern themselves with its affairs; they are by tradition and education its self-appointed guardians or reformers. They are the section of whom most is required or expected in public affairs, especially by themselves but also (though less now than heretofore) by others. They are therefore more inclined than others to accept the doctrine that wrong-doers are sick and unfortunate, to be pitied and helped, rather than wicked, to be punished and despised, and also less likely to be corrupted by it.

But this is only one hypothesis among others not less plausible. It may be that this doctrine has had little effect on the behaviour of any section of the community, and that all sections have changed in the ways I referred to earlier – ways not connected with the spread of this doctrine. There may be among them all a more widespread rejection of traditional or 'official' or widely held beliefs about right and wrong conduct, a greater indifference to blame and disgrace outside the circles in which they form and strive to realize their aspirations, their images of themselves as they would like to be. In all but the simplest, the most homogeneous, the most stable societies, there will nearly always be some degree of moral confusion, of incompatibility between any one person's ideas of what is right or desirable; and also some degree of social disharmony, of conflict between the values and aspirations of different persons. The larger, the more varied, the more quickly changing the society, and the greater the social mobility of individuals, the greater we should expect this moral confusion and this social disharmony to be.

We should expect to find confusion and disharmony in all sections of the community. But their effects may differ considerably from section to section. The educated and the well-to-do, traditionally more concerned with public affairs, and perhaps also more conscious of the utility of established laws and institutions and of the need to change them legally, may find it easier to be prudent and discriminating, to abandon old aspirations and to pursue new ones, or even to be morally at sea, without coming into conflict with the law. Among them there may be many who, judged by widely accepted standards, old or new, are every inch as 'corrupted' as the worst of the uneducated, though better able to evade the law or to make use of it for evil purposes. If we define 'the criminal type' in terms of the propensity to commit offences which are punishable in the courts, there may be, proportionately, more persons of this type among the poor, the uneducated and the stupid than among the rich, the educated and the intelligent; but if we define it in terms of the motives which cause men to hurt one another (and themselves), it may not be so. Whether or not the malicious, the defiant, the angry, the spiritually insecure, the abnormally vain, the morally insensitive, commit punishable offences must depend largely on the opportunities open to them and the skills at their command. It is a clumsy malice which stumbles into crime or seeks relief through it.

Punishment, where it is no cure for moral confusion or social disharmony, may yet be an .effective deterrent. Though we may know much more than we did about the causes of crime, punishment is not a whit the less necessary and justifiable, unless we contrive to use this knowledge to remove these causes or to devise more effective or cheaper remedies.

When we put our minds to such problems as these, it is good that we should have a large dose of the spirit of Montaigne, the spirit of uncensorious curiosity, but we need also something of the spirit of Bentham, who, believing that fear of suffering was among the most powerful of human motives, wanted it put to the best use. No one came closer than Montaigne to finding nothing human alien to him, even the stupid and the base. But Montaigne was a watcher by the wayside, and had little advice for busy men. Action, especially preventive action, to be effective, must be timely; and timely action is apt to be hasty, ruthless and short-sighted, an abrupt turning of the back on possibilities; it is executive, and understanding and sympathy are always, to some extent, its victims.

9 Freedom as Politics[1]

Bernard Crick

Need a student of politics apologize for a tedious obsession with the matter of freedom, particularly when so many people, both philosophers and the man at the back of the bus, appear to believe that freedom is keeping politics at arm's length?

My point will be that there is a reciprocity between freedom and politics, properly understood, not an animosity. Certainly freedom and government or freedom and order live always in tension and often in animosity; but insofar as any government responds to some political factors, this is then a sign of some freedom; and those comparatively few governments who govern in a manner systematically political are then properly called 'free governments' – which otherwise might seem empty rhetoric and a contradiction in terms.

Indeed, I am persuaded of the value, both moral and scientific, of an old and unfashionable way of looking at things which would link politics and freedom together, not merely in civil wedlock, but in permanent progenitive embrace. Politics is the collective need to bargain, to compromise and to conciliate between differing interests, whether conceived as material or ideal, whose existence is accepted, at least for a time, as natural. Freedom is the act of an individual making choices among all such relationships and activities; it cannot simply be regarded, as even some liberal philosophers and many artists have thought, as freedom from – or the successful avoidance of – politics and publicity. Put in its most abstract way, the very possibility of privacy depends upon some public action; and conversely public life is all just 'telegrams and anger' if it does not accommodate private happinesses.

This is not a very fashionable point I want to make. It may sound more like rhetoric than analysis. So I must insert some argument that freedom is *both* a value and an institutional precondition for any scientific study of society. Freedom, indeed, I will seek to show, need not be either just rhetoric or analysis; for being both a concept and an institution, it has a history. If it has no end, it has a fairly clear beginning; that is why students of politics have to go back to the *polis* of Athens. If the Greeks were not the first to experience it, they were the first to give lectures about it. To say that history is the unfolding of freedom, as would Hegel and Marx, may be meaningless or at times simply

---

[1] This is a slightly chastened version of an inaugural lecture delivered at the University of Sheffield in 1966.

false; but it is far from meaningless to say that the most important task for history and political studies, both intellectually and morally, is to write an account of the origins and conditions of freedom. The task is difficult but conceivable: Lord Acton was to be pitied for failing to complete his history of liberty, not blamed for the attempt.

That we in the West, where freedom grew, are sometimes simply too embarrassed to state the obvious can be seen by the clarity with which a brilliant Japanese contemporary, Professor Maruyama, sees that freedom is both, as it were, a fact and a value for political science (and is indeed in its origins as distinctively Western as science). 'It is unreasonable to expect any genuine social science to thrive', he says, 'where there is no undergirding of civil liberty.' He suggests that all forms of autocracy depend on the truth not being known about how they are actually governed. But equally, the other side of the coin, he says: 'The extent to which politics can become the object of free scientific inquiry is a most accurate barometer by which to measure the degree of academic freedom in a country.'[2] It is interesting that much the same answer to the same problem has recently been reached independently by someone else who has also lived under both autocracy and freedom. Professor Giovanni Sartori, in discussing Max Weber's famous demand that the social sciences should be *wertfrei*, value free,[3] points out that this is a very fine ideal which could only possibly be applied in a free society: modern totalitarianism persecutes both neutrality and objectivity and old-fashioned autocracy allows it only subject to censorship. And I think our instinct to go further is not wrong. The laboriousness of marshalling the evidence should inhibit us more than any embarrassment about the claim: that scientific advance itself is closely related to the history of liberty (though we then need to distinguish between science and technology).

So the matter is still important. So important indeed is the concept of liberty that we are all reluctant to define it too closely, wanting to apply it to everything we value. Other people's states of freedom, after all, commonly appear as either wilful self-deception or as anarchy – however gentle. Thomas Hobbes had quite a lot to say about liberty and anarchy; even 'conscience' to him was but 'a worm within the entrails of

[2] Masao Maruyama, *Thought and Behaviour in Modern Japanese Politics* (Oxford University Press, London, 1963), pp. 227–8 and 229.
[3] Giovanni Sartori, *Democratic Theory* (Praeger, London and New York, 1965), chapter III. See also W. G. Runciman's brilliant discussion of this problem in his *Social Science and Political Theory* (Cambridge University Press, 1963).

the body Commonwealth'. And then there are some who while they do appreciate what freedom is, better than some of its democratic champions, yet reject it either as an intolerable burden, too capricious, demanding and uncertain a companion, or else despise it as an unwanted brake, hindrance or obstacle to economic betterment and intensified nationalism. Erich Fromm wrote a psychoanalytic account of the origins of Nazism entitled *The Fear of Freedom*; and numerous authors have added wine to old hash by quoting Dostoievsky's sardonic words on those whose supreme need it is 'to surrender as quickly as possible the gift of freedom . . . with which they, unfortunate creatures, were born'. Thus freedom may always be rescued from platitude by observing the refugees from it and by mixing with its opponents. Acton once wrote to Mary Gladstone *à propos* the Jesuits:

> It is this combination of an eager sense of duty, zeal for sacrifice and love of virtue, with the deadly taint of a conscience perverted by authority, that makes them so odious to touch and so curious to study.

In not claiming too much, we must beware of not claiming too little. This, I think, Isaiah Berlin has done in his otherwise admirable, influential, bewitching and powerful *Two Concepts of Liberty*.[5] I want to argue with deep and genuine respect that, while he has shown a great skill in defending the nymph of Liberty from abuse, he has been unnecessarily modest in denying her exercise and is at fault in letting her languish with so little to do.

Berlin has argued, using 'liberty' and 'freedom' virtually as synonyms, that there are two fairly clear and distinct traditions of the use of the word and concept: 'negative liberty', which is freedom *from* constraint; and 'positive liberty', which is freedom *to* achieve some one good thing. 'Positive liberty' men thus commonly say of 'negative liberty' men that they are being 'just negative': liberty to them must consist in fulfilling the proper object of the good life. Berlin shows that 'negative liberty' is what is often called 'the liberal view'; and he argues that attempts to go beyond that, to assign a positive object to free actions, prove philosophically paradoxical and politically autocratic.

He makes no bones about 'negative liberty' being just 'negative liberty': that it is inadequate as an account of political activity, certainly of the alleged 'ends of political activity' or of 'justice'. He quotes

[4] *Letters to Mary Gladstone* (1st ed.), p. 251, quoted by Gertrude Himmelfarb in her edition of Acton, *Essays on Freedom and Power* (Free Press, Glencoe, Ill., 1948), p. 1.
[5] Isaiah Berlin, *Two Concepts of Liberty* (Oxford, Clarendon Press, 1958).

Bentham: 'Every law is an infraction of liberty.' Laws are plainly needed; but to be under the constraint of laws is not to be – as some positive liberty men would say – free or more free. He even quotes Bentham again, with evident approval, as saying: 'Is not liberty to do evil, liberty? Do we not say that it is necessary to take liberty from idiots and bad men, because they abuse it?'

'Positive liberty' is characterized as the valuing of freedom only as a means towards some end, identifying it with some good extrinsic object, even if just 'freedom from error'. Berlin quotes a dictum of the Jacobin Club: 'No man is free in doing evil. To prevent him is to set him free.' Here one agrees with Berlin wholeheartedly: agrees that there is such a theory of freedom and that its consequences are both linguistically self-contradictory and often morally obnoxious. Indeed, I would make so free as to slightly extend Berlin's analysis here to identify three common sub-groups of theories of positive liberty: there is a *moral* theory of positive liberty – as in the degrading confusion of either 'Oh God . . . whose service is perfect freedom' or 'the truth shall set you free'. There is a *material* or *economic* theory of positive liberty – as in Harold Laski's 'liberty is the existence of those conditions in society which enable me to become myself at my best'[6] (to which the answer is quite simply that not being unemployed etc., is not the same thing as being free). There is finally a *psychological* theory of positive liberty – as in Rousseau's argument that one must only will generally, that one must sink one's selfish self utterly in the general welfare and that he who does not see this 'must be forced to be free', for he is really denying his own chance of self-realization.

Plainly whatever freedom is, it is not being forced. But even if not being forced, freedom surely also appears pragmatically paradoxical, at least, if of one's own free will one puts oneself in a situation in which one's freedom of choice is radically diminished. Does it really tell us anything to say that a man is free to put himself under a discipline of silence, continence and abstinence from all worldly things? Or that those Germans who mistakenly voted for Hitler were still free at the moment of voting? If freedom simply means absence of constraint, then actions that destroy the possibility of exercising freedom are free actions. In a logical sense so they are; but in the same sense, so is everything else. Here I begin to get slightly restive and to feel that the subject is un-

[6] But compare several such formulations in chapter 4 of his *Grammar of Politics*, fifth edition (Allen and Unwin, London, 1948), with an explicitly negative formulation throughout his *Liberty in the Modern State* (Pelican, London, 1937), p. 49, for instance. Laski appeared to adopt whichever best suited his mood of the moment or 'the felt needs of the time'.

naturally restrained by Berlin's too purely linguistic analysis (or too purely contemporary?). Isn't it, in fact, more *informative* and *explanatory* to say that such people are rejecting freedom – often very consciously – rather than exhibiting it?

Berlin argues that we should realize that we cannot always be free and that there are always some things we think so valuable that we gladly sacrifice some liberty in order to achieve them: full employment and a decent standard of living, for instance. But let us not call this sacrifice, he says, freedom. In times of emergency, let us admit, he suggests that we *are* being repressive, otherwise the distinction is lost for ever between free and necessary actions (or actions deemed to be necessary); and we then end up by saying that 'freedom consists in the recognition of necessity'[7] or some such blinding nonsense. One agrees. Basically all advocates of 'positive liberty' are, at the very best, confusing the conditions of freedom with the thing itself. 'There cannot be freedom until X and Y' is very different from 'X and Y, here they are. So you're free – damn you.'

But in avoiding one error, Berlin walks too cautiously. He virtually separates the word from any possible social or political context. Can one really just 'be careful', as distinct from being careful about and for something? Is liberty simply an absence of constraint? I don't find this very precise or convincing even just as a matter of verbal usage. I would call such a condition simply 'isolation' or more often 'loneliness' – put more sympathetically, 'splendid isolation' or 'the self-reliant individual' (who is not human, but an anatomical abstraction, and put sociologically, impossible). The strange gap in such defensive battles as Berlin's against the arrogance of 'positive liberty' is any systematic recognition that freedom is, firstly, a peculiar type of relationship between people and, secondly, an *activity* by people.

Berlin can only tell us in the end that we are free to do what we are not stopped from doing: freedom consists of the infinite range of opportunities to act, not in a limited range of actual actions. Things move until they are checked. This is an analogy from physics and mechanics under the influence, remote, refined but precise, of Thomas Hobbes. But why draw one's analogies from mechanics? If one presses linguistic analysis into philology, both 'freedom' and 'liberty', both the German and the

---

[7] Engels, *Anti-Dühring* (Martin Lawrence, London, 1934), 128. But there is, admittedly, a certain melodrama in his use of 'necessity' where the argument of the whole passage plainly implies 'circumstance', 'conditions' or 'limitations' – something not, as it were, 'necessarily necessary'. Some criticism is purely verbal. How rarely do people mean 'necessity' when taken contextually.

Latin roots, indeed the Greek equivalents, had little to do with natural
science but were primarily 'status' words – words that described certain
legal and social rights. But back to this point later. What is missing in
Berlin's analysis, odd though it may sound to say so, is any analysis
of the link between freedom and political action – a typically liberal
lack, if a socialist may say so (though a Tory could say so equally well).
Freedom is being left alone from politics – is it?

He cannot indeed entirely avoid this impasse of triviality. He has to
cover it, as we all do, by exhortation. And as readers of Hume will know,
no one can exhort more forcefully than a prince of sceptics on a negative
tack:

> The 'negative' liberty that they strive to realize seems to me a
> truer and more humane ideal than the goals of those who seek
> in the great, disciplined authoritarian structures the ideal of
> 'positive' self-mastery, by classes, by peoples or the whole of
> mankind.[8]

Now, as much as one agrees with much of this, it seems to me not
very helpful to speak of 'negative liberty' as an 'ideal' which people can
'strive to realize'. How can one strive to realize a state of affairs in which
one is constrained as little as possible when everyone recognizes that
social and moral constraints are always present and, in fact, these re-
straints more often form the object against which men strive in order
to get them taken off themselves and put on others? Some content is
needed somewhere. While it seems dangerous and paradoxical to attach
freedom to particular objectives, yet it seems trivial and hopelessly incomplete to leave it purely negative.

I think certain positive things can be said. There is, for instance,
fairly general agreement about the formal condition in which it is held
to be justifiable to constrain people. Other things are sometimes tacked
on, like 'public decency', 'good taste', libel and slander, but the essential
condition is commonly held to be that even established and habitual
liberties may be justifiably constrained if their exercise threatens public
order – the fact of government at all. Governments govern and even in a
well-nigh perfect liberal state, presumably, things will be stopped when
they threaten the survival of the State. Abraham Lincoln put the matter
nicely:

> It has long been a grave question whether any government not
> too strong for the liberties of its people, can be strong enough
> to maintain its liberties in great emergencies.

Disputes flourish, of course, about what constitutes an emergency: Élie
Halévy once suggested that it was the distinctiveness of modern tyranny

to preserve artificially a 'state of emergency' from wartime on into what could well have been peace.[9] But this formal recognition that liberty depends upon order is neither trivial nor unimpressive. When we wonder whether Weimar Germany and Republican Spain did not cut their own throats by appearing to apply a liberal American 'clear and present danger' test to restricting the liberties of enemies of republican government, rather than using the harsher (though admittedly more speculative) Roman *'principiis obstat'*, we are shifting the argument, quite properly, from 'what does one mean by liberty?' to 'what does one mean by public order?'

Friends of 'negative liberty' do in fact tend rather hopefully to say, as it were, 'Locke until Hobbes', even if they can no longer quite believe in 'Locke after Hobbes': they recognize the difficulty, but seem unwilling to stop and talk to it. If there is this positive limitation of 'public order' on even such 'negative liberty', may we not be able to put a little flesh of historical and sociological circumstance onto the otherwise rather dry linguistic bones of liberty? Berlin himself says that 'to demand more than this [negative liberty] is perhaps a deep and incurable metaphysical need'.[10]

Indeed it is. Some synthesis is needed which will avoid the extreme of tyranny latent in 'positive liberty' and the anarchy or quietism of 'negative liberty' – if we take them to be political concepts at all. I am not criticizing Berlin's distinction as far as it goes. Down with positive liberty and two cheers for negative liberty! But the distinction is a dangerously incomplete account of what freedom has been and is.

At one point he himself comes near to the view I am about to suggest. At the end of a passage in which he points out that all ideas of 'natural rights' imply absolute values – which are never, in fact, clear, enforceable or universally agreed upon, he says:

> Perhaps the chief value for liberals of political – 'positive' – rights, of participating in the government, is as a means for protecting what they hold to be an ultimate value, namely individual – 'negative' – liberty.[11]

Berlin has to admit that 'negative liberty' at least needs positively asserting if it is to be political at all. He is at least close to the view that true freedom is something neither positive nor negative in his senses, but a relationship and an activity: an individual acting voluntarily in public or for a public – whether in art or politics.

Free actions, surely, are *actions* of individuals; but they arise from and

[9] *L'Ère des Tyrannies* (Paris, 1938), pp. 213ff.
[10] Berlin, *Two Concepts*, p. 57.
[11] *Ibid.*, p. 50.

affect the actions of others. Free actions are unpredictable, otherwise we would say that they are determined and necessary; a free action is an action of which it cannot be said that it must have happened. All public communication and actions are subject in some degree to constraints, both necessary ones which arise from the other people and the materials involved, and contingent ones of social circumstance; but it can never be said that there are no alternative actions possible, unless the person simply chooses – in Berlin's pure negative sense – not to act and then, presumably, to hope for the best.

In Thomas Mann's short story, or parable of Fascism, *Mario and the Magician*, he portrays the 'gentleman from Rome' as initially resisting the hypnosis of the charlatan in the seaside village, but eventually he succumbs. Mann wrote:

> As I understood what happened, the gentleman was beaten because he took up a posture for the struggle which was too negative. It would seem that the mind cannot live by not wanting to do something. It is not sufficient in the long run not to want to do something. Indeed there is, perhaps, such an uncomfortable closeness between the ideas of not wanting to do something and of not wanting to be bothered to make any longer the effort of wanting not to do it, i.e. being prepared to do what one is told, that between the two the idea of freedom is gravely endangered.[12]

Berlin really commits what logicians call a 'category mistake'. Freedom is not an attribute of all possible actions, it is one type of action; it is *political* action. Even Acton saw this in his famous definition – if I am correct in putting emphasis where I think it should be: 'By liberty I mean the assurance that every man shall be protected *in doing* what he believes his duty against the influence of authority and majorities, custom and opinion. . . .'[13] The Whig cart of consent is here put before the Tory horse of government, but at least they are together: participation and action are part of freedom, neither conditions nor consequences, but the thing itself.

Freedom, then, needs rescuing from the philosophers – or from a type of philosopher who construes usage too narrowly – and needs placing in its historical and sociological setting. The earliest words we have for freedom have little relation to words for 'absence of constraint' or 'unimpeded movement' of matter. They were social status words: one suspects that the mechanical words were in fact analogies from these – not *vice versa* as is usually supposed. After all it is a bold metaphor to

[12] Thomas Mann, *Mario and the Magician*
[13] Acton, *The History of Freedom and Other Essays* (London, 1907), p. 3.

say that the wheel is free, rather than the man who chooses to make it comes unstuck.

The Greek *eleutheros* means free in the sense of not a slave. Someone was *eleutheros* if his status was such and if he displayed the qualities which the Greeks associated with this status: disinterestedness and generosity – also a certain outgoing forcefulness.[14] A freeman would possess *arete*, like Homer's Achilles,[15] would be 'a doer of deeds and a speaker of words' – what the Romans called *virtus*, or in a debased and revived form, Tom Brown's 'manliness', or better what both Robespierre and Jefferson, liking it, or Dr Johnson, disliking it, meant by 'patriotism' – before that word became debased too: the active citizen moving freely from private to public in the common interest. The Latin *liber* and *liberalis* correspond almost exactly to the Greek. In time the social meanings of the Roman word grew less: from the constant contrast between the freeman and the slave and between the freeman and the barbarian (who did not know freedom), the ethical meanings came to dominate it: a man's character would become *liberalis* – as we still call people 'liberal-minded' and once called people 'liberal-handed'. The English word 'free', from the Anglo-Saxon *freora manna*, kept, in a feudal world, its social significance longer and its ethical significance appears more vague and empty, as in Chaucer's knight who had 'Trouthe and honour, freedom and courtesye'. Am I alone in fancying that the word 'freedom' even today carries a slightly more positive connotation, a status enjoyed or a status to be achieved, than does the gentler 'liberty'? At any rate, Berlin chose the word 'liberty' where I have chosen 'freedom'.

If we treat freedom, then, as a social-status word and thus susceptible to historical and sociological study, we can sensibly study the relationship between freedom and order – even though the result will be different in every circumstance. But I am naïve enough to see no general philosophical difficulty. It is not enough, though it may be occasionally necessary, to polemicize against 'determinism' or 'historicism' as does Karl Popper. I take 'freedom of the will' for granted – what else can one do? The problem remains of relating freedom of the will to action and to order. Indeed I can see two types of order in which constraints are not merely justified, in the nature of the activities, but may be sensibly felt positively to enhance liberty: politics and love. I simply limit my remarks to politics.

[14] See the section on 'Free' in C. S. Lewis, *Studies in Words* (Cambridge University Press, 1960).
[15] See Werner Jaeger's discussion of *arete* in vol. 1 of his *Paideia* (Blackwell 1947).

Politics, like freedom, very like freedom, is ubiquitous in some minimal and thin sense, but in thicker and richer senses is something highly specific and by no means universal. Politics cannot exist without government any more than freedom can exist without order: freedom is always freedom within a context. Some governments harry freedom and others nurture it. Government is the general ability to make decisions between different groups which can collectively be regarded as society for most purposes. Politics as an institution is the conflict of differing interests (whether ideal or material) in an acknowledged mutual context. Politics as an activity is the conciliation of these differing interests in the public context created by a state or maintained by a government. Politics as a moral activity is the creative conciliation of these interests.

Now perhaps some politics exists everywhere – even in the court of the Grand Mogul, the Kremlin or the Brown House. And by the same token *some* freedom must then exist – though the barber, the court jester or the second gravedigger may appear far more free than even the Grand Vizier, the Chief of Police or old Polonius. In a palace or a court they will dislike it, but will try to ignore it; but in the party headquarters of a modern one-party state they will commonly hunt it down: differences of opinion are a sign of insufficient dedication or of unpurged Jewish, bourgeois or colonialist decadence.

Politics as a *system*, however, only exists in relatively few states: those states which actually make their decisions in a political manner and encourage politics, which then becomes (the most vital distinction of all) public politics. These states, which I pedantically call 'political régimes', are commonly and misleadingly called democracies (which they all became during the First World War as casualties mounted); but *all* industrial and industrializing states are democracies, whether they allow free politics or not: they all depend on the consent of the majority, as peasant cultures never did, and most of them need the actual enthusiasm of the new class of skilled manual workers.[16] These states are perhaps better known by their more proud and ancient – and once more precise – name of 'republic'.

In such political régimes or republics, freedom varies in its scope and

---

[16] It seems to me quite unjustifiable (*vide* nearly all American political scientists) to deny the equal propriety and to miss the theoretical significance of the Napoleonic usage of 'democracy' rather than the Jeffersonian. Democracy can be an element in many different kinds of government, but no government can be democratic. See chapter 3 of my *In Defence of Politics*, and also C. B. Macpherson, *The Real World of Democracy* (Clarendon Press, Oxford, 1966).

content, but always it exists as a positive activity.[17] As both Montesquieu and Rousseau said, quite correctly, the stability of republics depends on the virtue of their citizens.

This was once seen more plainly than now, before the rhetoric of 'democracy' obscured the precise and limited sense of the word 'politics' which I find so useful; and before there began a kind of liberal panic at modern power which, fortified by literary aestheticism, turned freedom from participation in communal affairs into a conscious attempt to be left alone – which one never is. Just one example: Chief Justice Fortescue could write sometime in the 1470's in his *De Laudibus Legum Angliae:*

> A king of England cannot at his pleasure make any alterations in the laws of the land, for the nature of his government is not only regal, but political. Had it been merely regal, he would have a power to make what alterations and innovations he pleased in the laws of the kingdom, impose tallages and other hardships upon the people whether they would or no, without their consent, which sort of government the civil laws point out, when they declare 'Quod principii placuit legis habet vigorem'. But it is much otherwise with a king whose government is political, because he can neither make any alteration or change in the laws of the realm without the consent of the subjects, nor burden them against their wills with strange impositions, so that a people governed by such laws as are made by their own consent and approbation enjoy their properties securely, and without the hazard of being deprived of them, either by the king or any other.[18]

---

[17] I do not see that this sense of 'positive' offends Berlin's logical objections to 'positive liberty'. He objects to identifying liberty with any one goal or good; my objection is to identifying it with one particular goal or good. Freedom as human activity must always be attached to some object; what is objectionable is when it is held that there is only one true object for everyone. Freedom is choice-amid-clash of alternatives, not the absence of conviction. And it is a different matter, even, for individuals to hold 'positive liberty' views in our shared objectionable sense, than for the state power. The threat they then represent will be relative both to their influence and to the character of the ideal. Some of Professor Sir Karl Popper's objections, for instance, to 'essentialism' (the great killer) are fairly silly when one considers the character of most such folk and the context in which they act and react. Both Berlin and Popper seem to me profoundly unhistorical and unsociological in their imagery of, as it were, 'what would happen if things were taken to their logical conclusion'. When things were, it was not because of a mistake in logic.
[18] Quoted by T. F. T. Plucknett in his eleventh edition of *Taswell-Langmead's English Constitutional History* (Sweet and Maxwell, London, 1960), p. 218.

We may know that in such a passage the signification of 'a people' and 'subjects' who give their consent is narrower, very much narrower, than the words might suggest. But this does not alter the fact that, however small the aristocracy or élite concerned, the relationship was political, and that in so far as there was politics there was an experience of freedom – even if only within a governing class. That by itself is something. In history we must talk, like Edmund Burke, of 'liberties' rather than of liberty. Historically, indeed, liberty as we know it arose within aristocracies or the merchant oligarchies of the medieval free cities. It was practised in Parliament long before it was widely sought after or tolerated in the country. When men came to talk of a proletariat they were talking of a community shaped by oppression and dedicated to achieving justice by means of intense discipline and solidarity; individual freedom has seldom been even a working-class value, let alone something consciously proletarian. But this need only embarrass that kind of conservative who confuses the value of things with their origins. As a socialist, I can quite happily say that freedom was in England – and in most other countries – an aristocratic invention, but that it can, should and must be popular.

Hannah Arendt has written, with only slight exaggeration, that 'the *raison d'être* of politics is freedom and . . . this freedom is primarily experienced in action'.[19] As she herself comments, any attempt to derive freedom from the political must sound strange and startling because of two peculiarly modern fallacies. The first derives from the complete separation in many people's minds between the concepts of private and public – so that the very point of freedom is often thought to be an escape from the public realm (as if even lyric poetry did not need to be heard); the second arises because from at least the time of Rousseau we have thought that freedom is an activity of the will and of thought rather than of action. Sartre is one of the few moderns, besides Hannah Arendt and Simone Weil, who has seen this distinction clearly. In a review of François Mauriac's *La Fin de la Nuit* he wrote:

> We must understand that for M. Mauriac, freedom cannot construct. A man, using his freedom, cannot create himself or forge his own history. Free will is merely a discontinuous force which allows for brief escapes, but which produces nothing, except a few short-lived events.[20]

---

[19] In her essay 'What is Freedom?' in *Between Past and Future* (Faber, London, 1961), 151 – to which I am in debt. Exaggeration, for surely politics is the institutionalizing of freedom, possibly its justification, not literally a *raison d'être*.
[20] J.-P. Sartre, *Literary and Philosophical Essays* (Rider, London, 1955), p. 17.

Or as he said in his essay on Descartes, the 'experience of autonomy does not coincide with that of productivity'. Put in plainer terms, to mark the end of my criticism of Berlin, freedom is doing something with it, not just sitting pretty on it. Put in more complex terms, to show the importance of insisting that freedom is an activity, I would quote Arendt again:

> Political institutions . . . depend for continued existence upon acting men; their conservation is achieved by the same means as brought them into being. Independent existence marks the work of art as a product of making [she means, once made it is always there]; utter dependence on further acts to keep it in existence marks the state as a product of action.[21]

Where there is politics there is freedom. There is some freedom, even if limited to contesting aristocratic clans, wherever government recognizes by institutional means the need to consult with conflicting interests – whether (as I have argued elsewhere) through prudence (being unable to predict the outcome of coercion) or through principle (when, in some sense, the moral equality of individuals is part of the culture – whether in the manner of Jesus Christ or of Immanuel Kant).

'Freedom' can hardly be treated as a condition for a political system because, in a minimal sense, it is almost a pleonasm for politics; and because, in more elaborate senses, it is a derivative of an already existing political system or culture. A political system is a free system – though the order is thus: freedom depends on politics as politics depends on government.

It is notorious that political régimes will often consciously run risks with their very stability rather than curtail particular freedoms. Only anti-political régimes are for ever preparing the individual to sacrifice his freedom of action for the collectivity, or try to persuade him that freedom is not choosing between *and* making possible alternatives, but is the euphoria or transfiguration that comes from making the right choice in good company.

Some freedom in a negative sense may exist in the autocracies, between the gaps of the laws, the indifference of the ruler, and the inefficiency or corruption of the bureaucracy. But in totalitarian and ideological societies not merely are fields of free activity hunted down, even in spheres irrelevant to the mechanisms of control of traditional autocracies, like art and music, but free actions are, as part of the ideology, deemed to be impossible. Everything, in theory, is sociologically determined – whether by economic or by racial factors, the only real competitors in this league. But political societies neither enshrine such

[21] Arendt, *Between Past and Future*, p. 153.

fabulous theories, nor do they even imagine the need to claim that all human actions should submit to the test of public policy.

Freedom depends on some distinction and *interplay* between private and public actions, for it is neither isolation from politics (as the liberal often wants to believe), nor is it loneliness (as following the concept of being an 'intellectual' has often involved). Freedom and privacy both thrive when government is conducted publicly in the manner called political. Freedom, then, is neither isolation nor loneliness: it is activity of private men who help to maintain, even if not personally participating in, public politics. Privacy is itself a social relationship. Men who cease either to identify or to value politics usually lose and at the best weaken freedom. Politics is the public actions of free men; free men are those who do, not merely can, live both publicly and privately. Men who have lost the capacity for public action, who fear it or despise it, are not free, they are simply isolated and ineffectual. As Aristotle said, the man who seeks to dwell outside the *polis*, or the political relationship, is either a beast or a god.

'Political freedom' – as we may now call it, to distinguish it firmly from 'negative liberty' – is simply the habit and possibility of men as citizens acting freely. An absolutely unique and a reasonably private man says or does something unpredictable and uncommanded in public – or for a public – which has some effect, however slight, on others: that is a free action – whether in art or politics. Freedom depends upon people continuing to act freely in actual public affairs, and in being willing to run risks by speaking bluntly in public, not in constantly taking one's own temperature, according to some abstract standard laid down by god, don or judge, or according to the foundation myths of one's country, to see if one is still left free or not. Eventually the answer will then be – not. Freedom does not consist in being able to choose between pushpin and poetry, but in actually choosing. Although both choices are possible, neither is necessary or entailed.

By such purely negative conceptions of freedom, such people then discover, not surprisingly, that they are cut off utterly from society, are 'alienated', and then 'the whole system', nothing less will do, is blamed. This whole system must then be changed and freedom becomes the concrete service of some one single abstract idea. It is both sad and instructive to see how readily 'great individualists' fall victim to systems of thought and allegiance in which *nothing but* public values and social purposes are allowed. Such exciting extremes of unnecessary despair and unguarded hope come from a failure to accept freedom for what it is: a creative relationship between the private and the public, the assertion of both as complementary, not rival.

There is *fortuna* as well as *necessita* in politics – as the greatest of all republican apologists, Machiavelli, reminds us. We have been simply fortunate in England that the habit of acting freely in public affairs came so early, so that tolerance of the free actions of others became accepted as a condition of one's own. Tolerance is always relative, of course, but so it must be; for there are always some things, quite simply, which we should not tolerate.²² We should not tolerate, for instance, threats to toleration: we should not allow freedom to destroy freedom. And nor should we tolerate tyrants: tyrannicide is praiseworthy and is an essential part of the tradition of political thought.²³

I find these questions easy in principle – not worth an examination question even; the difficulties are entirely practical. Yet toleration was far stronger when it was accepted as one of the facts of political life than when it was finally and pompously espoused by the Victorians as a matter of principle – so as to remove it from the low company of compromising politicians. For tolerance became important and secure in England not because most men just believed, out of indifference or out of the exhaustion of ecclesiastical animosities, that many different things were not worth the discomforts and risks of public life, but because many of them believed that many different things were worth the risk. Tolerance arose from the clash of moralities, not from their absence. The means of conflict became more civilized, literally politicized, but the causes did not vanish. We tolerate opinions because opinions do matter: if not, it would be simpler not to tolerate them (the manner in which most governments of most countries do, in fact, act). Tolerance comes not through caring for nothing, but through caring for many things – just as freedom comes from *acting* freely, not from just being left alone or having some narrow 'everything' done for one.

Freedom and toleration supplement each other in one very important respect: they make it easier both to find out and to tell truths about human behaviour. Freedom implies, as in the scientist's use of hypothesis, creative speculation on goals and an exploration of alternatives. Tolerance implies, as in Coleridge's 'willing suspension of disbelief' for the literary critic, greater understanding. Valery's maxim seems to me as good for the practice of politics as for scholarship: 'The first task of anyone who would refute an opinion is to master it a little more

²² As recently argued with great brilliance in Robert Paul Woolf, Barrington Moore and Herbert Marcuse, *A Critique of Pure Tolerance* (Beacon Press, Boston, 1966).
²³ See Irene Coltman, *Private Men and Public Causes* (Faber, London, 1962). And Hobbes warned against reading the 'books of policy' of the Greeks and the Romans: 'From the reading, I say, of such books men have undertaken to kill their kings.'

surely than its ablest defenders.' Now it is an evident peculiarity of 'political régimes' or republics that they are the only type of government whose system of authority is not destroyed by allowing significant truths to be discovered and told about who actually rules and how. All governments try to hide things, both for lazy convenience and for *raison d'état*. But general censorship is only a necessary device in autocracies; political régimes can cheerfully admit that things are done as they are done, and for political reasons.

If consultation and compromise are to be effective, if it is possible at all to govern politically amid freedom, then it is necessary for a government to find out reasonably accurately what various interests want or are likely to put up with, and what is their relative strength. There must then be found people representative of these groups who are free to speak the truth. Representative institutions are fundamentally a matter of communication and not of rights. Aristotle remarked on how difficult it is for a tyrant to find people who will tell him the truth about what is going on. If this is to be done – and it surely contributes to the stability of any government – then the penalties of mistaken or unwelcome advice must not be too drastic. Particularly in complex matters of modern economic planning, it is helpful to any government for there to be some spheres of independent thought and action. The weakest of all justifications of the tyranny in some developing countries, for instance, is that economic shortages (including those of manpower) do not allow the 'luxury of public debate' on economic policy. One wonders how they can afford not to, since the consequences of mistakes must be so much more drastic. Of course, they do get independent advice – but in the only possible way that does not extend internal liberties and knowledge: from outside experts. This is related to an ancient device of autocracy, the recruitment of key advisors from abroad who are given a life of isolated luxury in the palace compound or the Grand Hotel.

The plea of 'necessity' is, indeed, the great enemy of freedom and of knowledge. Professor Ernest Gellner has recently suggested that there are in fact only two conditions needed in our times for a social order to make valid and rightful claims on members of the society – that: '(a) It is bringing about, or successfully maintaining, an industrially affluent society. (b) Those in authority are co-cultural with the rest of the society' (he is referring to nationalism).[24] This is a commendably short way, at least, to treat the problems of political obligation and justice. 'The question of how to retain or acquire liberty', he says, is only meaningful after 'the hump' of wealth is passed.[25] One ventures to suggest that in socie-

---

[24] Ernest Gellner, *Thought and Change* (Weidenfeld, London, 1964), p. 33.   [25] *Ibid.*, p. 38.

ties which do have such a simple view of government, the recognition of 'over the hump' will always be delayed. It is a view of government which arises naturally from, but which then can fatten unnecessarily upon, emergency. As Machiavelli argued, this is a view appropriate to state-founding or state-saving (in an emergency), but one not likely to preserve a state through time. In order to create or save a state, he implies in *The Prince*, 'concentrate power'; in order to preserve a state through time, 'spread it' (*The Discourses*). If Gellner's categories of industrial affluence and nationalism were indeed crystal clear, then freedom and politics might in practice be willingly squeezed out. But the ambiguities of these categories will lead to dispute, over means if not of ends; and it may again be dramatically discovered that some degree of freedom is a functional necessity for economic and social advance. To my mind this has nothing to do with capitalism or free-enterprise; state planning will inevitably arise in circumstances of war and emergency, of acute shortages or of acute aspirations. But effective planning must depend on the most public and honest gathering of information, discussions of how to evaluate it, criticism of plans and preparation of those likely to be affected by them. Planning is in no sense the necessary enemy of freedom; in many practical circumstances, it is a necessary precondition for its exercise.

That conscious control of an enviroment increases, not diminishes, the range of choices to be made was the theme of Malinowski's posthumous book, *Freedom and Civilization* (1947) – overshadowed by Popper's *Open Society and Its Enemies* but, I think, a greater work. He argued that freedom was to be seen as a cultural phenomenon before ever philosophers tried to say that this or that was private or public. Certain cultures had been able to make deliberate choices of what purpose to achieve, or what policies to adopt. These had in fact been the successful cultures, both economically and intellectually. Freedom was the capacity for adaptation, and so a clue to survival as well as to increased knowledge. So Malinowski, in terms less ponderous than Arendt, argued that freedom was not to be identified with any particular object, but with a type of process or activity which was self-critical, self-perpetuating and inventive, concerned with both means and ends. Since it is seldom read – and embarrasses most anthropologists for having gone somewhat beyond the evidences of field-work – let me quote two passages at some length:

> Those who attempt any definition of freedom in terms of negative categories are chasing an intellectual will-o'-the-wisp. Real freedom is neither absolute nor omnipresent and it certainly is not negative. It is always an increase in control, in efficiency,

and in the power to dominate one's own organism and the
environment, as well as artifacts and the supply of natural
resources. Hence freedom as a quality of human action, freedom
as increase of efficiency and control, means the breaking down of
certain obstacles and a compensation for certain deficiencies; it
also implies the acceptance of rules of nature, that is scientific
laws of knowledge, and of those norms and laws of human
behaviour which are indispensable to efficient co-operation.[26]

He concludes a chapter on 'The Semantics of Freedom'

. . . our conception of freedom is positive and objective; it is
essentially pragmatic, and implies a social and technical context.
It implies always the benefit from action and responsibility by
individuals and groups alike. The instrumentalities of freedom
we find in the political constitution of a community, its laws, its
moral norms, the distribution of its wealth, and the access to
such benefits as health, recreation, justice and religious or artistic
gifts of culture. To scour the universe for possibilities of freedom
other than those given by the organization of human groups for
the carrying out of specific purposes, and the production of
desirable results, is an idle philosophic pastime.[27]

All this has been very abstract. I have said little or nothing about the
actual history of freedom, about its conditions in the modern world,
nor about its relation to politics in Britain at the moment. All these things
need to be done and, in bits and pieces of gold, silver and lead, are
being done. But important and laborious enterprises usually go wrong
at the beginning, not at the end. If one asks the wrong question, one will
never get an answer. Thus 'negative liberty' is the wrong end of the
right stick; it only defines what we seek to avoid harming in others while
we act more positively ourselves. Without action, there is no liberty of
any kind. Even Lincoln was too negative in saying that 'the price of
liberty is eternal vigilance'. Better to have said that liberty is eternal
vigilance – if by vigilance is implied 'observer-participation'.

I have really returned to a view of 'freedom as citizenship' which was
current in the late seventeenth century and throughout the eighteenth,
but which hardly survived the mid-nineteenth century. It was swal-
lowed either by worship of the state – as in nationalism – or by alienation
from the state and a belief, among many liberals, that all power is
inherently evil.[28] This viewpoint did not centre so much on individual
rights against the state, but on those conditions which were necessary
to operate successfully the kind of state characterized as republican.
The viewpoint was often called 'Roman', or they spoke of 'the liberties

[26]Bronislaw Malinowski, *Freedom and Civilization* (Allen
and Unwin, London, 1947), p. 59.
[27] *Ibid.*, p. 95.
[28] See Preston King, *Fear of Power* (Frank Cass, London, 1967).

of the ancients' (as in the title of Benjamin Constant's famous essay).[29] But its genius was Machiavelli in his *Discourses*, where republican power is shown to be stronger and more stable and lasting than that of a *Principate* – given citizens who have not lost their *virtu*: the qualities of endeavour, involvement and audacity which hold states together – 'the native hue of resolution'.[30]

A recent author writing on Tocqueville, while using Berlin's categories of 'positive' and 'negative' liberty, points out that Tocqueville is not easy to understand in these terms: for there is an element of both positive and negative liberty in him, of social responsibility and of personal freedom. 'Both require, in his eyes', writes Mr Lively, 'the defence of politics against socially determined activity.' Tocqueville, he concludes, posed the 'essentially classical' idea of the free man as an active participant in communal affairs.[31]

Tocqueville was important not so much because he was the sayer of wise and quotable saws, but because he was among the first to appreciate the distinction between cause and condition in the writing of history. History does not determine the outcome of events, it narrows the range of alternatives. History presents us with alternatives: we are not just 'free to choose', we are not truly free unless we do choose. Freedom is thus moral freedom: it involves choosing and acting in such a way

---

[29] 'The Liberty of the Ancients Compared to that of the Moderns'. See the discussion of this in Bertrand de Jouvenel, ed., *Futuribles* (Droz, Geneva, 1963), 99–102.

[30] Oddly Berlin comes close to this view, but then shies away. He refers (*op. cit.* p. 45) to: '. . . what Mill called "pagan self-assertion" . . . Indeed, much of what he says about his own reasons for desiring liberty – the value he puts on boldness and non-conformity, on the assertion of the individual's own values in the face of the prevailing opinion, on strong and self-reliant personalities free from the leading strings of the official law-givers and instructors of society – has little enough to do with his conception of freedom as non-interference, but a great deal with the desire of men not to have their personalities set at too low a value, assumed to be incapable of autonomous, original, "authentic" behaviour . . . '

Now I am not saying that Mill was ever wholly consistent, but 'little enough to do with' indeed! Mill plainly meant what he said: such behaviour was freedom. 'Non-interference' is a necessary but not a sufficient condition for what Mill meant by freedom. 'Pagan self-assertion' was equally important. (Here is my whole difference with Berlin – perhaps in some circumstances a slight one: between being able to choose and actually choosing).

[31] Jack Lively, *The Social and Political Thought of Alexis de Tocqueville* (Oxford University Press, London, 1962).

that the area of free choices for others is not impaired – which it always will be if we do not act at all. Men may not always act that way, but Tocqueville is saying that if they choose to treat each other as men, then, very simply, they should.

There are no protective devices which can be minutely and precisely copied from one country to another; but to Tocqueville the American example (for him it was only an example) was sufficient to show that a conscious and rational allegiance to some laws and customs could restrain even the majority against itself. No laws work without the will; but good will is useless if it does not become an institution. So to Tocqueville it was plain that understanding and action must go hand in hand. The individual is only truly an individual when acting a part with other men. The central state is strong when its roots are local and when allegiance is conditional. American Federalism was not the antithesis of power; it was potentially among the strongest forms of power. Freedom is not the antithesis of authority; it is the only form of authority – except, again, love – which can be accepted without force or deception. All this was once embraced in the classical concept of 'republican liberties'.

I am happy to take such a classical – even pagan – stand on the matter of freedom. Progress is not always in the same direction in everything. We need to recover this lost relationship between common citizenship and freedom. More precisely, we need to extend it to the people before other forces in our society succeed in treating them entirely as masses. But to characterize the view as 'classical' is perhaps better to identify its origins than to characterize its present mode – which is, quite simply, social, or even socialist. It is socialist at least in the sense that it is both an inadequate account of freedom to think of it as being left alone, as the liberal implies, or as simply preserving the fruits of experience, as the conservative implies, for it does involve the constant need to do new things in a premeditated manner – the adaptation of man to circumstance and environment in such a way that his capacity for future adaptation is not impaired.

Schiller wrote in his *Aesthetic Letters:* '. . . a political administration will always be imperfect when it is able to bring about unity only by suppressing variety. The state ought to respect not only the objective and the generic, but also the subjective and specific in individuals.'

But, in the end nothing can be done if people do not wish to help in doing it themselves; the conditions can be provided, but it takes individual human action, since man is free, to bring about a result. Beaumarchais, good bourgeois though he was, still saw the dark side of this when he wrote in his *Notes and Reflections*:

Slaves are as guilty as tyrants. It is hard to say if freedom can more justly reproach those who attack her than those who do not defend her.

We live in a world in which so many not merely fail to defend freedom out of ignorance, indifference, laziness or cowardice, but can either scorn her, from the loftiest of mistaken motives, or else underestimate her by usage too narrow and pedantic.

10 Values and Collective Decision-making[1]

Kenneth J Arrow

I Values of a single individual

As an exercise in clarifying terminology, let us consider what can be said about the values of an imaginary, completely isolated individual. His personal skills and qualities and the physical world available to him jointly delimit a range of *actions* possible to him. To be precise, I shall so define the concept of action that alternative actions are mutually exclusive. An action, then, means a complete description of all the activities that an individual carries on, and two alternative actions are any two descriptions which differ in any relevant way. For example, an individual may describe his activities by indicating the amount of time he spends on each of the alternative modalities of performance available to him; thus, three hours at farming, three hours at hunting, four hours of violin playing, etc. A change in any one of these time allocations would represent a change in action. This particular definition is truly a formal choice of language, and does not by itself change the nature of the problem. It simply brings out formally that the basic question of the individual is a choice of actions.

1 *Values, Tastes, and Hypothetical Imperatives*

To an economist, and I suppose to most philosophers, a value system would, in these terms, be simply the rule an individual uses to choose which of the mutually exclusive actions he will undertake. If an individual is facing a given set of alternative actions, he will choose one, and there seems to be little interesting to talk about. However, the problem, at least to the economist, is put in slightly different form. Consider an individual who does not yet know which actions will be available and which will not. Let us term the set of available actions the *environment*. One might ask him what action he *would choose* if offered some particular environment. By repeating this question for many alternative environments we have obtained a description of his value system in the

[1] This paper is a slightly revised version of 'Public and Private Values', presented at a symposium on *Human Values and Economic Policy* at the New York University Institute of Philosophy in 1966.

sense of a rule giving his hypothetical choice for many or all possible environments.[2]

One might want to reserve the term 'values' for a specially elevated or noble set of choices. Perhaps choices in general might be referred to as 'tastes'. We do not ordinarily think of the preference for additional bread over additional beer as being a value worthy of philosophic inquiry. I believe, though, that the distinction cannot be made logically, and certainly not in dealing with the single isolated individual. If there is any distinction between values and tastes it must lie in the realm of interpersonal relations.

II *The Assumptions of Ordering*

The description of a value system as a correlation between possible environments and the hypothetical choices to be made from them is not by itself a very informative procedure. Economists have been accustomed to adding considerable strength (empirical restrictiveness) by specifying that the value system shall have a particular structure – namely, being derivable from an *ordering*. To define this concept let us first consider environments consisting of just two alternative actions. For such two-member environments we can find the one chosen, in accordance with the individual's value system, and we will speak of it as having been *preferred* to the other action in the environment. We may have to admit that the individual is equally willing to choose neither of the two actions, in which case we speak of the two actions as being *indifferent*. The assumption of an ordering means that certain consistency assumptions are postulated about the relations of preference and indifference, and it is further assumed that choices from any environment can be described in terms of the ordering, which relates to choices in two-member environments.

The first assumption is that of *connexity* (or connectedness, or completeness, or comparability). It is assumed that for each pair of alternatives, either one is preferred to the other or the two are indifferent. The second assumption is that of *transitivity*. Consider three alternatives, to be designated by x, y, and z. Then if x is preferred to y, and y

---

[2] For technical mathematical reasons one must admit that sometimes more than one action should be regarded as chosen in a given environment, by which is meant the individual does not care which of the chosen actions is in fact adopted in a particular set of circumstances. We must also allow for the fact that there may be no chosen action; for an example of the latter, consider an individual with a normal desire for money who can choose any amount of gold less than (but not equal to) one ounce.

is preferred to z, we assume that x is preferred to z. We can and must also include in the definition cases where some of the choices are indifferent; for example, if x is indifferent to y, and y is indifferent to z, then x is indifferent to z.

For later use we introduce some symbolic notation to express these ordering relations. Specifically, we denote alternatives by x, y,... . Then

xPy means 'x is preferred to y',
xIy means 'x is indifferent to y',
xRy means 'x is preferred or indifferent to y'.

If we start with the relation R (that is, only knowing for which ordered pairs of alternatives, x, y, the statement xRy holds), then we can define the relations P and I in terms of R:

xIy is defined to be xRy and yRx;
xPy is defined to be xRy and not yRx.

The assumption of connexity can be stated:

For all x and y, xRy or yRx.

(Here, and below, 'or' does not exclude 'and'.) The assumption of transitivity can be stated:

For all x, y, and z, if zRy and yRz, then xRz.

Finally, and perhaps most important, it is assumed that the choice from any environment is determined by the ordering in the sense that if there is an alternative which is preferred to every other alternative in the environment, then it is the chosen element. This is an additional assumption not logically implied by the existence of an ordering itself.

In symbols, let S be any environment (set of alternatives), C(S) the alternative (or alternatives) chosen from S. Then

C(S) is the set of alternatives x in S for which xRy for all y in S.

It is easy to see that if x^1 and x^2 are both in C(S) (both chosen alternatives in S), then x^1 I x^2.

Obviously, the assumption of ordering is by no means unreasonable. The notion of connexity carries the idea that choices have to be made whether we will or no. The idea of transitivity clearly corresponds to some strong feeling of the meaning of consistency in our choice. Economists have typically identified the concept of rationality with the notion of choices derivable from an ordering.

It may be worth while dwelling on the meaning of these two assumptions a little more, in view of their importance. It is not at all uncommon to find denials of the connexity assumption. Sufficiently remote alternatives are held to be incomparable. But I must say I do not find this line of argument at all convincing. If a choice has to be made, it has to be made. In most practical choice situations there is some *null* alternative, which will be chosen in the absence of what might be termed a positive decision. Thus, if there is dispute about the nature of new legislation, the pre-existing legislation remains in force. But this does not mean that no choice is made; it means rather that the system produces as its choice the null alternative. I think what those who emphasize incomparability have in mind is rather that if one is forced to make a choice between alternatives which are difficult to compare, then the choice is not apt to satisfy the assumption of transitivity.

The possibility of regarding inaction as an always available alternative is part of the broader question of whether social choices should be historically conditioned. It is here that the importance of transitivity becomes clear. Transitivity implies that the final choice made from any given environment is independent of the path by which it has been derived. From any environment there will be a given chosen alternative, and in the absence of a deadlock no place for the historically given alternatives to be chosen by default.

III *Independence of Irrelevant Alternatives*

Since the chosen element from any environment is completely defined by knowledge of the preferences as between it and any other alternative in the environment, it follows that the choice depends only on the ordering of the elements of that environment. In particular, the choice made does not depend on preferences as between alternatives which are not in fact available in the given environment, nor – and this is probably more important – on preferences as between elements in the environment and those not in the environment. It is never necessary to compare available alternatives with those which are not available at a given moment in order to arrive at a decision. It is this point which is being made when it is argued that only ordinal measures of utility or preference are relevant to decisions. Any cardinal measure, any attempt to give a numerical representation of utility, depends basically on comparisions involving alternative actions which are not, or at least may not be, available, given the environment prevailing at the moment.

IV *Omitted Considerations*

For the sake of economy of discussion we pass by many interesting issues. Most important, probably, is the relation between hypothetical choices and real ones. It is implied in the above discussion and below that a preference will in fact be translated into a choice if the opportunity ever comes. But the question may be raised how we can possibly know about hypothetical choices if they are not actually made. This is not merely a problem of finding out about somebody else's values; we may not know our own values until put to the crucial test.

Even the actual preferences may not be regarded as in some sense true values. An observer looking from the outside on our isolated individual may say that his decision was wrong either in the sense that there is some other standard of values to which it does not conform or in the sense that it was made on the grounds of insufficient information or improper calculation. The latter possibility is a real and important one, but I will simply state that I am abstracting from it in the course of the present discussion. The former interpretation I am rejecting here. For the single isolated individual there can be no other standard than his own values. He might indeed wish to change them under criticism, but this, I take it, means basically that he hasn't fully thought through or calculated the consequences of his actions and upon more consideration wishes to modify them.

II   Public Values

1 *Interpersonal Nature of Social Action*
The fundamental fact which causes the need for discussing public values at all is that all significant actions involve joint participation of many individuals. Even the apparently simplest act of individual decision involves the participation of a whole society.

It is important to note that this observation tells us all non-trivial actions are essentially the property of society as a whole, not of individuals. It is quite customary to think of each individual as being able to undertake actions on his own (e.g., decisions of consumption, production, and exchange, moving from place to place, forming and dissolving families). Formally, a social action is then taken to be the resultant of all individual actions. In other words, any social action is thought of as being factored into a sequence of individual actions.

I certainly do not wish to deny that such factoring takes place, but I do wish to emphasize that the partition of a social action into individual components, and the corresponding assignment of individual responsibility, is *not* a datum. Rather, the particular factoring in any given context is itself the result of a social policy and therefore already the outcome of earlier and logically more primitive social values.

In economic transactions the point is clearest when we consider what we call property. Property is clearly a creation of society through its legal structure. The actions of buying and selling through offers of property are only at a superficial level the actions of an individual. They reflect a whole series of social institutions, and with different institutions different people would be having control over any given piece of property. Furthermore, the very notion of control over one's 'own' property, as is apparent upon the most casual inspection, itself acquires its meaning through the regulations of society.

These are no idle or excessively nice distinctions. When it comes to racial discrimination, notions of liability and responsibility for injury to others, or the whole concept of a corporation and its special and complex relations to the world as a whole, economic and social, we know that social values have altered considerably the terms on which property can be used in the market-place or transmitted to others. Needless to say, the taxation system constitutes one of the strongest examples in which the state, as one aspect of society, makes clear the relative nature of ownership. Nor, in this context, should it be forgotten that the claims of society, as modifying the concept of ownership, are by no means confined to the state. Our particular culture has tended to minimize non-coercive obligations relative to the predominant role they have played elsewhere, but they are far from absent even today. There is certainly a whole complex of obligations implied in the concept of a 'good neighbour'. The use of one's real property is limited by more than legal conditions. As everyone knows – sometimes painfully – there are obligations of generosity and organized giving appropriate to an individual's income status and social position. In short, we argue that the facts of social life show clearly that there is no universally acceptable division of actions with regard to property into mine and thine.

To be sure, there is another category of actions, those which involve the person himself as opposed to his property. We have a stronger feeling here that there is a natural meaning to speaking of one's own actions as opposed to others. Presumably there is a meaningful sense in which we say that *I* am writing this paper – not anyone else. But of course even here the action is full of social interconnections. I am here in a conference arranged by others, using words which are a common part of the culture, expressing ideas which draw upon a wide range of concepts of others, and which embody my education.

To be sure, I am using my own capacities at some point in this process. But how logically do we distinguish between the capacities which somehow define the person, and those which are the result of external actions of a society? I may see well because my vision is intrinsically good or because I have glasses. Is the vision more peculiarly *mine* in one case than in the other? One may concede that there is more of an intrinsic idea of property here in certain personal actions, but I think this whole matter needs deeper exploration than it has received thus far. In any case, there are obviously very strong social obligations on personal behavior and the use of one's personal capacities, just as there are on the use of property.

To conclude, then, we must in a general theory take as our unit a social action, that is, an action involving a large proportion or the entire domain of society. At the most basic axiomatic level, individual actions play little role. The need for a system of public values then becomes evident; actions being collective or interpersonal in nature, so must the choice among them. A public or social value system is essentially a logical necessity.

The point is obvious enough in the contexts that we tend to regard as specifically political. The individuals in a country cannot have separate foreign policies or separate legal systems. Among economists the matter has been somewhat confused because economic analysis has supplied us with a model of factorization of social actions, that achieved through the price system. The system itself is certainly one of the most remarkable of social institutions and the analysis of its working is, in my judgment, one of the more significant intellectual achievements of mankind. But the factorization implied is a particular one made in a particular way. It is one that has turned out to be highly convenient, particularly from the point of view of economizing on the flow of information in the economic system. But at the fundamental level of discourse we are now engaged in we cannot regard the price system as a datum. On the contrary, it is to be thought of as one of the instrumentalities, possibly the major one, by which whatever social value system there may be is realized.

II *Individual Preferences for Social Actions*

The individual plays a central role in social choice as the judge of alternative social actions according to his own standards. We presume that each individual has some way of ranking social actions according to his preferences for their consequences. These preferences constitute his value system. They are assumed to reflect already in full measure altruistic or egoistic motivations, as the case may be.

Following the discussion in Part I, we assume that the values are expressed in the form of an ordering. Thus, in effect, individuals are taken to be rational in their attitudes toward social actions.

In symbols, we now let x, y,..., represent alternative social actions. Then the ith individual has an ordering among these actions which, as in I.II, can be represented by a relation, to be denoted by R_i:

xR_iy means 'x is preferred or indifferent to y in the view of individual i.'

As before, we can define P_i (preference in the view of individual i) and I_i (indifference in the view of individual i) in terms of R_i:

xP_iy is defined to be zR_iy and not yR_ix;

xI_iy is defined to be xR_iy and yR_ix.

We are face to face with an extremely difficult point. A standard liberal point of view in political philosophy, which also has dominated formal welfare economics, asserts that an individual's preferences are or ought to be (a distinction not usually made clear) concerned only with the effects of social actions on him. But there is no logical way to distinguish a particular class of consequences which pertain to a given individual. If I feel that my satisfaction is reduced by somebody else's poverty (or, for that matter, by somebody else's wealth), then I am injured in precisely the same sense as if my purchasing power were reduced. To parallel the observations of the preceding section, I am in effect arguing here that just as we cannot factor social actions so as to make each component pertain to a given individual, so we cannot factor the consequences of social actions in any meaningful way into separable consequences to individual members of the society. That is, let me make it clear, we cannot do it as a matter of fact. The interdependence of mankind is after all not a novel ethical doctrine. The man who questioned whether he was his brother's keeper was, according to an ancient source, not highly approved of. The general conclusion here is not one that I find myself entirely comfortable with. I do share the general liberal view that every individual should have the opportunity to find his own way to personal development and satisfaction. The question of interference with the actions of others has been raised most acutely in recent years in legal rather than economic contexts, specifically in the English discussion on laws regulating deviant sexual behaviour. Homosexual behaviour between consenting adults is probably a classic example of an action affecting no one else, and therefore should be exempt from social control. Yet many find themselves shocked and outraged. They would strongly prefer, let us say, the situation to be different. Similarly, I may be disturbed that the Negro is discriminated against and judge accordingly social actions which lead to this result.

One could of course say that the general principle of restraint in judging the affairs of others is an empirical assumption that people in fact do not care about (or strictly have no preferences concerning) matters which would in the usual terminology be regarded as none of their business. But of course empirically we know that this is quite false. The very fact that restrictive legislation is passed or even proposed shows clearly that people are willing to sacrifice effort and time because of the satisfactions to be received from seeing others' patterns of life altered.

The only rational defence of what may be termed a liberal position, or perhaps more precisely a principle of limited social preference, is that it is itself a value judgment. In other words, an individual may have as part of his value structure precisely that he does not think it proper to influence consequences outside a limited realm. This is a perfectly coherent position, but I find it difficult to insist that this judgment is of such overriding importance that it outweighs all other considerations. Personally, my values are such that I am willing to go very far indeed in the direction of respect for the means by which others choose to derive their satisfactions.

At this stage I want to emphasize that value judgments in favour of limited social preference, just as other value judgments emphasizing social solidarity, must be counted as part of the value systems which individuals use in the judgment of alternative social actions.

III   Welfare Judgments and the Aggregation of Preferences

The problem of social choice is the aggregation of the multiplicity of individual preference scales about alternative social actions.

1 *Welfare Judgments and Constitutions*

Classical utilitarianism specifies that alternative social actions be judged in terms of their consequences for people. In the present terminology I take this to mean that they are to be judged in terms of the individual preference scales. This by itself does not supply a sufficient basis for action in view of the multiplicity and divergence of individual preference scales. It is therefore at least implicit in classical utilitarianism that there is a second level at which the individual judgments are themselves evaluated, and this point has been given explicit recognition in a classic paper of Abram Bergson.[3] Let us call this second-order evaluation a *welfare judgment;* it is an evaluation of the consequences to all individuals based on their evaluations. If in each individual evaluation two social

---

[3] 'A Reformulation of Certain Aspects of Welfare Economics', *Quarterly Journal of Economics*, 52 (1938), 310–34; reprinted in A. Bergson, *Essays in Normative Economics* (Cambridge, Mass.: Harvard University Press, 1966), 1–49.

actions are indifferent, then the welfare judgment as between the two must also be one of indifference.

The process of formation of welfare judgments is logically equivalent to a social decision process or *constitution*. Specifically, a constitution is a rule which associates to each possible set of individual orderings a social choice function, i.e., a rule for selecting a preferred action out of every possible environment. That a welfare judgment is a constitution indeed follows immediately from the assumption that a welfare judgment can be formed given any set of individual preference systems for social actions. The classification of welfare judgments as constitutions is at this stage a tautology, but what makes it more than that is a specification of reasonable conditions to be imposed on constitutions, and it is here that any dispute must lie.

II *Social Decision Processes and the Notion of Social Welfare*

While I have just argued that a welfare judgment is necessarily a constitution or process of social decision, the converse need not be true, at least not without further clarification of the meaning of 'welfare judgment'. A welfare judgment requires that some one person is judge; a rule for arriving at social decisions may be agreed upon for reasons of convenience and necessity without its outcomes being treated as evaluations by anyone in particular.[4] Indeed, I would go further and argue that the appropriate standpoint for analysing social decision processes is precisely that they not be welfare judgments of any particular individuals. This seems contrary to Bergson's point of view.[5] In my view, the location of welfare judgments in any individual, while logically possible, does not appear to be very interesting. 'Social welfare' is related to social policy in any sensible interpretation; the welfare judgments of any single individual are unconnected with action and therefore sterile. In a more recent paper Bergson has recognized that there may be this alternative interpretation of the concept of social welfare; I quote the passage at length since it displays the issue so well: 'I have been assuming that the concern of welfare economics is to counsel individual citizens generally. If a public official is counselled, it is on the same basis as any other citizen. In every instance reference is made to some ethical values which are appropriate for the counselling of the individual in question.

---

[4] This point has been well stressed by I. M. D. Little, 'Social Choice and Individual Values', *Journal of Political Economy*, 60 (1952), 422–32.

[5] A. Bergson, 'On the Concept of Social Welfare', *Quarterly Journal of Economics*, 68 (1954), 233–52, reprinted in *Essays in Normative Economics, op. cit.*, 27–49, esp. pp. 35–6.

In all this I believe I am only expressing the intent of welfare writings generally; or if this is not the intent, I think it should be. But some may be inclined nevertheless to a different conception, which allows still another interpretation of Arrow's theorem. *According to this view, the problem is to counsel not citizens generally but public officials.* [Emphasis added.] Furthermore, the values to be taken as data are not those which would guide the official if he were a private citizen. The official is envisaged instead as more or less neutral ethically. His one aim in life is to implement the values of other citizens as given by some rule of collective decision making.'[6] My interpretation of the social choice problem agrees fully with that given by Bergson beginning with the italicized statement, though, as can be seen, this is not the view that he himself endorses.

IV   Some Conditions for a Social Decision Process and the Impossibility Theorem

---

The fundamental problem of public value formation, then, is the construction of constitutions. In general, of course, there is no difficulty in constructing a rule if one is content with arbitrary ones. The problem becomes meaningful if reasonable conditions are suggested, which every constitution should obey.[7]

1 *Some Conditions on Constitutions*

I suggest here four conditions which seem very reasonable to impose on any constitution. More can undoubtedly be suggested but unfortunately, as we shall see in Section II below, these four more than suffice.

Recall that a constitution is a rule which assigns to any set of individual preference orderings a rule for making society's choices among alternative social actions in any possible environment. Thus, for a given set of individual orderings the result of the process is a particular value system in the sense of Part I; that is, a rule for making selections out of all possible environments. The first condition may be termed that of COLLECTIVE RATIONALITY: For any given set of orderings, the social choice function is derivable from an ordering. In other words, the social choice system has the same structure as that

---

⁶ A. Bergson, 'On the Concept of Social Welfare', *op. cit.*, p. 242; *Essays, op. cit.*, pp. 37–8.
⁷ The analysis that follows is based on my book *Social Choice and Individual Values* (New York, London, and Sydney: Wiley: 1st ed. 1951; 2nd ed. 1963).

which we have already assumed for individual value systems. The next condition is one that has been little disputed and is advanced by almost every writer in the economic literature:

PARETO PRINCIPLE: If alternative x is preferred to alternative y by every single individual according to his ordering, then the social ordering also ranks x above y.

Notice that we can use the term 'social ordering' in view of the previous condition of Collective Rationality. The next condition is perhaps the most important as well as the most controversial. For my own part, I am less tempted to regard it as ultimately satisfactory than I formerly did, but it has strong pragmatic justification:

INDEPENDENCE OF IRRELEVANT ALTERNATIVES: The social choice made from any environment depends only on the orderings of individuals with respect to the alternatives in that environment.

To take an extreme case, suppose that individuals are informed that there are a certain number of social actions available. They are not even aware that there are other conceivable social actions. They develop their own preference systems for the alternatives contained in this particular environment, and then the constitution generates a choice. Later they are told that in fact there were alternatives which were logically possible but were not in fact available. For example, a city is taking a poll of individual preferences on alternative methods of transportation (rapid transit, automobile, bus, etc.). Someone suggests that in evaluating these preferences they also ought to ask individual preferences for instantaneous transportation by dissolving the individual into molecules in a ray gun and reforming him elsewhere in the city as desired. There is no pretence that this method is in any way an available alternative. The assumption of Independence of Irrelevant Alternatives is that such preferences have no bearing on the choice to be made.

It is of course obvious that ordinary political decision-making methods satisfy this condition. When choosing among candidates for an elected office, all that is asked are the preferences among the actual candidates, not also preferences among other individuals who are not candidates and who are not available for office.

Finally, we enunciate probably the least controversial of all the conditions,

NON-DICTATORSHIP: There is no individual whose preferences are automatically society's preferences independent of the preferences of all other individuals.

There is a difference between the first two conditions and the last two which is worth noting. The assumptions of Collective Rationality and the Pareto Principle are statements which apply to any fixed set of individual orderings. They do not involve comparisons between social orderings based on different sets of individual orderings. On the contrary, the condition of Independence of Irrelevant Alternatives and of Non-Dictatorship are assertions about the responsiveness of the social ordering to variations in individual orderings.

11 *Impossibility Theorem*

The conditions of Collective Rationality and of the Independence of Irrelevant Alternatives taken together imply that in a generalized sense all methods of social choice are of the type of voting. If we consider environments composed of two alternatives alone, then the condition of Independence of Irrelevant Alternatives tells us that the choice is determined solely by the preferences of the members of the community as between those two alternatives, and no other preferences are involved. Define a set of individuals to be *decisive* for alternative x over alternative y if the constitution prescribes that x is chosen over y whenever all individuals in the set prefer x to y and all others prefer y to x. Then the rule for choosing from any two-member environment has the form of specifying which sets of individuals are decisive for x over y and which for y over x. The majority voting principle, for example, states simply that any set containing a majority of the voters is decisive for any alternative over any other.

Then, if the social value system is generated by a social ordering, all social preferences are determined by the choices made for two-member environments, and hence by pairwise votes (thus systems like plurality voting are excluded).

Now it has been known for a long time that the system of majority voting can give rise to paradoxical consequences. Consider the following example. There are three alternatives, x, y, and z, among which choice is to be made. One-third of the voters prefer x to y and y to z, one-third prefer y to z and z to x, and one-third prefer z to x and x to y. Then x will be preferred to y by a majority, y to z by a majority, and z to x by a majority.[8]

[8] This paradox seems to have been first observed by the Marquis de Condorcet, *Essai sur l'application de l'analyse à la probabilité des décisions rendues à la pluralité des voix* (Paris, 1785). That a rational voting scheme requires knowledge of all preferences among the candidates and not only the first choice was already argued even earlier by Jean-Charles de Borda, 'Mémoire sur les élections au scrutin', *Mémoires de l'Académie Royale des Sciences*, 1781, 657–65. For a modern analysis of Condorcet's work on voting, see G.-G. Granger, *La Mathématique Social du Marquis de Condorcet* (Paris: Presses

One might be tempted to suppose that the paradox of voting is an imperfection in the particular system of majority voting, and more ingenious methods could avoid it. But unfortunately this is not so. The following general theorem may be stated:

There can be no constitution simultaneously satisfying the conditions of Collective Rationality, the Pareto Principle, the Independence of Irrelevant Alternatives, and Non-Dictatorship.

The proof is given in the following Section III.

This conclusion is quite embarrassing, and it forces us to examine the conditions which have been stated as reasonable. It's hard to imagine anyone quarrelling either with the Pareto Principle or the condition of Non-Dictatorship. The principle of Collective Rationality may indeed be questioned. One might be prepared to allow that the choice from a given environment be dependent on the history of previous choices made in earlier environments, but I think many would find that situation unsatisfactory. There remains, therefore, only the Independence of Irrelevant Alternatives, which will be examined in greater detail in Section IV below.

III *Proof of the Impossibility Theorem*

We assume the existence of a social choice mechanism satisfying the conditions of Collective Rationality, the Pareto Principle, the Independence of Irrelevant Alternatives, and Non-Dictatorship, and show that the assumption leads to a contradiction. Since the condition of Collective Rationality requires that social choice be derivable from an ordering, we can speak of social preference and social indifference. In particular, as defined in the last section, a set of individuals V is *decisive* for x against y if x is socially preferred to y whenever all individuals in V prefer x to y and all others prefer y to x.[9]

The proof falls into two parts. It is first shown that if an individual is decisive for some pair of alternatives, then he is a dictator, contrary to the condition of Non-Dictatorship. Hence, no individual is decisive for any pair of alternatives, and the Impossibility Theorem itself then follows easily with the aid of the Pareto Principle.

Universitaries de France, 1956, esp. pp. 94–129). For an English translation of Borda's work see A. de Grazia, 'Mathematical Derivation of an Election System', *Isis*, 44 (1953), 42–51. For a general history of the theory of social choice, see D. Black, *The Theory of Committees and Elections* (Cambridge, U.K.: Cambridge University Press, 1958), Part II.
[9] The following proof is quoted, with minor alterations, from Arrow, *op. cit.*, pp. 98–100.

We first distinguish one individual, called I, and introduce the following notations for statements about the constitution:

(1) $x\bar{D}y$ means that x is socially preferred to y whenever individual I prefers x to y, regardless of the orderings of other individuals;

(2) xDy means that x is socially preferred to y if individual I prefers x to y and all other individuals prefer y to x.

Notice that this notation is legitimate only because of the assumption of Independence of Irrelevant Alternatives. Note too that the statement, $x\bar{D}y$, implies xDy and that xDy is the same as the assertion that I is a decisive set for x against y.

Suppose then that xDy holds for some x and y. We will first suppose that there are only three alternatives altogether. Let the third alternative be z. Suppose I orders the alternatives, x, y, z, in descending order, whereas all other individuals prefer y to both x and z, but may have any preferences as between the last two. Then I prefers x to y, whereas all others prefer y to x; from (2) this means that xPy. All individuals prefer y to z; by the Pareto Principle, yPz. Then by transitivity, xPz; but then this holds whenever xP_iz, regardless of the orderings of other individuals as between x and z. In symbols,

(3) xDy implies $x\bar{D}z$.

Again suppose xDy, but now suppose that I orders the alternatives, z, x, y, whereas all other individuals prefer both z and y to x. By a similar argument, xPy and zPx, so that zPy.

(4) xDy implies $z\bar{D}y$.

Interchanging y and z in (4) yields

(5) xDz implies $y\bar{D}z$.

Replacing x by y, y by z, and z by x in (3) yields

(6) yDz implies $y\bar{D}x$.

Since $x\bar{D}z$ implies xDz, and $y\bar{D}z$ implies yDz, we can, by chaining the implications (3), (5), and (6), deduce

(7) xDy implies $y\bar{D}x$.

If we interchange x and y in (3), (4), and (7), we arrive at the respective implications

$$yDx \text{ implies } y\bar{D}z,$$
$$yDx \text{ implies } z\bar{D}x,$$
$$yDx \text{ implies } x\bar{D}y,$$

and these can each be chained with the implication (7) to yield

(8)   xDy implies yD̄z, zD̄x, and xD̄y.

Implications (3), (4), (7), and (8) together can be summarized as saying

(9) If xDy, then uD̄v are for every ordered pair u,v from the three
alternatives x, y, and z;

i.e., individual I is a dictator for the three alternatives.

We can extend this result to any number of alternatives by an argument due to Blau.[10] Suppose aDb holds, and let x and y be any pair of
alternatives. If x and y are the same as a and b, either in the same or in
the reverse order, we add a third alternative c to a and b; then we can
apply (9) to the triple a, b, c and deduce xD̄y by letting u = x,v = y.
If exactly one of x and y is distinct from a and b, add it to a and b to
form a triple to which again (9) is applicable. Finally, if both x and y
are distinct from a and b, two steps are needed. First, add x to a and b,
and deduce from (9) that aD̄x and therefore aDx. Then, again applying
(9) to the triple a, x, y, we find that xD̄y. Thus, aDb for some a and b
implies that xD̄y for all x and y, i.e., individual I is a dictator. From the
Condition of Non-Dictatorship it can be concluded that

(10) xDy cannot hold for any individual I and any pair x, y.

The remainder of the proof is now an appropriate adaptation of the
paradox of voting. By the Pareto Principle, there is at least one decisive
set for any ordered pair, x,y, namely, the set of all individuals. Among
all sets of individuals which are decisive for some pairwise choice, pick
one such that no other is smaller; by (10) it must contain at least two
individuals. Let V be the chosen set, and let the ordered pair for which
it is decisive be x,y. Divide V into two parts, V_1, which contains only a
single individual, and V_2, which contains all the rest. Let V_3 be the
set of individuals not in V.

Consider now the case where the preference order of V_1 is x,y,z,
that of all members of V_2 is z,x,y, and that of all members of V_3 is
y,z,x. Since V is decisive for x against y, and all members of V prefer x
to y while all others have the opposite preference xPy. On the other
hand, it is impossible that society prefers z to y since that would require
that V_2 be decisive on this issue; this is impossible since V_2 has fewer
members than V, which, by construction, has as few members as a
decisive set can have. Hence, yRz, and, since xPy, society must prefer
x to z. But then the single member of V_1 would be decisive, and we have
shown that to be impossible.

Thus the contradiction is established.

[10] J. H. Blau, 'The Existence of Social Welfare Functions',
Econometrica, 25 (1957), 310.

IV *The Independence of Irrelevant Alternatives and Interpersonal Comparisons of Intensity*

Modern economic theory has insisted on the ordinal concept of utility; that is, only orderings can be observed, and therefore no measurement of utility independent of these orderings has any significance. In the field of consumer's demand theory the ordinalist position turned out to create no problems; cardinal utility had no explanatory power above and beyond ordinal. Leibniz's Principle of the Identity of Indiscernibles demanded then the excision of cardinal utility from our thought patterns. Bergson's formulation of the social welfare function carried out the same principle in the analysis of social welfare. Social choices were to depend only on individual orderings; hence, welfare judgments were based only on interpersonally observable behaviour.

The condition of Independence of Irrelevant Alternatives extends the requirement of observability one step farther. Given the set of alternatives available for society to choose among, it could be expected that ideally one could observe all preferences among the available alternatives, but there would be no way to observe preferences among alternatives not feasible for society.

I now feel, however, that the austerity imposed by this condition is stricter than desirable. In many situations we do have information on preferences for non-feasible alternatives. It can certainly be argued that when available this information should be used in social choice. Unfortunately, it is clear, as I have already suggested, that social decision processes which are independent of irrelevant alternatives have strong practical advantages, and it remains to be seen whether a satisfactory social decision procedure can really be based on other information.

The potential usefulness of irrelevant alternatives is that they may permit empirically meaningful interpersonal comparisons. The information which might enable us to assert that one individual prefers alternative x to alternative y more strongly than a second individual prefers y to x must be based on comparisons by the two individuals of the two alternatives, not only with respect to each other but also to other alternatives.

Let me conclude by suggesting one type of use of irrelevant alternatives, which may be termed 'extended sympathy'. We do seem prepared to make comparisons of the form: Action x is better (or worse) for me than action y is for you. This is probably in fact the standard way in which people make judgments about appropriate income distributions; if I am richer than you, I may find it easy to make the judgment that it is better for you to have the marginal dollar than for me.

How is this consistent with our general point of view that all value judgments are at least hypothetical choices among alternative actions? Interpersonal comparisons of the extended sympathy type can be put in operational form. The judgment takes the form: It is better (in my judgment) to be myself under action x than to be you under action y.

In this form the characteristics that define an individual are included in the comparison. In effect, these characteristics are put on a par with the items usually regarded as constituting an individual's wealth. The possession of tools is ordinarily regarded as part of the social state which is being evaluated; why not the possession of the skills to use those tools, and the intelligence which lies behind those skills? Individuals, in appraising each other's states of well-being, not only consider material possessions but also find themselves 'desiring this man's scope and that man's art'.[11] The principle of extended sympathy as a basis for interpersonal comparisons seems basic to many of the welfare judgments made in ordinary practice. It remains to be seen whether an adequate theory of social choice can be derived from this and other acceptable principles.

[11] The moral implications of the position that many attributes of the individual are similar in nature to external possessions have been discussed by V. C. Walsh, *Scarcity and Evil* (Englewood Cliffs, N.J.: Prentice-Hall, 1961).